114188

THE GOLDEN CORE OF RELIGION

The Golden Core
of Religion

BY

ALEXANDER F. SKUTCH

London

GEORGE ALLEN AND UNWIN LTD

RUSKIN HOUSE MUSEUM STREET

© *Alexander F. Skutch*, 1970

ISBN 0 04 210003 8

PRINTED IN GREAT BRITAIN
in 11 point Ehrhardt type
AT THE ABERDEEN UNIVERSITY PRESS
ABERDEEN

TO PAMELA

Contents

Acknowledgements

I am grateful to Charles Scribner's Sons for permission to quote part of the 'Hymn to Aton' from *The Dawn of Conscience*, by James H. Breasted; to the Society of Authors for permission to reproduce John Masefield's sonnet, 'Here in the Self'; to William Morrow and Company for quotations from *Sex and Temperament in Three Primitive Societies*, copyright 1935 by Margaret Mead; and to J. M. Dent and Sons Ltd. for the lines from W. E. Leonard's translation of Lucretius' *On the Nature of Things* in chapter 13. I am equally grateful to all the other authors and publishers, ancient and modern, on whose works I have, without permission, drawn to enrich this book. They are listed in the footnotes.

A. F. S.

I

Introduction

We are religious because we love life and cling passionately to our conscious existence. The more we awake spiritually, the more we experience the values of such existence and dimly surmise its still unrealized potentialities, the more precious it becomes to us. The basic postulate of religion is that conscious life is desirable, worth preserving and fulfilling. Jesus understood this well when he declared: 'I am come that they might have life, and that they might have it more abundantly.'

Religion is life's ceaseless effort to preserve and perfect itself, become at last self-conscious, foreseeing and, in consequence, fearful amid the thousand perils that beset it. It was said of old, and has been reiterated by modern students of religion, that fear made the gods; but this is a half-truth. We fear only when that which we wish to preserve is threatened. Love of life, concern for the things that support and embellish it, is prior to fear. When we pursue our analysis far enough, it becomes clear that it is our attachment to conscious existence which made the gods. Religion begins at its natural starting point, the instinct of self-preservation, which has been called the first law of nature. Its function has been to deepen and broaden this natural impulse. Increase in depth leads to care for our character and spirit even more than for our organic bodies. Increase in breadth leads finally to concern for the whole of which we are a part.

The maintenance of life involves activities of various sorts, which bring us into relation with a multitude of things of diverse natures. Our first necessity is to feed, clothe, and shelter ourselves; and for these purposes we generally make use of things which we regard as inferior to ourselves, so that we may apply them to our purposes without considering their own feelings and desires, if such they have. Art has from ancient times been the most inclusive term for

9

all those activities whereby we exploit and turn to our use the materials and forces that nature provides. Nowadays we tend to restrict this term to the fine arts, such as painting, sculpture, and music, although we still speak of the culinary art or the art of horticulture. Technology is an advanced form of art that leans heavily upon scientific research. The names that we employ make little difference, so long as we recognize that the most primitive craft and the most advanced technology have this in common, that they transform for our use materials which make no recognized claim to our consideration.

In addition to things which we look upon as inferior to ourselves, the world contains beings that we regard as, in some sense, our equals. Even if we surpass them in strength, beauty, intelligence, or wealth, they make a claim to our consideration that we cannot disregard. We cannot treat them merely as instruments or means to our own ends, but must regard them as ends in themselves, and in this sense on a level with ourselves. The regulation of our dealings with beings whose rights or claims we recognize as valid is the province of morality. The scope of the moral community has varied immensely in different ages and cultures. The moral code of the primitive savage commonly failed to govern his conduct toward people outside his own tribe. To the slaveholder, the slave was a tool to be used, a sort of detached organ of his master's body obedient to the master's will, not a fellow man whose right to a full and happy life was equal to that of the master. In the West, animals in general have been regarded as objects to be exploited; although from ancient times, and especially in the East, a more exacting morality has demanded better treatment of them. In so far as we recognize in any creature a claim to our consideration which prevents us from exploiting it regardless of its own will or feelings, we admit it to our moral community.

To adapt to our uses, by art or technology, materials which we regard as inferior to ourselves and feel free to exploit, and to achieve satisfactory moral relationships with beings that we recognize as in some sense our equals, would, it seems, so occupy our intelligence and strength that we would have little time for anything else. Many men, indeed, appear to be satisfied if they can live comfortably and win the respect or good will of their neighbours. But from a remote epoch there have been those who feel that competence in the arts and moral conduct are not enough, because in addition to the things below us and those on the same plane with us in the scale of being, there is also something above us to which we must adjust our lives. To many, this higher order of being has been represented by the gods, or by God; but some thinkers have adopted the pantheistic view and regard the whole universe as divine. The essential point is that to be religious is to recognize something greater than our individual selves, greater even than humanity, and to strive to achieve a satisfactory relationship with it. Whether this greater thing with which religion is or should be concerned is a transcendent God or the whole of which we are parts, is a question that need not detain us now. For the present, it is enough to recognize three classes of activities, or three attitudes, appropriate to our dealings with three grades of being: art, for the exploitation of things that we deem inferior to ourselves; morality, for regulating our relations with things on the same plane as ourselves; and religion, to place us in the proper relationship with whatever we regard as higher than ourselves. Only when we achieve such a relationship do the things most precious to us seem secure.

Since man became man, religion has claimed a major share of his time, thought, energy, and wealth. After the effort to feed, clothe, and shelter ourselves, religion has probably received the greatest amount of human effort. Sometimes, comparing the stupendous constructions which men have, since prehistoric times, raised from religious motives with the hovels in which a majority have always lived, one suspects that more effort has been expended on religion than on the building of homes. In many countries, the priesthood or established church has received a large share of the total revenue; in some, religious institutions have owned a large portion of the arable land. Even today in the most enlightened countries, the churches have in aggregate an enormous income and claim the devoted service of countless people.

Sometimes one wonders what is the value of all this activity and outpouring of wealth. What is it worth to the individual? To society? In an age that is highly conscious of economics and insists upon efficiency, religion largely escapes that close scrutiny to which most other forms of human activity are subjected, probably because it is regarded as too personal, too sacred, or else too controversial, to have its productivity assessed. We do not live by bread alone; the values which religion offers are not of the economic order; and it seems difficult to establish a relationship between an expenditure of wealth or energy and the spiritual benefit it yields. Yet some such relationship must exist. In some cases, no doubt, a spiritual gain is too slight to justify a large material outlay; whereas in other cases the immaterial reward is immeasurably greater than the material outlay.

One bold enough to assess the value of religion might tackle his problem from various angles. In the first place, there is religion's claim to prepare the faithful for a blessed immortal life. Since there is no incontrovertible evidence that even a single person has achieved such an existence, the problem does not invite scientific inquiry. Religion's promise of immortality must be accepted on faith, or not at all. Secondly, one might examine the doctrines of religion, for their objective truth or even their internal consistency. But if, as in the present book, we are interested in religion as a whole rather than in some particular religion, the first thing that we notice is the lack of agreement among the various faiths. Judaism, Christianity, and Mohammedanism recognize a personal God; Jainism, and Buddhism in its original form, do not. These and other Eastern religions hold that the soul, or at least the personality, migrates from body to body before it is finally released; Judaism and the religions derived from it deny metempsychosis. These religions teach that each soul will finally appear before a divine judge, who will examine its conduct while in the flesh and either admit it to eternal bliss or condemn it to endless torment; the Indian religions see no need of a judge, because karma, operating as impersonally as a natural law, ensures that everyone will finally receive what he deserves. Christianity holds that men are saved by Christ's blood; the Buddha, in his final message, warned his disciples that their salvation depended on their own strenuous efforts—he claimed to do no more than to point out the way.

These are only a few of the crucial points on which the various major religions are at odds. There has been no lack of attempts to reconcile their so diverse teachings; they may be regarded as allegorical rather than literal, or, as in theosophy, as more or less garbled accounts of one pure doctrine taught by enlightened sages in the misty past. It is far from my purpose to undertake a critical comparison of religious dogmas; they are too controversial and involved in metaphysical perplexities which I wish to eschew. Besides, I hope that this book will make friends rather than enemies. Avoiding, so far as possible, the vexed subject of religious dogmas and even the assessment of religious ethics, I wish to examine the innate foundations of religion—of all religions worthy of the name. The method that we shall follow is primarily psychological rather than metaphysical. Why are we religious? What qualities of the human spirit find expression in religion? How adequately do existing religions satisfy those spiritual yearnings which gave rise to them?

I began this introduction by anticipating one of these questions. We are religious primarily because we love and wish to enhance life, and it is painful to contemplate its extinction. To anticipate still more the argument of this book: as we mature spiritually, that strong attachment to life in a beautiful world, which we inherit from prehuman ancestors, finds expression in appreciation, devoted care, and aspiration. Appreciation adds to simple enjoyment, such as we experienced as children and do still in our less reflective intervals, such overtones as wonder at our presence in a world that offers so much to delight us, gratitude to whatever we conceive it to be that prepared this boon for us, and a certain respect or tenderness toward the sources of our enjoyment, as though they were too precious or too sacred to be rudely touched or carelessly handled.

This feeling leads naturally to the second element in the religious attitude, devoted care. I use the word *care* in its widest sense, which includes *caring about* and *caring for*. To care about something is to be concerned for it, to wish it well, even if we can do nothing for it. The generous, thoughtful man cares about many things that he is quite unable to help; for example, he wishes all sentient beings to be spared pain and to enjoy such happiness as their nature permits, although for the vast majority of them he can do nothing. Caring about things would be only a sentiment if there were not certain things, animate and inanimate, that we can care for: shield from perils, nurse toward perfection, build or aid by our own strenuous exertion. It is caring for the few things within our reach that gives substance to our concern for the many things that we can only care about; such active effort is proof of our earnestness.

No matter how lovingly we care for ourselves or the things about us, we seem rarely to succeed in making anything all that we wish it to be. We would not appreciate existence in this world if it did not contain much that is good, yet at the same time we recognize, and suffer from, its vast evils. I doubt if anyone who assays himself truthfully will claim to be free from defects of body or character that he desires to overcome; and the same may be said of those whom we most love. We hardly pass a single day without some incident, great or small, to mar its perfection. We and all that we cherish are swept relentlessly toward final dissolution. Yet, with an intensity proportional to our capacity for religious feeling, we aspire to become better than we are, to make those we love better, to make a better world. Above all, we aspire to save something from the dissolution which common experience assures us will one day overtake our mortal frame, which astronomers predict will, ages hence, overwhelm our planet with all its living cargo. This aspiration for self-improvement, this hope of saving something from the disaster which threatens finally to overtake everything, has been persistently encouraged by every religion that has appealed widely to men.

Of these three basic elements which form the golden core of the religious life, devoted care occupies the most central position and serves as a link between the other two. Appreciation, when sufficiently strong, leads to it; without it, aspiration has nothing to stand on. Only the fool aspires for more without taking the best possible care of whatever advantages he has. By caring faithfully for what we are and have, we lay a solid foundation for what we aspire to become and to possess. Devoted care is the heart of religion.

It has been truly remarked that every man's interpretation of religion is based on his own inward experience of it rather than on his observation of what it is for others. Since it is unlikely that any man's religious experience is altogether unique, he will, no doubt, by diligent search succeed in finding in the religious expressions of others much evidence that the interpretation suggested by his own experience applies widely to the religious experience of mankind. But it is exceedingly difficult to find a definition that will do justice to everything that religion has been to everybody who might, by a liberal interpretation of the word, be called religious. Perhaps the statement that religion is a serious attitude toward the whole of our conscious existence, however far we believe it to extend, is the only one inclusive enough to cover the religious attitude to life in all its shades. Religion, then, is the attitude just the opposite of that expressed in the old, careless adage: 'Eat, drink, and be merry, for tomorrow you may die.' Even Schleiermacher's much-quoted interpretation of religion, as arising from our feeling of utter dependence on that which does not depend on us, will hardly apply to religion in its whole length and breadth; for in some of the more primitive religions, of which that of the Aztecs is a notable example, men and gods lived in reciprocal dependence: if men did not nourish the gods with sacrifices, the gods could not maintain the order of nature on which human life depends.

From this it is evident that to understand the essence of religion, what it has meant to mankind as a whole, one must consider not only those more advanced religions that flourish widely in the modern world but likewise the primitive religions to which, in their vast and bewildering variety, mankind was attached for a very much longer period. If we limit our attention to religions of the type of Christianity, modern Judaism, Islam, and the more advanced sects of that great *mélange* of religions known as Hinduism, we shall have a lamentably one-sided and inadequate view of the role that religion has played in the life of man. One who considered only these higher religions, and particularly their more mystical side, might conclude that religion is above all man's striving for union with God, when in reality this is only a special, late development. Religion is not even primarily an institution for the worship of God or the gods; its fundamental purpose, as I hope will become clear in the course of this book, is the protection of things precious to man—his life values—against perils that he could not adequately confront by ordinary, practical means. At a certain stage of intellectual development, man conceived that the mysterious processes that so strongly affected his welfare were controlled by supernatural powers, which were eventually personified as gods; he deemed it prudent to cultivate the good will of these gods as a means of safeguarding whatever was dear to him. Since these supernatural beings were as often envious as benign, it was of the utmost importance to placate them. Only after long ages did they become transformed into the supernal Being who was the personification of the highest values, the supreme object of the religious man's desire.

In the chapters which follow, we shall consider in detail the basic elements of religion—appreciation, devoted care, and aspiration—

examining their various expressions and tracing their development through the ages, from primitive to advanced religions. If in this study we fail to clear up, in definitive fashion, those main problems of religion, God and immortality, perhaps we shall learn something of value about ourselves, of our capacities and the direction our development has taken and may continue to follow. Since we are integral parts of the universe, composed of its substance and moulded by its dominant process, insight into our own nature should help us to understand that of which we are parts—and not the least revealing parts. Such knowledge of the grand movement in which we are involved should in turn shed fresh light upon our destiny and give direction to our strivings.

In recent years there has been a growing endeavour to bring the various religions closer together by emphasizing what they have in common and trying to reconcile their divergent doctrines. Along with diverse historical and cultural backgrounds, these doctrinal differences are the great obstacles to union. The more one insists on intellectual honesty, the more capable he is of appreciating metaphysical distinctions, the more serious these obstacles are recognized to be. If reconciliation is our aim, the only promising course appears to be that of digging down to prime foundations—to those elements in our human nature which make us religious—and building anew from this solid rock. Appreciation, devoted care, and aspiration are aspects of man's agelong effort to relate himself correctly to something greater and more enduring than mankind considered as a biological species. The true function of religion is to adjust us properly to the whole of which we are parts. Its tragedy is that, in the absence of adequate knowledge, it has been compelled to make guesses and assumptions about the things which transcend mankind, and all these assumptions or, to be liberal, imperfect glimpses of truth, have crystallized into hard dogmas; and the irreconcilability of these dogmas has stirred up fierce conflicts among men who should be united in a common endeavour, that of caring devotedly for the best that is in us and for the world which supports our bodies and enriches our spirits.

2

Appreciation

When we are young and thoughtless we enjoy life, but only as we grow older and more thoughtful do we become capable of appreciating it at all adequately. Probably few people ever sufficiently appreciate the privilege of living on a planet as beautiful as ours, with a body so well equipped with delicate sensory organs to make us aware of all its wonders. Without appreciation, the religious attitude can hardly exist. One who lives without enjoyment, finding nothing to admire in the starry heavens or the verdant earth or the accomplishments of mankind, who is insensitive to beauty and devoid of love, develops toward all things a cynical outlook which is the antithesis of religion.

Animals, like children, appear to enjoy life without appreciating it. One who observes them closely can hardly doubt that they find pleasure in eating, basking in the sunshine, gambolling and frolicking, and associating with their mates. Indeed, the more I reflect upon the matter, the more I doubt whether anything has ever existed quite barrenly, with no slightest satisfaction in existence, or only for the sake of some other being that was far in the future. Possibly even atoms, and the protons and electrons of which they are composed, feel with an intensity commensurate with their minute size. But this is a speculation which need not detain us here.

Although appreciation can hardly arise in the absence of some sources of enjoyment, it is much more than enjoyment. Like gratitude, to which it is allied, it flowers only in a finely organized, warmly responsive mind. Rude, insensitive people are rarely grateful for what others do for them. To be adequately grateful for a favour requires a vivid realization of the magnitude of the effort that was made on one's behalf and of the love or good will which prompted it. In a mind capable of gratitude, appreciation grows with understanding. The more one knows of the history of the earth, of the aeons of slow transformation that were required to prepare it to support life, of the long evolution that was needed to create man, the more capable he is of appreciating the wonder and the privilege of being here.

Because to appreciate the earth and to be grateful for the boon of life are among the higher mental developments, one would hardly look for expressions of this attitude among the more primitive religions, which were little more than magic and tribal ritual. The pre-agricultural savage, living precariously in a small group in a state of constant hostility toward neighbouring groups, was too concerned about his next meal to think deeply about himself and his world. According to some anthropologists, his predominant emotion was fear—fear of hunger, of the fury of the elements, of wild animals, of the ghosts of the dead, of the sorcery no less than the weapons of his enemies. The finer sentiments hardly flourish in such stony soil. Yet even to the most miserable savage, life must bring some joys and satisfactions, without which he would lose the will to preserve it. And doubtless if one searched diligently through the vast anthropological literature, he would find traces of dawning appreciation even among men of the most primitive cultures.

Among the higher religions one seeks more profitably for expressions of appreciation of life and the world which supports it. Let us begin with the scripture most familiar to Western readers, the Bible. In the very first chapter of the Old Testament, the account of each day's accomplishment by the Creator is followed by the comment 'God saw that it was good'; and when the whole fabric of heaven and earth and all its living creatures was completed, the final judgment was 'behold, it was very good'. Although the Lord is represented as approving his own handiwork, we can hardly doubt that the anonymous author(s) of these verses concurred with this appraisal. Whatever their faults, the post-exilic Jews who are responsible for the Old Testament in its present form were certainly not lacking in grateful appreciation of the world in which they lived. The dominant thought which runs through the Hebrew scriptures is that a beneficent Deity created a good world, and only man's perverse wickedness prevented his continuing to live in the lovely paradise where he first awoke.

The Psalms, which often repel the modern reader with their reiterated appeals for vengeance upon enemies, delight us with their expressions of appreciation of God's blessings to man. 'When I consider thy heavens, the work of thy fingers, the moon and the stars, which thou hast ordained; what is man, that thou art mindful of him? and the son of man, that thou visitest him?' Psalm 104 is a long and appreciative recital of God's beneficent works, written by a poet who was evidently a close observer of nature:

> He sendeth the springs into the valleys, which run among the hills.
> They give drink to every beast of the field: the wild asses quench their thirst.
> By them shall the fowls of the heaven have their habitation, which sing among the branches.
> He watereth the hills from his chambers: the earth is satisfied with the fruit of thy works.
> He causeth the grass to grow for the cattle, and herb for the service of man; that he may bring forth food out of the earth;
> And wine that maketh glad the heart of man, and oil to make his face to shine, and bread which strengtheneth man's heart.
> The trees of the Lord are full of sap; the cedars of Lebanon, which he hath planted;
> Where the birds make their nests: as for the stork, the fir trees are her house.
> The high hills are a refuge for the wild goats; and the rocks for the conies.
> He appointed the moon for seasons: the sun knoweth his going down.

Finally, in an outburst of grateful wonder, the psalmist exclaims:

> O Lord, how manifold are thy works! in wisdom hast thou made them all: the earth is full of thy riches.

As noticed by Breasted, the foregoing verse seems to be a paraphrase of one in a hymn to Aton, the Sun-God, composed by the Egyptian Pharaoh Ikhnaton or a member of his court in the fourteenth century B.C. This ruler's brave attempt to establish a universal monotheism, with the sun as God, was fiercely resisted by the entrenched Egyptian hierarchy, which after his death did its best to obliterate not only all traces of his too-advanced reforms but his very name. Egyptologists have estimated him variously, some praising him as an inspired idealist, others condemning him as a fanatic who ruthlessly swept aside time-hallowed institutions and rites dear to the people, who neglected the administration and defence of his far-flung empire, in his preoccupation with religious and artistic innovations. For us, the important point is that he was capable of religious appreciation in no small degree, as is evident from the following verses of a hymn to Aton, which was resurrected by archaeologists after remaining hidden for more than three millennia in a cliff tomb at Tell el-Amarna:

> Thou risest beautifully, O living Aton, Lord of Eternity;
> Thou art glittering, beautiful, strong;
> Thy love is great and mighty,
> Thy rays furnish vision to every one of thy creatures,
> Thy glowing hue brings life to the hearts of men,
> When thou hast filled the Two Lands with thy love.
> O God, who himself fashioned himself,
> Maker of every land,
> Creator of that which is upon it:
> Even men, all herds of cattle and the antelopes,
> All trees that grow in the soil,
> They live when thou dawnest for them,
> Thou art the mother and the father of all that thou hast made.
> As for their eyes, when thou dawnest,
> They see by means of thee.
> Thy rays illuminate the whole earth,
> And every heart rejoices because of seeing thee,
> When thou dawnest as their lord.[1]

Despite the terrible afflictions which befell them, in part a consequence of their situation between more powerful warring nations and in part because of their own wayward, intractable character, the ancient Jews never lost the belief that their God had created an excellent world, while their prophets continually reminded them that their sufferings were their own fault. The entrancing vision which the more inspired of these prophets, such as Isaiah, held before them was not of some far-off mysterious heaven but simply of this solid earth beneath their feet, purged of all the evils which man's wickedness had brought upon it, and blessed with a peace so pervasive that the most radical conflicts, such as that between the carnivorous wolf and the defenceless lamb,

[1] James H. Breasted, *The Dawn of Conscience*, Charles Scribner's Sons, New York and London, 1950, p. 287–8.

would be overcome, and all creatures would dwell together in idyllic friendship—as they had done in the beginning, when the Creator, resting after the completion of his week-long task, surveyed the newborn world and found it 'very good'.

The 'kingdom of heaven' which Jesus died to bring about was apparently just such a redeemed and purified world as had been foretold by the Hebrew prophets whose work he had come to complete. The New Jerusalem of the Apocalypse would descend from a new heaven to a new earth, to replace the historic city that would be destroyed along with the old earth. It would be built of transparent gold; its walls would be garnished with all manner of precious stones; and—a more important point—it would be inhabited only by righteous citizens, who would live in glory, beholding the countenance of their God. If Jesus, who was at heart a poet, ever composed a hymn in praise of his Father's creation, it has not been preserved for us. Yet scattered through his recorded speeches are expressions, such as the parable of the lilies, which suggest that he was keenly appreciative of natural beauty. He would have been untrue to the whole Hebrew tradition, of which he was the finest product, if he had regarded the visible world as other than fair and good, the work of a beneficent Creator.

It seems paradoxical that the most articulate people of the ancient world, the Greeks, had no sacred scriptures. Homer and, at a much later date, the great dramatic poets, took the place of the scriptures of other lands in moulding the sentiments of the people; and it would be difficult to find a more elevating influence than the reverent, thoughtful tragedies of Aeschylus and Sophocles and the moral fervour of the sceptical Euripides. The absence of a sacred book does not imply that the Hellenes were uninterested in religious questions; they created philosophy, which has always been preoccupied with the same problems that religion has professed to solve: the origin of the world and of life; man's nature and destiny; the good which he should seek; how he should treat his neighbours.

Religion and philosophy differ not in scope so much as in method. Every successful religion has, sooner or later, developed a ponderous establishment, upheld by men whose comfortable living would be endangered by any radical change in the venerable traditions which have become firmly rooted in the people whose spiritual destiny they undertake to control. Philosophy, on the other hand, has always, except in its decadent periods, resisted such a crystallization of belief. Free inquiry is its lifeblood; and the greatest philosophers have typically felt it necessary to build anew from first principles. For religion, salvation lies in unexamined faith; for philosophy, in examined truth. The philosopher's firm determination not, if he can avoid it, to be deceived has led him to examine questions, such as how we know and the validity of knowledge and the structure of the language by which it is passed from mind to mind, which matter little to priests committed to the preservation of a hoary tradition. These foundational studies which the philosopher undertakes in order to avoid error may so engross his attention that he neglects the superstructure which philosophy has from the beginning striven to raise upon a sound theory of knowledge. But whenever philosophy loses interest in the grand questions which from the first it has shared with religion, it abandons the bold curiosity which made it a momentous undertaking and is reduced to the status of a timid academic exercise.

Let us, then, see how the Greek philosophers evaluated the world. Did they, whose minds were too active and original to be shackled by traditional outlooks and beliefs, appreciate the visible creation as much as their Semitic contemporaries? Although religious myths often pass for well-established knowledge, a philosopher sometimes finds it convenient to present tentative conclusions in the form of a myth. Thus Plato, well aware of the difficulty of accounting for the origin of the world, gave a mythical dress to his thoughts on the subject, and he placed his creation myth in the mouth of Timaeus of Locri:

> Let us, then—said Timaeus—state for what reason becoming and this universe were framed by him who framed them. He was good; and in the good no jealousy in any matter can ever arise. So, being without jealousy, he desired that all things should come as near as possible to being like himself. That this is the supremely valid principle of becoming and of the order of the world, we shall most surely be right to accept from men of understanding. Desiring, then, that all things should be good and, so far as might be, nothing imperfect, the god took over all that is visible—not at rest, but in discordant and unordered motion—and brought it from disorder into order, since he judged that order was in every way the better.

Now it was not, nor can it ever be, permitted that the work of the supremely good should be anything but that which is best. Taking thought, therefore, he found that, among things that are by nature visible, no work that is without intelligence will ever be better than one that has intelligence, when each is taken as a whole, and moreover that intelligence cannot be present in anything apart from soul. In virtue of this reasoning, when he framed the universe, he fashioned reason within soul and soul within body, to the end that the work he accomplished might be by nature as excellent and perfect as possible. This, then, is how we must say, according to the likely account, that this world came to be, by the god's providence, in very truth a living creature with soul and reason.[1]

One recognizes several similarities between this account and that in the first chapter of Genesis. Like the Hebrew God, Plato's Demiurge took over a universe of discordant, unordered motion—chaos—and gave it form and order. Plato, no less than Genesis, insists that the Creator made a good world—the best that he could make. Indeed, why should God make a world that was anything but the best? But Plato the philosopher introduced into his creation myth a refinement that is absent from the simpler account of the old Hebrew priest or scribe. According to the *Timaeus*, the visible, tangible things which the Demiurge created in this world were copies of the immaterial Forms or Ideas that exist eternally in a supersensuous realm. The natural objects that we see about us, from the sun and stars to the living things that inhabit the land and sea, are good because they are copies of these supernal objects; yet the copies can never quite equal the originals in excellence. In his famous simile of the Cave, in the seventh book of the *Republic*, Plato compared visible things to shadows cast by firelight on the wall of a cavern, and asked us to imagine the glories that we should behold if we, who are chained in the cave in such a way that we cannot look outside, could turn around and see the statues which cast these shadows as they are carried in procession past the cave's mouth. But this is impossible, because these statues stand for ideal Forms that are invisible to our corporeal eyes and can be seen only by disembodied intelligence.

[1] Plato, *Timaeus*, 29D–30C. F. M. Cornford's translation.

Platonism, as the master left it, was half philosophy and half religion; its later offshoot in the Graeco-Roman world, Neo-platonism, was less than half philosophy and more than half religion. Six centuries after Plato's death, we find Plotinus, the Neoplatonist, upholding the value of the world against Gnostics who despised it as the inferior creation of a degenerate deity:

> Nor must we grant them that this world was produced in an evil condition, because there are many molestations in it. For this arises from forming too exalted an opinion of this sensible world, and conceiving it to be the same with that which is intelligible, and not the image of it. For what more beautiful image of it could have been generated? What other fire could be a better image of the fire which is there, than the fire which is here? Or what other earth than this, of the earth which is there? What sphere, also, could be more accurate and venerable, or more orderly in its motion [than that of this sensible universe], after the comprehension which is there of the intelligible world in itself? And what other sun after the intelligible sun, can be prior to this which is the object of sight?[1]

Plato's pupil Aristotle, holding that a philosopher should follow truth even at the price of dissenting from his friends, disagreed with his master in the matter of the intelligible Forms, because he could find no creative potency in them. To him, the visible world was no copy of something else, but a fabric that had existed independently without beginning. Aristotle, the naturalist-philosopher, appreciated nature for its own sake. His parable of the Cave, contained in a lost dialogue 'On Philosophy' but fortunately preserved for posterity by being quoted by Cicero in the second book of *On the Nature of the Gods*, contrasts significantly with the corresponding parable in the *Republic*:

> If there were beings who had always lived beneath the earth, in comfortable, well-lit dwellings, decorated with statues and pictures and furnished with all the luxuries enjoyed by persons thought to be supremely happy, and who though they had never come forth above the ground had learnt by report and by hearsay of the existence of certain deities or divine powers; and then if at

[1] Plotinus, *Enneads*, II, 9. Thomas Taylor's translation.

some time the jaws of the earth were opened and they were able to escape from their hidden abode and to come forth into the regions which we inhabit; when they suddenly had sight of the earth and the seas and the sky, and came to know of the vast clouds and mighty winds, and beheld the sun, and realized not only its size and beauty but also its potency in causing the day by shedding light over all the sky, and, after night had darkened the earth, they then saw the whole sky spangled and adorned with stars, and the changing phases of the moon's light, now waxing and now waning, and the risings and settings of all these heavenly bodies and their courses fixed and changeless throughout all eternity,—when they saw these things, surely they would think that the gods exist and that these mighty marvels are their handiwork.[1]

I do not quote these passages from ancient psalmists and philosophers for the sake of their conclusion, that the beauty and wonder of the universe prove that it was made by God or the gods. Even Aristotle, in his extant works, developed a concept of God and of nature which seems incompatible with the view expressed in this fragment of a lost dialogue intended for the general public. Before we concede that the universe was created by a beneficent Deity, we must take account not only of the many excellent things that it contains but also of the vast amount of evil, not only in the human world but in the rest of nature, where it arose long before man appeared. In ancient times there existed no developed theory to compete with the only explanation of the form and order in nature that occurred to primitive man's groping thought, that it was placed there by a being who was but a magnified image of himself. Yet even before Aristotle lived, Greek thinkers like Empedocles were wrestling with the concept of evolution, which was to require millennia to be wrought into an acceptable form. My purpose in quoting the foregoing passages is simply to present evidence— which could be multiplied a hundredfold if it seemed desirable— that at the very sources of our Western religions and thought, in ancient Judaism and Hellenic philosophy, we find deep-rooted, sincere appreciation of the beauty and glory of the world in which we dwell. Indeed, one acquainted with the visual arts of ancient

---

[1] Cicero, *De Natura Deorum*, II, 95. H. Rackham's translation in Loeb Classical Library.

Greece would hardly expect anything different from her philosophers.

In this matter, Christianity has not always been true to its sources. The ascetic movement, which began with St Anthony late in the third century and continued in full force throughout the Middle Ages, encouraged a very different outlook upon the world. Although Christianity destroyed the Gnostic sects, Gnostic disdain of the world permeated Christianity to its roots. To countless men and women dwelling as monks and nuns in convents or as hermits in the wilderness, the world became, not a wondrous fabric to be admired and appreciated as the handiwork of a beneficent Creator, but a delusion and a snare, fit only to beguile men from their true vocation, the salvation of their immortal souls. The very senses that make us aware of the world around us were regarded as instruments of evil, whose operation should be suppressed.[1] The 'mortal frame' that supports these senses was treated with the utmost rigour and harshness, starved, exposed to the elements, flagellated, lacerated with self-inflicted wounds. Likewise, all those mystics who, like St John of the Cross, followed the *via negativa*, trying to empty their minds of every content so that God might fill it, averted their senses from God's fair creation.

Such harsh and narrow ascetics seem devoid of all appreciation of the familiar world. But are they? Whence comes their burning desire to win a mode of existence so immeasurably superior to earthly life that all present sufferings, all stern denials of attainable satisfactions, are a small price to pay for it? How can they know that conscious existence is worth having, except from their past and present experience of it? It is just because they have found a certain sweetness in life that they cannot bear the thought of its extinction. What they really desire is a kind of existence in which joys they have already experienced—they can imagine none that are totally different—are enhanced a thousand-fold, while all the toils and pains inseparable from our organic life are excluded. They too, appreciate life, in their own peculiar way. We need not pause at this point to consider whether to deny ourselves all the joyous and precious experiences which terrestrial life affords is the proper way to prepare ourselves for some superior mode of existence; whether

[1] See, for example, Walter Hilton, *The Ladder of Perfection*, Penguin Books, 1957, especially Book I, Ch. 78, etc.

our spirits are best prepared for whatever heaven may await them by contracting or by expanding them.

In addition to that stern, intransigent mysticism that tries to find God by excluding from the mind every external impression and every thought of transient things, there is a milder, more amiable variety of mysticism that seeks God in and through nature. For certain minds, the value of things visible lies not so much in themselves as in the supposed fact that they are replicas of, or were created by, something greater than themselves. As we have already noticed, Plato regarded the Creation as good because it was a copy of a far more excellent model that existed, eternally and changelessly, in the transcendent intelligible realm. Plotinus held the same view, with the elaboration that the intelligible realm, which he called *nous*, was more explicitly the emanation of something still higher, the Good or the One. In much the same vein, John Milton, centuries later, asked:

> What if earth
> Be but the shadow of heaven, and things therein
> Each to each other like, more than on earth is thought?

To the Christian nature-mystic, the world revealed to our senses is precious chiefly because God created it; he may regard it as the visible garment of Deity. To quote the fine expression of Inge, who in *Christian Mysticism* treated this type of mysticism in some detail, he 'has learnt to see the same God in nature whom he has found in the holy place of his own heart'.[1]

Certainly to applaud and love the natural world because it is regarded as the handiwork of God or a copy of a transcendent model is an attitude far more generous and wholesome than to despise or condemn this world as unworthy of the attention of the God-seeking man; but perhaps it is not quite fair to the world. Is the universe and all it contains any less beautiful and worthy of our admiration if it is a natural development than if it is the work of a supernatural Creator? And is it not just as religious to respond with grateful appreciation to the wonder of creation, considered as the result of a natural process, as to feel such gratitude when creation

---

[1] William Ralph Inge, *Christian Mysticism*, Charles Scribner's Sons, New York and London, 1899, p. 285.

is viewed as God's handiwork? For natural theology, which deduces the existence of an intelligent Creator from the order and beauty of the universe and the manifold adaptations which living things exhibit, it seems essential to begin by appraising the universe on its own merits.[1] To start by saying that the universe is excellent or wonderful because God created it, then to conclude that because the universe is fair and marvellously ordered it must have been made by God, is a viciously circular argument.

We love and admire the universe not only because it supports our lives and the lives of those dear to us but, above all, because it contains so much beauty. If we nowhere discerned beauty, if every signal that fell upon our senses, although meaningful, was as drab and uninspiring as the ticking of the telegraph, it is questionable whether we would care to live another day. Yet what is the essence of beauty? Can any common feature be found in the vast variety of things that we call beautiful, ranging from the starry heaven to some tiny blossom peeping forth from barren rocks, from a snow-crowned peak to a human face, from a symphony of a hundred instruments to the clear voice of a bird, from the sheen on a beetle's shard to the fragrance of a flower? It is doubtful whether some specific quality of beauty exists in each of the multitudinous and often strongly contrasting objects that we designate as beautiful. Things do not please us because of their possession of some mysterious quality of beauty; on the contrary, we call them beautiful because they please us through our senses, especially that of sight. Beauty is our delighted awareness, directly by means of sensation, of other beings, often at a great distance from ourselves. Whatever enriches or enhances our lives through sensuous awareness we are apt to call beautiful, and metaphorically we apply this term to intellectually apprehended objects and relations that have the same elevating effect.

The analysis of beauty provides the secret clue to the social law that underlies our spiritual life—perhaps all life. Awareness of other beings which coexist harmoniously with ourselves is intrinsically precious to us. The fundamental law that the interpretation of beauty suggests, is that the existence of every being is enhanced by

---

[1] The passage from Aristotle on p. 24 is a small sample of the method of natural theology. The whole second book of Cicero's *De Natura Deorum*, from which this quotation is taken, is probably as good an exposition of natural theology as one can find.

harmonious coexistence with other beings. The world process appears to result from the effort to achieve such coexistence on a universal scale.

The consideration of beauty brings us to the sensory organs which reveal beautiful objects to us. To the sense of vision we owe awareness of shapely forms and of the colours that make them more delightful. Colour, as the physicists point out, exists not in material objects nor yet in the luminous vibrations that they emit or reflect, but it is added by our sensory apparatus or our minds to an intrinsically colourless world. Similarly, we owe the melodies that enchant us to the organization of our sense of hearing no less than to the complex atmospheric vibrations, stirred up by voice or instrument, that impinge upon our ear-drums. Senuous beauty exists not in external objects nor yet in our minds, but arises through the interaction of an appropriate external object with our whole psycho-physical organization; so that an experience of beauty may be regarded as the fruit of a marriage between an appreciative spectator and a harmoniously formed object. The perception of beauty is never a passive state, although it may appear so to the conscious mind; when our senses are appropriately stimulated, we give birth to beauty, instantaneously.

Although many birds have more acute vision and many mammals have a keener sense of smell, it would be difficult to find any animal whose sensory equipment as a whole is superior to ours. Our ability to manipulate things, to fashion matter into innumerable useful or beautiful forms, far exceeds that of any other animal. None seems able to communicate with its fellows, by voice or other means, as adequately as we can, and none seems able to make records of its thoughts and experiences for future years, as we can do. Moreover our bodies, if properly cared for, last longer than those of most mammals, including many that are much larger than ourselves. We did not create all these advantages in ourselves; we cannot deliberately increase them in our children. With growing self-consciousness, men slowly awake to the realization of their superb endowments; and whether we attribute them directly to a divine creator or to the slow course of evolution, they are equally worthy of our gratitude. Our appreciation of the world would be incomplete if it failed to extend to the marvellous organization of our bodies and minds which is the indispensable counterpart of all external beauty; without which, indeed, there would be, for us, no beauty anywhere.

We sometimes hear it said, resignedly or accusingly, that we dwell in a purposeless universe. Although I do not believe that this is true, to demonstrate cosmic purpose is a difficult undertaking; so let us provisionally admit the contention and see what we can make of our condition as purposeful beings in a supposedly purposeless universe. Must we, as some do, give way to despair in the face of our loneliness in an alien world?

Imagine a traveller who, in the midst of a vast wilderness, stumbles unexpectedly upon a splendid mansion, elegantly furnished, and set in a beautiful garden. Birds and butterflies embellish the grounds, animals disport in the trees and feast on their fruits; but the traveller searches in vain for the mansion's owner, or for any human occupant who might tell him who built it or for what purpose it was erected. When continued investigation fails to reveal that the dwelling was built, and is claimed, by some intelligent being, he feels justified in regarding it as his own, enjoying its comforts and beauty as long as he wishes. Thereby the traveller gives significance and value to that which, as far as he could discover, was hitherto devoid of purpose, an empty, barren shell.

If we believe that the world was quite without purpose until man arose, we are in much the same situation as the traveller who found the uninhabited mansion. Lacking any earlier purpose that might conflict with our own, the universe is free to receive whatever purpose we choose to give it. Its purpose will be whatever we like, its meaning that which it pleases us to impart to it. Just as a single drop of some concentrated dye colours all the water in a large vessel; so a single purpose, if wide and strong enough, can give significance to a whole world. It can reach to the farthest visible galaxies, if only it have reference to them, as by trying to follow their evolution and to understand them.

What nobler and more worthy purpose could we introduce into a universe which, although apparently devoid of purpose, contains many marvellous and beautiful things, than that of knowing and joyously appreciating all that it contains? Such a purpose would stabilize our lives, for only by taking proper care of our bodies and minds can we keep them fit instruments for perceiving, understanding, and enjoying the world. It would bind mankind together in a common endeavour, for to know and understand a world as vast and complex as this requires many eyes, many minds freely communicating with each other. Such a purpose would replace our prevalent selfish acquisitiveness by unlimited sharing, for we can impart our knowledge and insights to many others while preserving them entire for ourselves, as we cannot do with the material possessions for which men fiercely compete. The purpose of knowing and appreciating the world in which we live would give meaning and dignity to our own lives and significance to the whole universe, as far as our knowledge embraced it; for that which is known and enjoyed no longer exists quite barrenly. A beautiful universe that contains intelligent beings who appreciate and strive to understand it, who are thankful for their existence in it, is no longer a purposeless universe, even if we suppose that it once was so. Intelligence and love have arisen and discovered a purpose that embraces the whole.

Appreciation seems an inevitable development in a world like ours. First there was the evolution of inorganic and then of organic forms. When animals arose, they needed to develop awareness of the forms that surrounded them in order to fill their vital needs and avoid disaster. With the refinement of their sensory organs and the rise of aesthetic sensibility, this awareness became a potential source of delight. That the appreciative understanding of the universe and all it contains is a proper end of human existence seems to be demonstrated by the lives of those who devote themselves to the study and contemplation of the natural world. On the whole, they live long and contentedly; even if they belong to no church, they often have an attitude toward existence that is essentially religious; yet they avoid the anguished crises that so frequently afflict those who seek a hidden God while condemning the visible world; and they rarely envy their neighbours. To go forth into the wilderness to contemplate the beauty of nature with joyous appreciation is to make a religious pilgrimage, certainly no less meritorious or spiritually rewarding than a pilgrimage to Rome, Jerusalem, Mecca, or Banaras.

It is not only the grandeur of our planetary abode beneath the revolving stars and the beauty of nature that call forth the grateful appreciation of the pious man. He is thankful, too, for such homely blessings as his daily bread, the water that assuages his thirst, the fire that warms him in the cold season, the home that shelters him, his loving wife and bright happy children. Doubtless those who dwell close to the sources of the things that support their lives, who watch their crops grow and mature beneath sunshine and showers and fell the trees that furnish their firewood, who are aware of all the hazards between the sowing and the harvest, tend to be more appreciative of life's prime necessities than city people who rarely know whence they come. The old-fashioned habit of saying a grace at mealtime at least served to remind us to be thankful; although, like all habitual acts, it was too likely to be repeated mechanically, without feeling. One who deeply appreciates his life and all that supports and embellishes it bears within his heart the seed of true religion, which he will do well to nourish tenderly, even if he can find no formal creed that seems credible to him.

How charmingly simple and satisfying would be a religion founded upon grateful appreciation alone, and expressing itself in such willing service as a benevolent Creator might require of us, without all the harassing complications which fear, sin, doubt, and despair have introduced into our actual religions! Would it have been impossible for a wise and powerful Deity to have established and preserved such a beautifully direct and friendly relationship with his creatures, if he had so desired?

Appreciation is so closely linked with natural piety that it seems impossible for a religion to grow up without it; yet in Buddhism we have an example of a world religion of which the point of departure was the very opposite of appreciation. The first of the four Noble Truths which the Buddha expounded to his five disciples, in the very first sermon that he preached after he attained enlightenment beneath the Bodhi-tree, was the truth of pain. As he declared: 'Birth is pain, old age is pain, sickness is pain, death is pain, union with unpleasant things is pain, separation from pleasant things is pain, not getting what one wishes and pursues is pain; the body is pain, feeling is pain, perception is pain, the mental elements are pain, consciousness is pain, in short, the five groups of grasping are pain. This, monks, is the Noble Truth of pain.' The other three Noble Truths revealed that the cause of pain is desire or craving; how pain could be eliminated by the extinction of desire; and how to accomplish this by following the Noble Eightfold Way.

If an ancient Stoic could have been present to hear this one-sided account of our mortal state, he doubtless would have replied:

'The door is open. Nature gives us no choice as to how we enter this world, but she permits us to leave it in many ways. One who finds life too painful may choose his mode of departure.' To one without preconceptions, this solution of the problem posed by the first Noble Truth is so obvious that the Buddha could never have built a religion on his life-denying attitude alone. But firmly embedded in the tradition which Gautama inherited were certain beliefs which prohibited the easy way out. According to the doctrine of karma, the suicide would be reborn in a worse condition than before, and so on endlessly, unless he chose more adequate means to escape from the wheel of existence. Without righteous conduct, final release from the pains of embodied life could never be achieved. When we reflect that the whole purpose of morality is to safeguard the positive values of life, it seems paradoxical that a world dominated by pain should be governed by an immanent moral principle. Nevertheless, it was on karma, far more than on the first of the Noble Truths, that the Buddha built a religion which, with later elaborations that he might not have approved, has brought consolation to untold millions of men.

That life is painful is a partial truth which needs to be complemented by another partial truth, that life is joy or happiness. Not all of those who followed the Buddha's Eightfold Noble Path were insensitive to life's sunnier side. Some of the world's earliest appreciative nature poetry was composed by Buddhist eremites who dwelt in Indian forests. One who found such delight in the free woodland life as is expressed in the following verses by a monk called Ekavihariya could hardly have been impatient to escape from it into the mysterious realm of Nirvana:

> Yea, swiftly and alone, bound to my quest
> I'll to the jungle that I love, the haunt
> Of wanton elephants, the source and means
> Of thrilling zest to each ascetic soul.
> In Cool Wood's flowery glades cool waters lie,
> Within the hollows of the hills; and there
> I'll bathe my limbs when hot and tired, and there
> At large in ample solitude I'll roam.
>
> .   .   .
>
> I'll bind my spirit's armour on, and so
> The jungle will I enter, that from thence

33

I'll not come forth till every canker's waned.
I'll seat me on the mountain top, the while
The wind blows cool and fragrant on my brow,
And burst the baffling mists of ignorance.
Then on the flower-carpet of the wood,
Anon in the cool cavern of the cliff,
Blest in the bliss of liberty I'll take
Mine ease on three, old Fastness of the Crag.[1]

[1] Mrs Rhys Davids, *Poems of Cloister and Jungle; A Buddhist Anthology,*
John Murray, London, 1941, p. 41.

3
Caring for the Self

Care, as was said in the Introduction, has two aspects, caring for or taking care of things, and caring about or being concerned for the welfare of things, even if we can do nothing practical for them. In the evolution of animal life, caring for certainly preceded caring about, which is an attitude that requires some of the higher mental faculties. We lack proof that any animal, other than man, cares about things beyond its reach, although a bird or mammal, forcibly separated from its young, may do so. Caring for things, however, is widespread in the animal kingdom, and we inherit the habit from our prehuman ancestors. This activity, with its associated attitudes, appears to be the natural root from which religion has sprung.

In the natural sequence, an animal must first of all take care of itself, for unless it preserves its own life it cannot propagate its kind. Self-preservation includes finding a suitable habitat, procuring enough food, and escaping enemies. Many animals, including insects, mammals, and birds, spend much time caring for the covering of their bodies, removing dirt or moisture, grooming fur or feathers, ridding themselves of vermin. To care for their wonderful garment of feathers, birds devote a considerable part of each day, arranging their plumage, waterproofing it with oil secreted by the gland at the base of the tail, bathing in water or in dust, which probably helps to control parasites. In the daily care of their feathers some birds assist their mates or other companions, each preening parts of the other's plumage difficult for its own bill to reach. Similarly, horses lick each other's necks and shoulders, inaccessible to their own tongues, and social insects like ants may groom each other.

In the most diverse groups of animals, care for self includes the preparation of shelters that afford protection from the elements or concealment from enemies. Even apart from nests built for holding eggs or rearing young, the nests or shelters that animals make for their own comfort and safety are of amazing diversity. They include the subterranean burrows of many worms, insect larvae, reptiles, and mammals; the silken tubes that amphipods construct among seaweeds; the rolled leaves or tents made of foliage bound together with silk in which caterpillars live singly or in groups; the untidy piles of dead leaves and other trash which such mammals as squirrels and opossums collect in trees; the neater nests that some birds, especially in the tropics, build to sleep in when they are not breeding; the holes which woodpeckers and barbets carve in trees for the same purpose. A degree of foresight seems to enter into the preparation of some of these shelters, as of those which birds make by day for use in the following night, sometimes with the provision of alternative dormitories which they can occupy if they are disturbed or threatened as they are about to retire into one at nightfall.

In many animals, care for progeny goes no farther than depositing the eggs in a spot suitable for the development of the young that will hatch from them. Other animals not only guard the eggs until they hatch but give more or less care to their growing young, as is true of many species of crustaceans, insects, fishes, amphibians, and reptiles, and of all birds except the curious megapodes of Australia and neighbouring islands. In viviparous mammals, the nutrition and development of the embryo within the maternal body are processes of which the parent may be no more aware than of any other internal function, but after birth the young must be suckled, cleaned, and protected. In a few insects, a number of fishes and mammals, and most birds, the two parents cooperate in the care of the offspring, while in some fishes, amphibians, and birds, the male alone attends the eggs and young. The habit of caring for offspring, especially when this includes the cooperation of both parents and perhaps of other individuals as well, and the persistence of family groups after the young have become self-supporting, has had the most momentous consequences for the living world. From the activities and the emotions associated with the care of offspring and life in families have grown our societies, our morality, our altruistic sentiments, and our religions.

In some of the more social animals, care extends not only to self and progeny but to the social group. As every country-dweller knows to his own cost, colonial bees and wasps may vigorously defend their nest by stinging, a practice which costs the worker bee her sting and her life. Birds warn their companions of the approach of danger, and those which nest in colonies may unite in repelling objectionable intruders. When a herd of horned ruminants, such as buffaloes, is threatened, the old males surround the bunched females and young, presenting their horns to the enemy. In his book on the red deer of Scotland, Darling described how carefully the leading hind, the matriarch of a company of females and young, watches over the safety of her band.[1] In baboons and the great apes, the mature males are guardians of the troop. The leader of a herd or troop of larger mammals often behaves in a way that suggests altruism.

There can be no doubt that the capacity for caring, especially for self, for progeny, and for social companions, is one which men share with a wide variety of animals. Our present task is to trace the growth of caring to include an ever wider range of beings, until finally the realm of things which enlist our care extends beyond those we can *care for* to those we can only *care about*. It seems natural to begin with caring for self. The word 'self' has many connotations, and in the literature on Eastern religions has acquired a quite special meaning; but for the present we shall confine our attention to the physical and social self, that is, to man as an animal with certain biological requirements and a craving for recognition by his fellows. Moreover, we need not concern ourselves with details of procuring food and providing shelter, which even among the most primitive peoples are usually group activities, but can concentrate on those aspects of care for self which have religious or quasi-religious significance. Possibly some of the practices which we shall notice as being employed by primitive men to ensure their personal safety or advancement are not properly religious, but they shade into his religious beliefs and rites in such a way that it is difficult to separate them. In a later chapter we shall consider care for that part of ourselves which, in the higher religions, is held to be immortal.

First we may notice the ancient belief in the guardian spirit or supernatural protector of the individual. The guardian angel whom, according to the official catechism of the Catholic Church, God has given to each person for his special protection, and to whom we

[1] F. Fraser Darling, *A Herd of Red Deer*, Oxford University Press, 1937, Ch. V.

should pray when tempted or in peril, is a late survival of this comforting notion. Many readers will be familiar with the daemon of Socrates, who from time to time warned him of impending dangers to himself or his friends; its role was to prohibit improper activity rather than to initiate action.[1] Otherwise we hear little in classical literature of daemons who served as personal guardians: the term is more often applied to the blessed souls of the good men of the Golden Age, who wandered over the earth veiled in clouds, observing justice and injustice, dispensing riches like kings; or else it designates an inferior order of gods.

In ancient Rome, the supernatural guardian was the genius. Especially important was the genius of the paterfamilias or head of a family, to which libations of wine were poured as to a god, and by which oaths were sworn by members of the family. This object of household worship was regarded as the mysterious power that ensured the continued existence and prosperity of the *gens* or clan. Every man was held to have a genius, a sort of spiritual 'double' that represented the higher or more godlike part of his personality. The corresponding protecting spirit of a woman, known as her Juno, was the personification of the mother spirit of the female, as the genius was of the father-spirit of the paterfamilias. The notion of the genius was extended to places, institutions, and groups of men, such as a legion, each of which was believed to have its unseen guardian, standing in the same relation to it as the genius of the paterfamilias to his family. In the imperial age, the genius of the emperor was worshipped with divine honours, a ritual which the Romans considered important as a cement to bind together the heterogeneous peoples of their empire; as, in a later age, the sovereign of Great Britain became the centre of allegiance of an even vaster realm.[2]

In ancient Egypt, the guardian spirit of each individual, known as his *ka*, accompanied him throughout his life and, when he was about to die, preceded him to the land of spirits, where it helped him to become adjusted to a new mode of existence.[3] In old Persia,

---

[1] See Plato's *Theages*, and especially the introduction to this dialogue by W. R. M. Lamb in Loeb Classical Library.

[2] John Murphy, *The Origins and History of Religions*, Manchester University Press, 1949, p. 226-7.

[3] Breasted, *op. cit.*, p. 49-50.

the disembodied doubles or protecting spirits called *fravashis* belonged only to the righteous; wicked people lacked them. These guardian angels were essential for promoting birth; they nourished animals and plants, even bodies of water, no less than men; they guarded the moon and stars; they accompanied their protégés into battle and brought them victory. In time of drought, the *fravashis* vied with each other to procure water, each for its own household, clan, or village. After death, a man's soul united with his *fravashi*; for these spirits of their ancestors pious Persians set out food and drink and raiment, in a special festival that continued for ten days.[1]

The religions of ancient Greece, Rome, Egypt, and Persia had, as everyone knows, gods far mightier than the daemons, genii, *kas*, and *fravashis* that watched over individuals, households, and the like. But to succour them amidst life's trials and perils, men everywhere have turned to some unseen friend and helper closer and more intimate than the highest god, who often seems too aloof, too preoccupied with grander affairs, to pay attention to the humble suppliant. In religious India, the supreme God Brahman appears to have only one or two temples, while Vishnu, Shiva, and lesser deities have many. The primitive Alacaluf Indians of Tierra del Fuego are said to have refrained from any worship of their high god, because his very perfection rendered vain any attempt to change his will. In certain Catholic countries, Jesus is invoked more often than God, Mary even more than her son; while the saints are called upon as protectors and their images are carried as talismans. The more human and closer to man the supernatural being, the better fitted it seems to serve as his protector, or at least as his intercessor with a higher power. It was probably because their religion recognized no deity closer to them than the mighty and jealous Yahweh that the ancient Jews so often turned to the humbler gods of their neighbours, thereby exciting the thundering denunciations of the Hebrew prophets. Although in the Protestant sects and other modern religions men are encouraged to pray directly to God when in trouble, the proper approach seems to be to request no particular favour of Omniscience, but to beseech that in his supreme wisdom he do what is best for us.

[1] James Hope Moulton, *Early Zoroastrianism*, Williams & Norgate, London, 1913, Lecture VIII.

Turning now to a more primitive religion which seems to have lacked a high god, we find the cult of the guardian spirit well developed among the Manus of the Admiralty Islands north of New Guinea. According to Dr Margaret Mead, who lived among these Melanesians in the third decade of the present century, their religion was a special combination of spiritualism and ancestor worship. The skull and finger bones of a dead male of the family were suspended in a carved bowl from the thatched roof of the dwelling, so that his spirit might become its guardian and censor. On all important occasions, the desires and preferences of this household spirit were duly consulted, usually through a female medium whose dead son served as messenger boy. This spirit was, in the first place, the stern upholder of the moral code, insisting above all on rigorous conformity to the sexual behaviour prescribed by this rather puritanical race, strict compliance with their intricate economic commitments, and adequate maintenance of the house built on piles over a tidal lagoon. The household guardian might punish laxity in any of these matters in various tragic ways, such as afflicting a newborn baby with colic or causing the death of an elder; but when everyone in the family conducted himself as he should, they counted on the spirit's watchful care. He was the special guardian of the male head of the household, and unless requested to stay at home he would accompany the father on a voyage to the mainland or on a fishing expedition. In the latter case, he was expected to provide a good catch as well as to preserve the lives and limbs of the fishermen against the machinations of evil spirits.

If some serious disaster befell the Manus household, the chief guardian spirit was held responsible. He was either demoted to the rank of guardian of some youth or small boy or else expelled from the house, to roam futilely around the village and finally degenerate into some lowly marine animal. Some other deceased male of the family was then chosen to grace the household with his skull and finger bones and serve as its mentor and guardian. When four or five years old, boys were usually given unseen guardians, who might be the spirits of dead boys, or the demoted tutelary spirits of their fathers, or else children born to other spirits—for the departed philandered, married, and begot progeny in their own shadowy realm. Although these guardians were supposed to attend the small

40

boys everywhere, the latter took little account of them until they grew old enough to have responsibilities. Women and girls lacked personal guardians, and therefore did well to avoid dangerous situations.[1]

In many totemic societies, the totem, usually an animal but less often a plant or some other object, was the supernatural guardian of all the members of the clan which claimed descent from it, or some less specific relationship with it. Among the Indians of the New World, especially the North American tribes, the notion of the supernatural guardian was widespread. Unlike the Roman genius, the Egyptian *ka*, and the Persian *fravashi*, which seem to have been the birthright of every individual, or at least of every one who was destined to be righteous, the supernatural helper in many tribes of North American Indians had to be won by personal effort, often of a heroic sort. To obtain the vision that would indicate the role, that of warrior or medicine man or sorcerer, in which he might achieve success, the Indian of the Great Plains went out alone into the wilderness, determined to wait until the vision came. Often it was recalcitrant; and to force its appearance the suppliant might torture himself mercilessly, lacerating his body, cutting off a finger, or swinging from a tall pole by straps inserted under the muscles of his shoulders. For days together, he took neither food nor water. By such drastic practices, he reduced his vitality to that low ebb at which visions are most likely to appear to an exhausted mind that has long been fixed upon and expecting them. Often the visitation was by an animal, who came in human form, talked to the suppliant, gave him a song or a formula, then revealed its true form as it departed. Exhausted by his long vigil, often bleeding from self-inflicted wounds, the Indian returned satisfied to his lodge, to follow the course in which he could rely upon supernatural power to guarantee success. If he had failed to reduce his mind to that passive state in which visions most often appear, his future seemed bleak to him.[2]

Self-torture as a means of increasing holiness or drawing closer to God is a practice by no means confined to the more primitive

[1] Margaret Mead, *Growing Up in New Guinea*, William Morrow & Co., New York, 1930, Ch. 6.
[2] Ruth Benedict, *Patterns of Culture*, Houghton Mifflin Co., Boston, 1934, Ch. IV.

societies but is often found in the higher religions of both the East and the West. Among the American Indians, as among other peoples, it has been used not only to induce visions of the supernatural but likewise for the sake of more special advantages. The Indians of Guiana believed that by lying on a nest of stinging ants, or exposing themselves to the attacks of angered wasps, they refreshed and strengthened their bodies, increased their proficiency in hunting or fishing, and gained immunity from disease. Boys and girls who had reached puberty and were about to become full-fledged members of the community were often subjected to this ordeal, not to test their courage so much as to strengthen and protect their bodies. Among the same Indian tribes, flagellation was often used with similar intent, not only in puberty rites but also as part of the preparation for a foray against an enemy. New householders and the mourners at a funeral feast were likewise flogged, apparently as a means of purification. Over much of South America, the aborigines believed that by pricking and cutting themselves they could dispel fatigue and strengthen themselves. The magical effect of this procedure depended on the instrument used to draw the blood, which in the Chaco was often an awl made from the bone of a rhea or jaguar, and in fishing tribes might be the tail of the stingray. Even small children were encouraged to jab themselves for their own supposed good.[1]

The way men have abused the human body—their own or another's—makes one of the saddest chapters in the human story. For advantages far more often imaginary than real, the savage scarifies, lacerates, and mutilates himself and his children, often most horribly. For ritual purposes, he starves or drastically purges himself; he exposes himself to extremes of cold or heat; he dances to the point of exhaustion. He seems to take a fierce delight in demonstrating the punishment he can take, the pain he can endure. In somewhat higher cultures, where self-mutilation is reduced, criminals and prisoners of war are subjected to the most appalling mutilations, often while the gaping populace looks on, morbidly fascinated. Ascetics of the most diverse faiths imagine that the more they abuse their 'vile body', the more squalid and scabrous they

[1] Julian H. Steward, editor, *Handbook of South American Indians*, vol. 5, *The Comparative Ethnology of South American Indians*, Smithsonian Institution, Bureau of American Ethnology, Bull. 143, 1949, p. 581.

permit it to become, the nearer they approach their God—as though what is loathsome to the healthy human mind could be pleasing to him! It seems that only in advanced civilizations, as in classical antiquity with its ideal of a sound mind in a sound body, does a due respect for the human body begin to emerge. Yet even in the highest civilizations that men have so far attained, continuing warfare, in which men, women, and children become objects to be carved or blown to pieces on the largest possible scale, is proof that we do not yet adequately appreciate the marvellous structure and functioning of the human body. Perhaps fully to appreciate the human organism—or any animal body of comparable complexity— one must be a biologist who has studied its slow evolution through millions of years, its elaborate structure, its intricate functioning and capacity for self-regulation. Adequately to appreciate its perceptive powers, one must be a poet.

One reason for this deficient respect for our bodies is that moralists and religionists have so often regarded them as evil. The greed and lust that they attribute to the body are in large measure faults of the mind, which craves the pleasures that it derives from sensation and excites the organism by its uncontrolled imagination. From the ethical point of view, a healthy body is neutral, capable of becoming good or bad according to the moral purpose of the in-dwelling mind, which gives its own colour to the supporting organism, like a drop of dye in a clear liquid.

Another reason for the widespread abuse of our bodies is that they are regarded as expendable—instruments to be used in the pur-suit of some higher goal, then cast off like worn-out garments. Cer-tainly by no known procedure can they be made to last indefinitely; but like any finely wrought machine, they will give longer and more satisfactory service if treated with loving care than if knocked about, overworked, or deprived of proper maintenance. Finally, there is the danger that by treating the body too tenderly we fall into sybaritic luxury, which is hardly less injurious than the hardships and mutilations to which it is subjected by savages, whose life span is generally short. Already in ancient times we had the spectacle of civilizations, with primitive austerity not far behind them, that had fallen into a revolting voluptuousness which led to their dissolution. To follow the middle way between harmful austerity and harmful indulgence is not easy, but it is well worth trying.

To regard the body as the spirit's temple, to be kept clean and garnished, carefully guarded against all polluting intrusions and defiling excesses, is one of the highest of religious conceptions. Although the ritual purity prescribed by religions for participation in their ceremonies often includes practices of doubtful value, we may recognize a physiological purity, which consists in cleanliness and abstaining from harmful or unnecessary substances, and likewise an ideal purity, which consists in avoiding practices that seem intrinsically unfitting. An example of the latter is provided by the ancient Pythagorean, Apollonius of Tyana, whose admirers regarded him as not inferior to Jesus of Nazareth. When, as a lad of fifteen, Apollonius went to live in a temple of Asclepius, he resolved to eat no flesh, to drink no wine because it clouds the spirit, to wear only linen garments and to go barefoot, because skins torn from slaughtered animals seem inappropriate as a covering for any part of a pure living body.[1]

It is through the windows and doors of the temple which is our body that we became aware of whatever in the larger world is worthy of our admiration, love, and gratitude. If the windows are clouded and the doors obstructed, we receive only confused, distorted images of the surrounding world. If they were tightly closed, we should live in utter darkness, with never a ray to illuminate the mind, if indeed a mind could develop at all in such profound isolation from every influence that might stimulate intelligence. How completely, in our present existence, we depend upon the body and its sense organs for the revelation of all that the world contains of beauty and wonder is finely expressed in the following sonnet by John Masefield:

> Here in the self is all that man can know
> Of Beauty, all the wonder, all the power,
> All the unearthly colour, all the glow,
> Here in the self which withers like a flower;
> Here in the self which fades as hours pass,
> And droops and dies and rots and is forgotten
> Sooner, by ages, than the mirroring glass
> In which it sees its glory still unrotten.
> Here in the flesh, within the flesh, behind,
> Swift in the blood and throbbing on the bone,

[1] Philostratus, *The Life of Apollonius of Tyana*, Book I, viii.

Beauty herself, the universal mind,
Eternal April wandering alone;
The God, the holy Ghost, the atoning Lord,
Here in the flesh, the never yet explored.

How shall we regard this self of ours, this microcosm that mirrors the macrocosm and is all that we can ever directly know? Should we cherish as something precious our selfhood, our individuality, our uniqueness and distinctness from all the rest of the creation; or should we, as many deeply religious men have held, bend all our efforts to shake off this sense of 'I,' this feeling of distinctness and personality, and try to merge ourselves without a remainder in a vaster whole? This latter course has been advocated, with numerous quotations from saints and mystics, by Aldous Huxley in an erudite book, *The Perennial Philosophy*, in which he maintains that the highest goal of man's existence is to attain unitive knowledge of the divine Ground of all being.

This problem can be tackled from various angles. In the first place, we reflect that individuality is the product of an immensely long evolution. An individual, in the strict meaning of the word, can neither be divided into two or more individuals nor lose its identity by fusion with other individuals. It is only in the living world that true individuals exist; inorganic bodies, like rocks and crystals, can fuse together or be fragmented with no essential change in their properties. Moreover, many plants can hardly be called individuals; they can be separated into parts each of which will continue to grow; and in numerous cases shoots of two or more plants can fuse into one by grafting. Even among animals, protozoons which multiply by fission, and invertebrates such as worms which can be cut into pieces each of which will regenerate the organs it lacks and continue to live, are only by courtesy called individuals. Individuality, in its organic aspect, belongs chiefly to the higher animals, while in its psychic aspect, which we call personality, it is still more restricted. Personality, or uniqueness in outlook, temperament, and modes of behaviour, is to some extent present in the higher vertebrates, but it is well developed only in man and increases with his level of culture. If selfhood, the product of many millions of years of evolution, is of so little worth that holiness consists in getting rid of it, the world process has evidently been going in the wrong direction, so that we can only regard it as a tremendous mistake or an unfortunate cosmic accident. The effort to divest ourselves of our individuality or selfhood is an effort to cancel or reverse the whole course of development that made us what we are.

In the second place, we reflect that it is only as selves or individuals that we know, enjoy, love, appreciate, care, and aspire. If we stay close to experience, our only safe guide, we have no warrant for supposing that any of these can exist apart from conscious individuals, so that we must doubt whether a world devoid of selves could have any value at all. Only as individuals can we be generous, helpful, and compassionate. On the other hand, it is as individuals that we hate, envy, and suffer, that we are selfish, malicious, and cruel.

This evil side of selfhood is associated with its exaggeration, with viewing it as absolute when it is only relative. The truth of our individuality and uniqueness must be complemented by the truth of our universality and sameness, by the recognition that we are inseparable parts of a greater whole. We are made of the universal substance; the universal energy flows through us, supporting our activity and thought. We are shaped by the same evolutionary process that fashioned every other living thing. In the structure of our bodies and the operation of our minds, we share the universal features of humanity; and we have much in common with the other vertebrate animals. The most unique man is but a special configuration of universal elements. Our selves are as islands in an archipelago, which on the superficial view are quite distinct from each other, but in reality are only the projecting summits of one continuous land mass covered by a shallow sea.

Our individuality and our universality, our uniqueness and our sameness with the beings that surround us, are equally precious and worthy of careful cultivation; for each of these two aspects of ourselves gives most, if not all, of its value to the other. If we were utterly unique, we should be utterly isolated; if we lacked all individuality, we should be indistinguishable from the things around us. Our sameness permits fruitful intercourse with other beings; our uniqueness is our priceless contribution to the whole. Spirituality is above all the simultaneous awareness of our uniqueness and our universality. We cannot lose sight of either of these complementary aspects of our being without falsehood and spiritual deterioration. To neglect our universality, which binds us to others, is to become unsympathetic, hard and cruel, selfish in the worst sense of the word. To neglect our uniqueness is to diminish the value of life to ourselves and our worth to society. Despite all that the mystics may say, to attempt to divest ourselves of our unique selfhood would be disastrous in this world, and a dubious advantage in the hereafter.

To this simultaneous perception of our uniqueness and our universality, the foundation of our spiritual life, we must cling with all our strength. Perhaps we can clutch it most firmly if we symbolize it; and the most adequate symbol is an organ of a living body, which is the same as the rest of the body yet different from it. Only by sharing the common or universal life of the organism to which it belongs can an organ remain alive and perform its peculiar function, yet this function depends upon its unique structure. Its separation from the body not only causes the death of the organ but likewise impairs or even kills the organism. If our eyes were composed of skin and flesh like the rest of our face, we would be immensely impoverished; their priceless contribution to our existence depends on their unique configuration no less than on their being integral parts of our body. Each of us is related to the universe as an organ to the organism which it serves, and the whole value of our lives depends on this relationship. Each of us is an organ of the universe, one of the myriad unique parts by which the creative energy finds expression. And one of the chief functions of these organs which we are seems to be to know and appreciate the universe, to respond feelingly to its beauty and wonder, thereby giving significance to its existence—and to our own.

4

Caring for the Family and Tribe

In the natural sequence, care for self is followed by care for progeny, then for the families, clans, and larger groups which arise as children grow up, marry, and produce a succession of generations. As Herbert Spencer pointed out, primitive man lived in small groups which displayed internal amity and external enmity; each tribesman regarded all the rest of mankind with suspicion or hatred. Even amity within a group rarely amounted to true friendship, which depends, as Cicero so finely said, on having within one's own soul that which makes us worthy to be loved. The savage, who rated his fellows by the number of enemies they had slain or their prowess as huntsmen, rather than by such relatively modern virtues as honour, veracity, justice, and compassion, had not yet developed that ideal of character which is the foundation of noble friendship. The amity within the group was simply such solidarity and cooperation as was indispensable to its survival in an often harsh environment, surrounded by enemies. It was not unmarred by jealousies, bickerings, and occasional murders. Hence in primitive societies, even as in our own, we rarely find that concern for the welfare of neighbours which we would have if we loved them as ourselves.

In pleasing contrast to the harshness of many primitive societies stand the Mountain Arapesh of north-eastern New Guinea, as seen by Dr Mead, who lived among them and studied their culture in the early 1930s. These Papuans, who wore only scanty clothing and were careless how well it covered them, inhabited a mountainous terrain so rugged and broken that only on the backs of the ridges could they find a little fairly level land for their tiny settlements of crudely built huts. In the surrounding hills they grew taro, yams, plantains, and sago palms, often on slopes so steep that fencing

48

their gardens against their wandering pigs presented an almost insoluble problem. Their provision patches were scattered widely through the brushland, amid which the men hunted tree kangaroos, wallabys, opossums, and cassowaries. These coastal mountains were too unproductive to be coveted by neighbouring tribes, thus freeing the Arapesh of the necessity of preserving a warlike character in order to defend their homeland and permitting them to develop gentler ways.

In an easy-going, non-acquisitive, uncompetitive society, the Arapesh

see all life as an adventure in growing things, growing children, growing pigs, growing yams and taros and coconuts and sago, faithfully, carefully, observing all of the rules that make things grow. They retire happily in middle age after years well spent in bringing up children and planting enough palm-trees to equip those children for life. . . . The duty of every child is to grow, the duty of every man and woman is to observe the rules so that the children and the food upon which the children depend will grow. Men are as wholly committed to this cherishing adventure as are women. It may be said that the rôle of men, like the rôle of women, is maternal.

Not to amass wealth, not to outshine one's neighbours or to dominate them, but to care for things, watching them grow and develop, seems to be the ruling passion of every typical Arapesh man and woman. Despite their niggardly environment—or possibly because of it—the Arapesh developed an almost Utopian attitude to life.

The Arapesh believe that the father and mother contribute equal amounts of material to the formation of the 'egg' from which a baby will develop. Not until the swelling and discoloration of the mother's breasts show that the embryo has been formed is the father's procreative task deemed to be complete; thereafter, he must strictly refrain from intercourse, so that the developing child may sleep undisturbed in its mother's womb, placidly absorbing its nutriment. To ensure the proper growth and easy delivery of her baby, the mother must abstain from certain foods, such as the bandicoot, which would make her die in hard labour, the frog, which would cause too sudden a delivery, and the eel, which would bring on premature birth. The father must not be present while the baby is delivered in a special hut, but after it has been washed and brought up into the village, he begins a complicated and exacting ritual, for the new life is as closely joined to his as to the mother's. For the first day, both parents lie on the ground beside the newborn baby, fasting and abstaining from water and tobacco. Together the parents perform small magical rites, to ensure the infant's welfare and their ability to care for it. In one of the most significant of these rites, the father cuts a large yam into small pieces, each of which he names after a small boy of the village. Then, taking up the pieces in reverse order, the mother gives them the names of little girls. Finally, the father throws the bits of yam away. This charm ensures that the infant will grow up to be hospitable and friendly toward neighbours, a prime consideration in the education of an Arapesh child.

The father of a first child is in a situation even more delicate than that of the mother. For five days he remains in strict seclusion with her, not touching tobacco with his hands, scratching himself only with a stick, and eating all his food with a spoon. Then he is taken to a pool for an elaborate ritual bath. Returning to the village, he and the mother perform more ceremonies to lift the taboos surrounding childbirth. Later they make a feast for the midwife and the other women who fed them during their confinement.

To ensure the welfare of the growing baby, the father must sleep each night beside it and the mother; yet, until the child begins to walk, he must strictly avoid intercourse with her, as with his other wife, if he has one. (Among the Arapesh, a married man may take his brother's widow as a second wife.) This prohibition prevents the strain on the mother's strength which would result from closely spaced pregnancies, as likewise the necessity of weaning the child too soon. Whenever possible, it is nursed at the breast until it is three or four years old, and has gradually become accustomed to eating solid food. Both boys and girls are treated throughout childhood with the most tender affection. They are taught to love and trust all relatives on both sides of the family, to look upon all neighbours as friends—only the Plainsmen, who are arrogant, warlike, and practise black magic to the detriment of the Mountain Arapesh, are regarded with suspicion and dread.

Dr Mead described a unique custom of these mountain people:

An Arapesh boy grows his wife. As a father's claim to his child is not that he has begotten it but rather that he has fed it, so also a man's claim to his wife's attention and devotion is not that he has paid a bride-price for her, or that she is legally his property, but that he has actually contributed the food which has become flesh and bone of her body. A little girl is betrothed when she is seven or eight to a boy about six years her senior, and she goes to live in the home of her future husband. Here the father-in-law, the husband, and all of his brothers combine to grow the little bride. Upon the young adolescent husband particularly falls the onus of growing yams, working sago, hunting for meat, with which to feed his wife. In later years, this is the greatest claim that he has upon her. If she is dilatory or sulky or unwilling, he can invoke this claim: 'I worked the sago, I grew the yams, I killed the kangaroo that made your body. Why do you not bring in the firewood?' And in those exceptional cases when the arranged marriage falls through from the death of the betrothed husband, and the girl is betrothed again after she has attained her growth, the tie is never felt to be so close . . .

The Arapesh believe that parents should be able to control their children whom they have grown, and on the same principle, they believe that husbands should be able to control their wives; they have grown them, they are responsible for them, they are older and have better judgment. The whole organization of society is based upon the analogy between children and wives as representing a group who are younger, less responsible, than the men, and therefore to be guided.[1]

When the Arapesh boy is thirteen or fourteen years of age, his father selects his future wife, trying to find a girl with many male kindred, men who are successful gardeners and hunters, wise and slow to anger. With his brothers-in-law the boy will make widely scattered provision patches, working here with one gardening-partner and there with another. The little girl goes to live in the home of her betrothed, where she works with her future mother-in-law and plays with her sisters-in-law, behaving in all respects like one of them, and coming to feel as warmly toward her future

[1] Margaret Mead, *Sex and Temperament in Three Primitive Societies*, William Morrow & Co., New York, 1935, Ch. 6.

husband's family as toward her own. To him she is another small girl, his special small girl, whose hand he takes as they go along rough trails. Not until she reaches puberty and has gone through the rites that accompany the first menstruation does the marriage take place with a simple ceremony; and only some time after this, in the normal course of events, do these two young people, who have long known that they belonged to each other, lie together as husband and wife.

When he reached puberty, long before his marriage, the boy was initiated into adult status and made a full-fledged member of the community by one of those 'rites of passage' which figure so prominently in the rituals of primitive peoples. The idea underlying this rite is that the adolescent lad dies as a child, to be reborn as a man. The older males of many tribes appear to resent this intrusion of the youngsters into their ranks, and they have made the passage so long and severe, including such features as starvation, exposure, flagellation, scarification, and circumcision, that some of the initiants succumb. The Arapesh, on the contrary, welcome rather than resent the admission to full tribal status of the boys they have so lovingly grown, yet they retain some of the typical features of primitive initiation ceremonies. For two or three months, the initiants live separated from the company of women in special quarters, usually in small groups; although sometimes the son of an important man goes through the lengthy ritual alone. The boys are incised, and they must run the gauntlet between two rows of men armed with stinging nettles—severities which are supposed to help the novices to grow. A sacrificial meal of the blood of older men is held to have the same beneficial effect. The boys are shown the cult objects of the tribe and taught their esoteric meaning. Although the initiants observe special food taboos, they are fed liberally by the older men who sponsor them; they are taken daily to bathe in a stream; and at the end of their period of seclusion they return to their mothers and sisters splendidly attired, shining with health and vigour.

The men of certain savage tribes keep their females in awed subjection by means of a supernatural being that noisily proclaims its presence, often by means of bull-roarers. To intimidate their women would be contrary to the whole spirit of the Arapesh, who regard the sexes as equal partners with complementary functions.

Yet when there is a big feast, and distant flute-notes herald the approach of the mysterious *tamberan*, the women run down the steep slopes at the edge of the village, carrying their infants in net bags and dragging the toddlers who cling to their mothers' grass skirts. The fleeing women are careful not to look behind, for some dreadful calamity would befall the one whose eyes fell on the forbidden thing. Only after the imaginary being has disappeared into its gaily decorated little house are the fugitives called back to cook and participate in the feast. The *tamberan* cult, and the harsher features of the boys' puberty rites, appear to be archaic survivals that have become incongruous with the Arpesh culture but have been retained, and crudely fitted in by means of reinterpretation, because such relics of an earlier age are so hard to cast off. Such persistent archaism has dogged most cultures and religions, making it difficult for them ever to conform to the most enlightened contemporary thought.

The religion of the Arapesh, as revealed in our source, is quite simple. They believe in spirits called *marsalais*, who inhabit high waterfalls, quicksands, or waterholes and manifest themselves in the form of an oddly-coloured snake or lizard or less often some larger animal. There are also ghosts of ancestors who hover over and protect the ancestral lands and have some ill-defined connection with the *marsalais*.

The Arapesh seem to have no shamans; but in a fit of anger or resentment one of them may procure a bit of the 'dirt' of the person who offended him and place it in the hands of a sorcerer among the neighbouring Plainsmen, who by sympathetic magic can cast a withering spell upon the person who carelessly dropped some half-eaten food, a cast-off rag, or something else intimately associated with himself. If, perhaps after a long interval, sickness or some other calamity befalls the one who was placed in the sorcerer's power, the betrayer, having long ago forgotten his dudgeon, is said to be sorry.

Despite the primitive character of their religious notions, the Arapesh have an attitude toward life that would be creditable to a higher religion. Did some illiterate, forgotten genius of the spiritual life—some unchronicled Laotse or Jesus—teach these savages to be gentle and cherishing, loving and forgiving; or did their ideal of life develop by imperceptible degrees through the generations?

However this may be, we can hardly doubt that the peculiar traits of the Arapesh owe much to their environment, a mountainous land too lean to tempt neighbouring warlike tribes, thus permitting these mountaineers to develop a pacific temper, while the difficulty of producing food prevented their sinking into enervating luxury.

The Arapesh father who, surrounded by prohibitions, lies beside his wife and newborn child, is practising a sort of couvade. Typical couvade was formerly practised in such widely separated regions as eastern Asia, the Pyrenees, and western North America, but it was most prevalent among the Indians of South America. In contrast to the situation among the Arapesh, the couvadist father may spend several days in his hammock or bed, as though recovering from an exhausting experience, while the mother gets up and goes about her daily work a day, or even a few hours, after the delivery of her baby. When not even the mother is confined, the behaviour of the father can hardly be regarded as a symbolic lying-in; more probably, he keeps to his hammock because he is so hedged about by taboos that he can hardly do anything else. In any case, the practice of couvade springs from the belief that father and newborn child are joined by so close a bond that any improper activity of the former would be harmful to the latter in its present helpless state.

During the mother's pregnancy, the parents, or in some tribes only the father, must strictly abstain from eating, or even touching, certain animals or plants which would, by occult sympathy, transmit undesirable traits to the child, or cause a difficult delivery. The dietary restrictions on the father, which in certain South American tribes permitted him to eat little more than cassava cakes, continued for a variable period after the birth, sometimes only a day or two, more frequently until the navel cord fell from the baby, and in extreme cases for more than three months. For part or even all of this long period, he lived in confinement and of course could do no work. Even when permitted to move about more freely, the father must refrain from a number of activities which might in some mysterious way harm the baby. For three or four months after the birth, Macushí parents of both sexes ate only cakes and soup made from cassava (manioc) and did no work. Since the use of sharp instruments of any kind, even at a distance, would have imperilled the infant, the father had to give up hunting, fishing, felling trees, carving wood, and similar activities for this long interval. In another

South American tribe, the Galibi, the new father permitted himself to be whipped and stung by venomous ants. Until his first-born child was nearly a year old, a father among the Island Carib refrained from eating turtles lest his offspring become deaf, from parrots lest its nose grow too big, from crabs lest its legs become too long, and from many other animals for reasons of the same order.[1]

It might be questioned whether all these practices, which to the modern reader appear so absurd, fall properly within the scope of religion. They first appear at a stage of cultural evolution when men's activities were not divided into neat compartments, when magic and religion and myth and tribal rules were so interwoven that it was hardly possible to separate them. Certain practices of this character were to become embedded in the more advanced religions, where they survive to this day. Although many of the prohibitions surrounding childbirth and the care of babies are founded on belief in sympathetic magic, the motive that prompted them is no less religious than that behind infant baptism: to ensure the most favourable prospects for the newborn child. And the motive, not the ridiculous restrictions themselves, is all that need concern us here. That, for the welfare of his child, the savage was willing to submit to so many inconveniences and hardships, to starve and confine himself, even to shed his blood, speaks well for his capacity for caring. Primitive man's willingness to deny himself pleasures for the welfare of his progeny might put many moderns to shame. If we could combine this self-sacrificing devotion with our present scientific understanding of which practices are effective and which are futile, we might go far toward solving some of the most vexing problems that confront mankind.

One of the most common ways in which primitive man showed his care for himself, his family, and his fellow tribesmen was by the observance of taboos, or prohibitions applied not only to certain acts regarded as having undesirable consequences, but to contact with certain people or things possessed of dangerous potency. It is hardly possible to grasp the significance of the taboo in its whole range without some understanding of the primitive notion of agency or power. To any object, living or inanimate, which stood out from its class because of its size or activity, as to any phenomenon

---

[1] Alfred Métraux *in* Steward, *op. cit.* p. 369–74.

which strongly aroused the savage's interest yet for which no naturalistic explanation was available, he was likely to ascribe a mysterious potency which anthropologists call 'mana'. The term is of Melanesian origin, but it designates a way of thinking that appears to have been universal among men at a certain stage of intellectual development. Mana may be possessed by people, especially those with some exceptional ability, such as a warrior who slays many enemies, a medicine man unusually successful in his cures, or a craftsman of outstanding skill. Mana is also present in artifacts, such as the canoe that out-distances others, the bow that shoots farthest, the axe of superior quality. To the plant that yields an unusually abundant crop or a superior variety of fruit, mana may be ascribed, as likewise to an animal of extraordinary strength or cunning. Even such things as stones or bits of wood of arresting shape, talismans of all kinds, are believed to have mana.

This mysterious potency, which may inhere in a wide variety of things, was not originally attributed to spirits; belief in mana appears to have preceded the concept of spirits. The object in which mana was detected seems to have been viewed as possessing just enough life, will, and power to produce its arresting effects, without being endowed with sufficient personality to be considered a spirit. The notion of mana or mysterious power belongs to that fecund matrix of man's thought from which both magic and religion were to become differentiated as alternative methods for dealing with situations where ordinary human means are unavailing.

This inexplicable power which our uncritical ancestors detected in so many people and things is not, primarily, either friendly or hostile to men. Like fire or electricity, to which it has been compared, its effects depend largely on how it is handled. The fire which cooks our food and warms our houses may consume them and us if permitted to get out of control; the electric current that lights our homes and performs a thousand other useful services may kill the man who carelessly makes contact with it. It is exactly the same with supernatural power; everything depends upon the way it is treated. The taboo was, in effect, an effort to control this fire, to insulate this electric charge. Hence it must be regarded as an institution for safeguarding the people, an expression of care for the welfare of one's neighbours. It is a manifestation of moral concern among people who have not yet developed sufficient generality of thought to make ethical maxims of wide application, but require a special rule for every different situation.

As is to be expected, the things tabooed were just as diverse as those to which mana or mysterious power was ascribed. Many examples are given in Sir James Frazer's great collection of primitive lore, *The Golden Bough*. Kings, chiefs, and priests were often surrounded by taboos, lest the common man be hurt by contact with their superior power. In many nations, ranging from Persia to Japan and Mexico, the divine ruler could not touch the earth; in his palace, he walked on finely wrought mats or carpets; when travelling abroad, he rode in a chariot, in a litter, on horseback, or on the shoulders of bearers. Like electricity, the magical potency with which he was charged might drain away by contact with so good a conductor as the earth; or traces of it, lingering on the surface, might blast or destroy the common man who carelessly set his foot where divinity had trod. Even the names of sacred persons, like those of gods, were in many cases so charged with power that to utter them was dangerous, and accordingly tabooed.

Practically worldwide in tribal societies was the taboo on menstruating women and those in childbirth, who had to remain isolated, often in special huts, until they could be cleansed of the potency which primitive man detected in fertility and rendered safe for other people to approach. Blood, as the vehicle of the mysterious life power, was heavily charged with mana which those who shed it could absorb, thereby becoming dangerous to their fellows until they had undergone ritual purification; hence the taboos surrounding warriors and manslayers. Among lifeless things tabooed in various tribes were iron, sharp weapons, hair and nails, spittle, knots and rings, and many kinds of foods. The foods might be prohibited either permanently or in special situations, as we noticed while discussing the couvade.

In man, the instinct of self-preservation seems to be more strongly developed than in any other animal; he clings to life more stubbornly and tenaciously. Other animals do all they can to escape present and recognized dangers, but they are largely oblivious of remote or hidden perils; and the inevitability of death seems not to perturb them. Man anticipates threats to his existence; he fears unseen powers that may harm him no less than visible dangers; he rebels with every fibre of his being against the extinction of his conscious life. If we may assume, as is reasonable, that the tenacity with which an animal clings to life is a measure of the value which life has for it, then we may conclude that for man life is a richer, more rewarding experience than it is for other creatures. Or at least we may conclude that it is potentially so; and although many of us pass through the world with our potentialities most inadequately realized, we hold fast to our miserable, thwarted lives in the persistent hope that somehow we shall at last come into full possession of those capacities for significant existence that we dimly feel to be latent in us.

Throughout the long course of man's spiritual and intellectual evolution, there has been growing awareness, by no means equally developed in every individual, that the value of the life to which each individual so passionately clings does not depend on that life alone. Even if a single individual could somehow maintain himself on an otherwise lifeless planet, he would find his existence there poor and barren, with little to sweeten it. The value of our lives depends on the lives that surround us, not only those of our own species and perhaps the other species on which we rely for subsistence, but on the many kinds of living things that embellish and give interest to the world. Thus the instinct of self-preservation would be sadly inadequate if it did not extend beyond the self. To preserve our lives in the fullness and richness they are capable of attaining, we must preserve much more than our lives. Accordingly, as man has matured in spirit, his care has extended ever farther from his individual self, to his family and tribe, to the shades of his ancestors and the gods, to the plants and animals that surround him, and finally to humanity and the whole world, as far as his influence on them could extend. In the following chapters, we shall trace this expansion in the scope of man's caring.

5

Caring for the Dead and
the Gods

Many animals care for their helpless offspring; man alone cares for his aged and his dead. Although men attend their slowly developing young for a longer time than other animals, certain other vertebrates, especially birds, nurture their progeny with equal devotion, sometimes working with such intensity that to continue for many months would exhaust them. In all those animals whose young are born or hatched in a dependent state, parental assistance is indispensable for the survival of the species. The more efficient the care, the more successful the species will be; hence parental solicitude will be promoted by natural selection. But the aged, who can no longer produce, or attend, young, contribute little to the survival of a species, except in social animals which can profit by the experience or wisdom of their elders. The dead contribute nothing at all, unless they are eaten by their own kind, as has happened in certain tribes of men. Hence the usual processes of evolution, random variation and natural selection, can hardly give rise to any special methods for dealing with the dead. Only when it develops such psychic qualities as affection, sympathy, foreboding, fear, and, above all, imagination, is an animal likely to pay much attention to its lifeless companions. Since these are among the mental attributes that have given birth to religion, it is no accident that care for the dead is closely associated with religion's earliest stages. Indeed, those thinkers who see in the cult of the dead the origin of the idea of God can present a strong case for their thesis.

It might be argued that methods for dealing with the dead would be promoted by natural selection because of hygienic advantages. Prompt disposal of the corpse should help control disease. The advantage of prompt and efficient disposal, as by burial or burning, would be considerable only in a fairly dense, sedentary population. When populations are thin and nomadic, when there is no lack of scavenging animals to clean the flesh from the bones, the biological advantage of isolating or promptly destroying the human corpse might be too slight to compensate for the considerable effort involved. Yet man began to take special care of his deceased comrades at a time when his food-gathering or hunting-and-fishing economy could support only sparse populations, and, moreover, the methods he followed were often far from hygienic. The survival value of his mortuary practices can hardly account for their origin, for which we must look to psychic factors.

To discover the most primitive methods of disposing of the dead we may turn, not only to the archaeological records of prehistoric epochs, but also to those retarded tribes which have persisted, until recent times, in the more remote parts of the earth. There is evidence that, in the Paleolithic Period, Neanderthaloid men already took special care of their dead. At Le Moustier in France, during the Ice Age, the deceased were interred in the same caves where the living found refuge from the harsh climate. Beside the dead person were placed food, weapons for hunting and tools for digging, the ornaments he had worn; then flat stones were laid above the corpse, especially over the head. One youth was buried lying on his side, his head resting upon a heap of flint points for spears or arrows, a finely wrought hand-axe within his reach.

It is evident that even at this early period men believed that their life would somehow continue after they died. But it required long ages to develop the concept of an immortal spirit or soul, with a nature and mode of being wholly distinct from that of the material body. In the minds of our remote ancestors, after death men continued to exist much as before, preserving the familiar form in which from time to time they appeared in dreams to their surviving companions, still needing food and weapons and all the other appurtenances of living, still delighting to adorn their unsubstantial bodies—all in a vague and shadowy region, difficult to reach.

Not only in caverns, but even in dwellings erected by human hands, men have not infrequently kept the dead in the abodes of the living. House burial was frequent in many parts of the earth, and probably still persists in remote parts of the Amazon Valley. If the deceased had been a chief, the house was likely to be abandoned; but a humbler family might continue to inhabit the hut beneath whose earthen floor the corpse was interred, sometimes too shallowly to seal in the odour of decay. In some cases the burial was omitted, the corpse simply being kept in the occupied dwelling while it dried or decayed, meanwhile receiving offerings of food, even the kisses and caresses of a bereaved wife or mother, who might speak affectionately to it.

Another primitive method of disposing of the corpse was to lay it in a tree or on a raised platform, often with food or a weapon beside it, until it decayed. Or it might be buried shallowly, perhaps with the head exposed above the ground, until the bones were clean. In this case, the skull was often brought into the house, to be preserved as a talisman or oracle and receive occasional symbolic offerings from surviving relatives. Or a woman might hang from her neck her husband's skull or that of the child whom death had snatched prematurely from her. Other bones were sometimes carried about in the same fashion. Animals, too, occasionally treat the dead as though they still lived. Monkeys and apes have been known to cherish a dead baby until it decayed or dried up, after which it was dropped; a cow given a stuffed calf-skin to replace her lost calf licked it fondly; and birds may continue, sometimes for days, to bring food to a nest where their young lie dead, or from which they have been taken by a predator.

When so little care is taken to separate the corpse from the living, when the fleshless bones are kept close to the warm body of a bereaved survivor and receive demonstrations of affection, it is evident that the dead inspire neither fear nor repugnance in those who remain behind. Apparently the primitive mind has not yet grasped the full significance of death: its irreversibility; the vast chasm which, as we now see it, it interposes between ourselves and those most dear to us. To these simple children of nature, death is but another passage on life's path, like that from the womb to the outer air or that from boyhood to manhood, to be celebrated with appropriate rites.

At a somewhat more advanced stage of culture, we meet a different attitude toward the dead, which finds expression in more effective ways of separating them from the living. Now they are buried in deep graves, over which a heavy slab may be laid, or which may be covered with a cairn of stones or a massive mound of earth.

Elsewhere they are laid to rest in natural or artificial grottoes in a cliff, which are carefully sealed. That the object of such laborious methods of interring the dead was to prevent their returning to familiar scenes is evident from certain special practices that travellers and anthropologists have recorded. The limbs of the corpse might be securely tied, as among the Tupi Indians of South America, so that it cannot rise up to trouble the living. The body may be sewn up in an oxhide, as among the Damara of Africa. The spine of the corpse may be broken; it may be securely nailed to the coffin; or the grave may be enclosed by a fence too high to jump over—all for the purpose of preventing the dead person's return to the abodes of the living.[1]

Such burial practices were prompted by fear of the ghost. Those banished by death to a shadowy land were believed to be jealous of relatives who still enjoyed all the solid satisfactions of life in the flesh, and to be capable of harming the living. Why this change from the trusting, at times clearly affectionate, attitude toward the deceased that marked the earlier stage? Paul Radin's *Primitive Religion* contains an interesting suggestion. The prototype of the returning ghost is the shaman or medicine-man, who in primitive societies serves as intermediary between his less imaginative neighbours and the supernatural. The shaman is typically a man or woman of epileptic tendencies who has learned how to bring on self-induced trances, in which his ghost or spirit seems to wander afar, picking up desired information. Although the tribesmen call upon the shaman at crises in their lives, as in sickness, or when the rains fail or game is scarce, they hate and fear him, because he so often takes advantage of his supposed supernatural power to intimidate his neighbours and fleece them of their property. Since the dead man and his ghost are associated in the primitive mind with the avaricious shaman and his wandering spirit, they are, not unnaturally, viewed with the same distrust that the shaman inspires. Thus, from an early period, shamans and priests, playing for their own selfish ends on man's superstitious fears, have influenced the development of religious thought to a degree that it is now hardly possible to assess.

To prevent the dead person from troubling the living, it was not enough to seal him in a tomb, to bury him deeply in the ground with a massive pile of earth or stones above him, or to burn his

[1] Grant Allen, *The Evolution of the Idea of God*, Ch. 3 and 4.

corpse on a pyre. To send him to the realm of the shades and keep him contentedly there involved expensive procedures. It is difficult to learn to what degree a son who gave his parents a costly burial, and for years carried on the exacting cult of the dead, was motivated by fear, and to what degree he acted from filial piety, affection, and similar feelings. Doubtless his attitude toward his dead parents was ambivalent, as those of children toward a living parent commonly are. Good children love a kind, affectionate parent; but when they have been disobedient and expect punishment, they fear him. After they outgrow parental authority, a more purely affectionate relationship may prevail between the son or daughter and the respected parents who gave them a happy childhood; but where, as in patriarchal societies such as ancient Rome, even a grown son is subject to paternal authority, a trace of fear might long persist in his attitude toward his father. Probably in all cultures which had a continuing cult of the dead, the attitude toward ancestors whose rites were obligatory varied with the temperament of the individual and his former relationship to the deceased. Certainly in many cases men cared lovingly for their dead; yet, especially if the customary rites were neglected, disquietude or fear might arise.

Even in the advanced civilizations of ancient Greece and Rome, archaic rites and beliefs respecting the dead and their mode of existence persisted until they were tardily, and far from completely, changed by the Greek Mysteries and the spread of Christianity. From classical literature we learn the tremendous importance that was attached to giving the corpse a proper burial or cremation. As Aeneas, on his descent to Hades with the sibyl, approached the Stygian Lake bearing the Golden Bough, he was accosted by the shade of Palinurus, his former pilot. This unfortunate Trojan had slipped and fallen overboard while attending the helm, and after three nights in the water had reached the Italian shore, only to be murdered by the savage inhabitants. Now his bones lay scattered along the beach, and his ghost was doomed to wander disconsolate on the hither shore of Styx, denied passage to the abode of the dead, until his remains were buried—which the sibyl promised would soon be done.[1]

Antigone, that paragon of a sister and daughter, defying the order of her uncle Creon who ruled in Thebes, spread dust over the

[1] Virgil, *Aeneid*, Canto 6.

corpse of her brother Polynices, lying neglected outside the city walls where he had died in battle, and for this pious yet audacious act was immured alive in a tomb by Creon's order.[1] In historic times, the Greeks considered it a religious duty to permit the burial of foes fallen in battle; to deny the shade the rest that could be won only by means of due performance of the funeral rites was too terrible a vengeance to inflict upon enemies. The outraged Athenians sentenced to death their victorious commanders who had failed to recover the corpses of fellow citizens killed in the naval engagement with the Spartans at Arginousae. Athenian law required that every one, except condemned criminals and traitors, be given proper burial, at the expense of the community if need be. As Rohde remarked, more than sanitary considerations or simple piety was involved in this rule: unable to rest until its mortal remains are interred with due rites, the ghost may sorely afflict the land in which it is detained against its will.[2]

One of the most widespread of customs, among all peoples throughout the earth except those who have accepted the more advanced religions, is that of sending off the dead with everything needful in a new existence conceived as not greatly different from the old familiar one. A king or important noble was sometimes interred with immense treasure, a chariot and animals to pull it, and a whole retinue of guards, musicians, and other attendants, either murdered for the occasion or else buried alive, as in the great death-pit of the Chaldees[3] uncovered by Sir Leonard Woolley at Ur. The widespread practice of sacrificing the wife to accompany her deceased husband persisted until our own time in the Hindu suttee. Important Egyptians were sealed up in cliff-tombs with wonderful works of art, but not with servants killed for the occasion.

For the realistic method of sending the dead grandee's actual slaves and attendants with him into the realm of the shades, the Chinese long ago substituted the more humane procedure of furnishing his tomb with ceramic figures, including those of servants, guards, dancing girls, actors, and even concubines, which figures, especially in the T'ang Dynasty, were beautifully modelled in the

[1] Sophocles, *Antigone.*

[2] Erwin Rohde, *Psyche: The Cult of Souls and Belief in Immortality among the Greeks*, Routledge & Kegan Paul, London, 1950, p. 163.

[3] Sir Leonard Woolley, *Ur of the Chaldees*, Pelican Books, 1952, Ch. 2.

round and of high artistic merit. Nothing necessary for the comfort and pleasure of the deceased could be omitted, for unless the model were placed in the tomb, its spiritual counterpart could not serve the dead.[1] In warlike societies, the deceased warrior was often sent to the abode of the dead along with his horse, his dog, and all his armour. Humbler people everywhere had, perforce, to dismiss their dead less lavishly equipped; but to inter the corpse along with food, drink, clothing, ornaments, and the weapons or tools appropriate to its sex, was a common practice. In some primitive societies, all the dead man's possessions were buried with him, and if he was interred in his dwelling, the house or hut might be abandoned.

The vast sacrifice of wealth involved in these mortuary practices must arouse the wonder of anyone who reflects how eagerly, in the more advanced civilizations of both ancient and modern times, heirs look forward to their inheritance, how often they quarrel privately or in the law courts over its division. What mental attitudes, what sentiments, impelled the survivors to seal up treasures of art where they were never expected to be seen again; to relinquish weapons, tools, or household utensils that it would be laborious to replace; to skimp the food of the living in order to nourish the dead, as must frequently have happened in primitive economies that could barely make ends meet? Was superstitious fear, or mechanical adherence to established custom, or pride in a lavish funeral display, or genuine affection for the deceased, the impelling motive? Doubtless, as in most human undertakings, the motives were more often mixed than single. Yet I surmise that the offerings were laid by loving hands in the poorer graves more frequently than in the wealthy ones. The powerful monarch might, during his lifetime, command the erection and furnishing of the pyramid or mausoleum where he would one day rest; the provisioning of a humble burial often represented a genuine sacrifice by the bereaved relatives.

We can hardly imagine what benefits the dead derived from the articles interred with them, but we cannot doubt that two other classes of people have profited immensely from these mortuary practices. The first consists of the grave-looters, who were already active in ancient times, making it desirable to wall up or to guard the richer tombs. Without their activities through the ages, a substantial proportion of the world's gold might now lie hidden in

[1] Murphy, *op. cit.*, Ch. XXXI.

the burial places. Even today, in Latin America, hunting and excavating old Indian graves is a popular pastime and for some men a lucrative occupation. The second class of beneficiaries consists of the archaeologists and historians, who have learned much about the arts and mode of life of vanished peoples from what they have found in graves. The intention to equip the cherished dead with what they would need in another world has actually provided fascinating information for us who live in a world inconceivably different from that which held these old rites and beliefs.

To bury or burn the dead along with whatever they might need for comfort or pleasure in the realm of the shades was still not sufficient. They had constantly to be remembered, with gifts more substantial than the occasional wreath or bouquet of flowers which is all that our modern dead receive. Unless they were nourished by repeated offerings of food and drink, unless the traditional rites were duly carried out by their descendants, the ghosts would return to plague those who were remiss. Where, as in prehistoric Europe, a massive stone was laid over the grave, animals were sacrificed on it, their blood permitted to trickle down into the soil beneath which the deceased rested. The gravestones often contained hollows that were evidently made to hold blood or other liquid offerings, such as honey or wine. Often the whole carcase of the sacrificial animal was burnt, so that the subtle essence of the animal might become available to the subtle being who inhabited the grave. This ghostly being was believed to remain closely associated with its material body, living underground, sallying forth unseen to eat and drink the offerings left at the grave for it. Even after the Greeks and Romans had developed the belief in Hades and the Islands of the Blest, where the shades of the departed lived on in such happiness or suffering as they had earned for themselves while on earth, they continued to offer food at the tomb, as though the ghost still lingered there. The simultaneous existence of contradictory beliefs, or the discrepancy between belief and practice, will surprise no one familiar with the history of customs, religions, and popular superstitions.

Among the Indo-European peoples from Italy to India, the cult of the dead was in ancient times the family religion. In these strictly patriarchal cultures, the priesthood of this private religion passed from father to son. To beget sons was tremendously important to the men of old, for if the family became extinct in the male line, no one would remain to carry on the ancestral rites, to provide the food and drink deemed indispensable to the happiness of the deceased. A man not blessed with a son might adopt one to inherit his name and property, along with the duty of attending his grave and those of his forefathers with all the customary rites. If a man failed to take this precaution, not only he, but the whole line of his male ancestors, would be left without that support which the dead required of the living.[1]

Although usually strangers could not participate in the family cult of the dead, which might be profaned by their presence, in exceptional circumstances they could substitute for lineal descendants. After the defeat of the Persians at Plataea, the Plataeans undertook the care of the Greek soldiers who had died and were interred on the field of battle. Each year, at a fixed date, the citizens of this small town, accompanied by their chief magistrates and bearing jars of milk, wine, oil, and ointments, marched in solemn procession to the cemetery. Laying these offerings among the tombs, they sacrificed a black bull and, with supplications to Zeus and Hermes, called the valiant dead to come forth and enjoy their repast. As Plutarch records in his biography of Aristides, this ceremony was still faithfully performed in his day, six centuries after the battle.

At Athens, the legislation of Solon curbed the ancient extravagance of the funeral rites. Immoderate manifestations of grief, such as tearing the cheeks and beating the head and breast, were forbidden, as likewise the sacrifice of animals before the procession to the grave. After the funeral ceremony, the members of the bereaved family, having by solemn rites purified themselves from contact with death, adorned themselves with garlands and began the funeral feast, at which the soul of the deceased was felt to be present, even as playing the part of host. On the third and ninth days after the funeral, a meal was served to the dead person at his grave. This by no means ended the obligations to the deceased, which it was the sacred duty of the surviving male head of the family to fulfil. Among these were a traditional feast for the dead on the thirtieth

[1] Numa Denis Fustel de Coulanges, *The Ancient City: A Study of the Religion, Laws, and Institutions of Greece and Rome*, Doubleday & Co., Garden City, N.Y., 1956, Books 1 and 2.

of the month, as likewise the celebration of his birthday with sacrifice and libations, much as though he still lived. In addition, there was an annual festival at the end of the Dionysiac feast of the Anthesteria, when all the citizens of Athens honoured the dead, each family taking appropriate gifts to the graves of its own deceased members. On this day, the souls of the departed were supposed to swarm up into the world of the living and into the houses where they formerly dwelt. But the temples of the gods were closed against them, and citizens chewed hawthorn leaves and smeared their doorposts with pitch as magical precautions against mischievous ghosts. At the end of the festival, the souls were summarily dismissed from their homes with the injunction: 'Begone, ye Keres; Anthesteria is over.' In the words of Rohde:

> If we wish to form some idea of the way in which (under the influence of a civilization that tended to reduce all primitive grandeur to mere idyll) the worship of the dead altered its character in the direction of piety and intimacy—we need only look at the pictures representing such worship (though rarely before the fourth century) on the oilflasks which were used at funerals in Attica and then laid by the side of the dead in the grave. These slight sketches breathe a spirit of simple kindliness; we see the mourners decking the grave monument with wreaths and ribbons; worshippers approaching with gestures of adoration, bringing with them many objects of daily use—mirrors, fans, swords, etc. for the entertainment of the dead. Sometimes the living seek to give pleasure to the spirit of the dead by the performance of music. Gifts, too, of cakes, fruit, and wine are being made—but the blood of the sacrificial animals is never spilt.[1]

From the cult of the dead, which with endless variations of the same theme was practically world-wide, two developments of the highest importance have been traced. The first of these is agriculture, the foundation and support of every civilization. The origins of cultivation are so densely shrouded in prehistoric mist that many races have ascribed its introduction to a god or mythical culture hero. Of more recent theories, one of the most convincing is that developed by Grant Allen in *The Evolution of the Idea of God.*

[1] Rohde, *op. cit.*, p. 169.

Allen pointed out that pre-agricultural savages have little occasion to stir the ground—other than sporadically when they gather edible roots—except when they dig a grave for their dead. To this grave they periodically bring offerings of food, which sometimes include an animal that is slaughtered upon it, so that its blood may seep into the ground, and which is perhaps afterward burnt as a sacrifice. Edible wild fruits and grains were probably often included among the food left upon the grave. In the loosened, bare soil above and around it, some of the seeds might lodge and germinate. In this earth enriched by blood, ashes, and decaying food, and doubtless also kept clean of competing growths, the seedlings of the edible plants might thrive, and finally yield a modest harvest that would be welcome to the attendants of the dead. To repeat this gratifying result, an acute attendant might have deliberately sown seeds on or around the grave. He might even, in an experimental mood, have loosened the surrounding ground to plant more seeds; and if these grew well, he would in subsequent years have extended his little plantation more widely around the grave as a centre. He would have become the world's first agriculturist.

Alternatively, the first step toward agriculture may have been taken by food-gatherers who cared for, especially by freeing from competing growths, wild stands of useful plants. Actual sowing may have been started by somebody who noticed that seeds of wild plants sometimes grew when cast, along with other refuse, on a rubbish heap. Our modern cultivated plants sometimes flourish amid kitchen refuse rich in organic matter, and doubtless their hardier wild ancestors would grow even better. But removing competing vegetation from spontaneous stands, or finding useful plants growing on a midden heap, might not suggest to the primitive mind the advantage of working the ground, as seeing valuable plants flourish on a recently dug grave would do. Moreover, these alternative theories furnish no clue to the origin of the fertility rites that were so widespread in the earlier ages of agriculture and have survived in remote corners of the earth down to our own time, and in attenuated form have persisted, at least until quite recently, even in the most civilized countries of Europe.

The primitive people, whoever they were, who first sowed seeds on, and then around the graves would, by the inevitable association of ideas, attribute the success of their agricultural venture to the mana of the dead man who rested below, and perhaps also to the magical potency of the blood they poured out for his nourishment. They were quite capable of killing a man, a war captive or slave if not a victim selected from their own tribe, just for the sake of starting another garden on his grave. As we know only too well from contemporary experience, one of the penalties of successful agriculture is that, by supporting an expanding population, it creates the need for ever more agriculture. This was probably true from the beginning. After a while, the burial places, even including those of the special victims, no longer provided enough land to produce as much food as the people needed. Still obsessed by the idea that association with human blood was indispensable to make their crops grow well, prehistoric farmers hit upon the expedient of ritually murdering, at planting time, a human victim, hacking the warm body into small pieces, and distributing these gory fragments among the husbandmen of the district, so that each might squeeze some of the blood on the seeds he was about to sow, or else bury his bit of human flesh in his field for its magical potency. In some cultures, an animal was substituted for the human victim and treated in the same manner. This gruesome prelude to the spring planting once prevailed in regions so widely separated as Mexico and India. The theory that agriculture began at the grave, that caring for plants grew out of caring for the needs of the dead, provides an explanation for the whole complex of practices involved in primitive agriculture, as no other theory does.

The second momentous outgrowth of the cult of the dead is the idea of God. The ghosts or spirits of ancestors were the earliest gods, each a deity to his own descendants. No matter whether a man had lived righteously or wickedly, to them he was holy and blessed, to be honoured and worshipped with filial piety. For had not the progenitor possessed the supernatural power of giving life to others, which to primitive man was one of the greatest of mysteries? After his passage to another stage in the ordered sequence of human existence, he dwelt in the tomb where he was interred, or else hovered over his burial place, remaining closely linked with his descendants, dependent upon them for the food and drink which was his chief pleasure, taking an interest in their fortunes. If attended with due reverence, he remained the protector of the household, bringing prosperity, warding off impending evils, perhaps appearing in dreams to counsel his children or grand-children. If neglected and deprived of the customary offerings, the deified ancestor might become irritable or even malignant, sending disease or death to the household, causing the harvest to fail or the animals to sicken—just as, in ancient Israel, Yahweh blessed his people so long as they obeyed his commandments and worshipped him faithfully, but became terrible in his wrath when they turned to other gods—just as, even today, countless people expect divine blessings when they are righteous, divine punishment when they sin.

As, not only in barbarous tribes but even at Athens while Plato and Aristotle taught, parents died to become the gods of a family religion transmitted from father to son; so the ancestors of the chief or ruler became the gods and protectors of a tribe, to be worshipped in common by all its members. The gods of nations were created by the same process as the familial deities, the *daimones* of the Greeks and the manes of the Romans. In Egypt, as in ancient Peru, the king was the descendant and earthly representative of the sun-god; Romulus, the founder and first ruler of Rome, was the son of Mars, the special patron of the city. A case can be made for the derivation of Yahweh, who became the God of all Christendom, from the ancestral deity of a Hebrew patriarch, represented by a stone carried in the Ark of the Covenant.

It is certain that the omnipotent, omniscient Lord of the whole universe developed by slow degrees from the irascible, bloodthirsty godling of a tribe of land-hungry Semitic nomads; but the earlier stages of this process can hardly be reconstructed without a large measure of conjecture. Likewise, it is doubtful whether the countless nature gods of all races, from the local guardians of springs and hills to magnificent Apollo and earth-shaking Neptune, are ulti-mately derived from defied ancestors. The important point is that dead men, with the mysterious powers ascribed to them by the primitive mind, provided the prototype of deity, and their supposed needs set the pattern of worship. Once the idea took hold, there was no end to the gods that man's fertile fancy could create.

Just as deified ancestors were the first gods, so from the cult of the dead were derived many of the rites and adjuncts of religion. The central feature of this cult, the provision of nourishment for the unseen spirits of the ancestors, became the central feature of practi-cally every religion the world has known, except a few of the more recent and spiritual of them. The High God, whether Olympian Zeus, or Hebrew Yahweh, or Aztec Tezcatlipoca, was nourished by the sacrifices, which all too often were of human victims. In a sophisticated age, Aristophanes could deal humorously with the notion that the birds, led by the wily Athenian Peisthetairus, might starve the Olympians into submission by intercepting the smoke and incense that ascended to them from Grecian temples; but the Aztecs, and many another barbarous nation, believed that the very lives of the gods depended upon the regular performance of the sacrifices. If the gods lost their strength from malnutrition, they could not keep the sun in its course, bring the rains, or preserve the regular succession of the seasons, on which in turn the survival of the people depended; so that if the sacrifices were neglected, the nation would fail.

When, in the fourth century, the Emperor Julian, moved by love of all that was fine in classical culture as well as by hatred of his wicked relatives who had made Christianity the state religion of the Roman Empire, re-established the worship of the Grecian deities, he felt it necessary to restore the sacrifices. Since, at this late date, it was scarcely possible for an educated man to maintain that the gods were nourished by the victims, he had recourse to the mystical doctrine that only a living being, such as the sacrificial animal, could serve as intermediary between a living worshipper and his living god. Moreover, as his friend Sallustius pointed out, prayers without sacrifices are only words, with sacrifices they are live words; the word gives meaning to the life and the life animates the word.[1]

Although the Hebrew prophets declared again and again that Yahweh preferred righteousness to sacrificial victims, and the author of Psalm 50 had made God ask: 'Will I eat the flesh of bulls, or drink the blood of goats?' the restored temple at Jerusalem remained a gilded slaughterhouse until finally destroyed by the Romans in the year A.D. 70. Probably it was only the fortunate circumstance that the God of Judaism and the religions derived from it accepted sacrifices only at his temple on Zion, that the bloody custom did not follow the Jews of the diaspora, and perhaps even expanding Christianity, all over the globe. So far-reaching

[1] Sallustius, *On the Gods and the World*, appendix to Gilbert Murray, *Five Stages of Greek Religion*, Watts & Co., London, 1946.

have been the consequences of the belief that dead men require nourishment from their living descendants!

As the practice of sacrificing to the gods was derived from that of sacrificing to deified ancestors, so the altar on which the sacrifice was made developed from the gravestone. When the grave was enclosed in a flat-topped dolmen, the animal or human victim was doubtless immolated directly upon the tomb. When, as frequently happened, an upright stone or menhir marked the grave, this was smeared with the victim's blood. Idols or statues of the gods, which in the ancient Mediterranean world became such splendid works of art, are probably lineal descendants of upright gravestones or of the worshipped images of dead ancestors. The derivation of religious structures and rituals is a fascinating but controversial subject which would lead us too far from our main theme. Few people today recall that the altar, which in modern churches and temples is hardly more than an ornate lectern to hold the bible and the preacher's notes, was originally used for a more sanguinary purpose.

In *Ancient Art and Ritual*, Jane Harrison pointed out a quite different route by which gods may originate. One of the chief pre-occupations of men in the earlier stages of culture was to ensure their usually precarious food supply. In parts of the world which are periodically either cold or dry, the growth of plants, and even the multiplication of animals, depends on the regular alternation of the seasons. Instead of waiting passively for an event over which even today man exercises no control, primitive peoples expressed their strong desire for the return of the growing season by means of ritual, an important feature of which was the death and carrying out of the old year and the bringing in of the new, which might be represented by either an animal, a youth, or a maiden. Typical of these seasonal rites was the spring festival of ancient Greece, in which a holy bull often symbolized the spirit of fertility. From the succession of these holy bulls, that died only to live again, there gradually arose the image of a Bull-Spirit, a Bull-Daimon, and, finally, a Bull-God. In much the same way, Dionysos, the perpetually youthful god of fertility, vegetation and, more specifically, the vine, grew out of the succession of youths with the first down on their cheeks who figured in the tribal initiation rite—the rite of the new, the second birth. 'When once we see', wrote Miss Harrison, 'that out of the emotion of the rite and the facts of the rite arises that

73

remembrance and shadow of the rite, that *image* which is the god, we realize instantly that the god of the spring rite *must* be a young god, and in primitive societies, where young women are but of secondary account, he will necessarily be a young *man*.'[1]

Miss Harrison's theory, no less than that of Herbert Spencer and Grant Allen, finds in human beings the prototypes of gods, the principal difference between these two theories being that the former derives deities from a succession of living people who figured in recurrent rites, whereas the latter derives them from the carefully attended dead. Both theories are well supported and probably true, but they refer to different gods. The important point that emerges clearly from our study is that religion was not born of the belief, whether reached by induction or through divine revelation, that there is a beneficent God in heaven who created and preserves the world and ourselves, hence deserves our adoration. Religion, in all its more developed forms, began at the opposite pole. Not because there is a powerful Deity who cares for men, but because men care greatly for whatever preserves and enhances their lives, did religion arise. The capacity for caring was ascribed by living men to their dead ancestors, thence transferred to the ever more powerful gods who, with man's developing thought, grew out of his belief in the survival of the dead.

Sometimes, when we read the history of religions, with their frequently absurd or childish beliefs, practices as horrible as they are futile, intolerance and fiendish persecutions, we become ashamed of being men. Especially in generous and romantic youth, knowledge of what religion has taught and done is likely to drive us into the ranks of the opposition, of which Lucretius is the eloquent mouthpiece. Yet, if we delve deeply enough beneath the glitter and the fanfare, beneath the elaborate ritual and flowery language, beneath the scheming of fanatical or avaricious priests, beneath all the cruel and bloody rites of earlier ages, we uncover something of which we can be proud—our human capacity for caring about things beyond our individual selves and our helpless offspring. Entangled with man's selfish and violent impulses, misled by the befuddled thoughts of his inchoate intellect, exploited by those greedy for wealth or power, this precious capacity has had many lamentable

[1] Jane Ellen Harrison, *Ancient Art and Ritual*, Oxford University Press, 1951, p. 113.

74

consequences. Yet it has always been there, the golden core around which religions are built, from which they may be reconstructed.

One final point, before we end this chapter. Religion and agriculture are, as we have seen, associated developments. Whether or not we accept the theory, which has much to recommend it, that man's earliest plantings were on or around his graves, there can be no doubt that, until relatively recent times, agricultural practices were closely linked with rites of a religious character. Today scientific agriculture, wholly divorced from religion, bears ever more heavily upon the natural world, which it threatens ultimately to despoil. Unless agriculture, along with other forms of exploitation of nature, are brought back into relationship with the religious capacity for caring—caring about things beyond our immediate material interests—our topheavy civilization will collapse, our teeming populations will dwindle, with the wreck of the natural world that supports them.

6

Caring for Plants and Animals

Religion was born with man's growing awareness that the world contains more than his senses reveal to him. Perhaps other animals have a dim intuition of this truth, but in man it becomes more explicit and more strongly influences his behaviour. Yet to recognize that there is a hidden or transcendent reality is not the same as knowing its nature, so that imagination is left to compensate for the lack of solid information. It is hardly an exaggeration to say that religion arose when man began to view his world imaginatively. When the mind attempts to penetrate the transcendent side of reality, the only hint it has to work on is its awareness of its own thoughts and feelings. Although we firmly believe that other people and at least the higher animals are conscious much as we are, and we speculatively admit that sentience extends far lower in the scale of being, perhaps even to the least particles of matter, consciousness, other than our own, is hidden from each of us, so that, if we admit that it is widely diffused through the world, it forms a vast transcendent realm. It is, indeed, our best example of such a realm, the only transcendent realm of which we can form any conception. Hence it was inevitable that as, with growing thoughtfulness, man strove to fathom that hidden side of reality of which his senses told him nothing, he did so on the model of that side of himself which was hidden from all his companions, his consciousness, his spirit, his *anima*. He became an animist, attributing to all the things that surrounded him, or at least to those whose activity strongly arrested his attention, a conscious life, a soul or spirit, somewhat like his own.

At the period when the earliest religious sentiments grew up, man lived in closest association with the natural world; he was, indeed, part of the fauna in a way that his modern descendants have ceased to be. Since he not only depended upon plants and animals for the satisfaction of his vital needs but was constantly menaced by such creatures as carnivorous quadrupeds and venomous snakes, he was strongly interested in the living things around him. That he attributed to the animals minds much like his own is not surprising; unless trained in animal psychology, we moderns tend to do the same. But for early man, at a certain stage of his long intellectual pilgrimage, even plants were conscious and had indwelling souls or spirits, which could leave and return to the body, as his own soul seemed to do when he dreamed. These views gave him a brotherly feeling toward living things of all kinds which many of our contemporaries have unfortunately lost. From many parts of the world, there is evidence that early man felt uneasy about depriving any creature, vegetable no less than animal, of its life.

When discussing man's relations with other living things, including other individuals of his own species, it is important to bear in mind that his treatment of them has been determined by several motives which are often in sharpest conflict. On one hand, there is sympathy with them as living beings more or less akin to himself, having wants and feelings somewhat like his own. Opposed to this is the need, real or supposed, to use their flesh for food, their skin for clothing, or other products of their bodies for manifold purposes. And opposed to this again is the fear of vengeance, of the harm which these victims of man's material needs may wreak upon him by natural or supernatural means. In broad terms, we may recognize a religious motive, working toward the preservation of other creatures, and the motive of self-preservation, which often leads to their destruction. The latter is included in what in modern terminology we call the economic motive, which embraces not only the striving to fill our basic necessities but also our attempts to satisfy that exaggerated acquisitiveness into which primary vital needs have so frequently hypertrophied.

We who call ourselves civilized often find it extremely difficult to reconcile these two motives in our lives, the religious and the economic, the altruistic feeling which prompts us to seek harmony with a larger whole and the egoistic drive that impels us to feather our own nest regardless of the consequences to other beings. Primitive man experienced a similar conflict, which he strove to

77

resolve with logic less penetrating than ours, with feelings less delicate and refined. His efforts in this direction were often ineffectual, resulting in beliefs that seem absurd to us, in rites which strike us as stupid, grotesque, and often highly revolting. If we view these rites as an alien onlooker, they can only fill us with scorn and contempt; but if we recall that the savage, like ourselves, is trying to harmonize elements in his life which are perhaps radically incompatible, we shall look upon them with sympathy and understanding, with pity rather than with ridicule. Moreover, it is well to remember that complete internal harmony, logical no less than affective, so precious to the sage and the saint, is not indispensable for the survival of man or other animals. A balance of opposing attitudes, the ability to shift swiftly from one emotional state to another as external circumstances demand, is all that is necessary for the preservation of life.

Primitive man's tenderness toward other living things was, as we have seen, directed toward the vegetable no less than the animal kingdom. In particular, those grandest of vegetable forms, the giant trees so much statelier, older, and more enduring than man himself, inspired him with awe, reverence, and wonder. The worship of trees was widespread among the European branches of the Aryan race; among the Germans, natural woods were the earliest sanctuaries. The intensity of the feeling inspired by trees may be inferred from the severity of the penalty prescribed by the old Germanic laws for anyone who dared to peel the bark from a living tree. The culprit's navel was cut out and fastened to the spot whence the bark had been removed, then he was driven around and around until his entrails were wound about the trunk. Thus the offender replaced with his own vital parts the bark of which he had so thoughtlessly deprived the living tree. Even in civilized Athens, as we learn from Aristotle's work on the Athenian constitution, anyone who dug up or cut down a sacred olive tree was tried by the Council of Areopagus and, if found guilty, punished with death. This law was no longer enforced in the philosopher's day.

In these and similar instances, the modern reader is likely to remark that the laws imply greater regard for the life of an animal or plant than for that of a man. This is to miss the essential point. Most legal codes, down almost to modern times, decreed penalties which we now consider ruthlessly harsh for misdemeanours that we now regard as venial. The severity of the punishment was determined not so much by the magnitude of the crime as by the fact that it violated a tribal taboo or outraged a ruler's decree, with all the disastrous effects that might follow from disrupting the tribe's solidarity and exposing it to supernatural evils, or from undermining the royal authority. It was not so much that animal or vegetable life was valued more highly than human life, but that, as in ancient Rome, the sanctity of law and custom, upon which depended the preservation of society, was placed above any individual life.

In that vast treasure-house of information on the customs and beliefs of primitive man, Sir James Frazer's *The Golden Bough*, we find numerous instances, drawn from all parts of the world, of the sanctity which, in cultures long dead or fast disappearing, attached to living trees. Before their conversion to Christianity, the Lithuanians worshipped trees and preserved about their villages or houses holy groves, where even to break a twig would have been a sin. They believed that one who cut a bough in such a grove would, through some mysterious agent of retribution, lose his life or at least be maimed in limb. The Indians along the upper reaches of the Missouri River revered the great cottonwoods that grew in the river bottoms and were the most impressive trees of the region. They would not cut these trees for the logs they needed, but depended for their supply upon such trees as had fallen. The Ojibways 'very seldom cut down green or living trees, from the idea that it puts them to pain, and some of their medicine-men profess to have heard the wailing of the trees under the axe.' The Wanika tribe of East Africa believed that every tree was the abode of a spirit. The coconut palm was held in special reverence, and the destruction of one of these trees was regarded as the equivalent of matricide, because the palm gives men life and nourishment, as a mother her child.

Among numerous peoples, when a tree was about to be felled for timber, special ceremonies were performed at its foot for the propitiation of the indwelling spirit, lest it take revenge upon the despoilers of its abode; or apologies were offered, and expressions of regret that the living tree was about to be sacrificed to man's necessity. When the Toboongkoos of Celebes prepared to clear a tract of forest to make a rice field, they built a tiny house and furnished it with food, miniature clothes, and some gold. Then they beseeched the woodland spirits to quit the area of forest destined for the axe and fire, and to take up their abode peacefully in the dwelling that had been made and provisioned for their accommodation.

In these and numerous other examples that have been collected by ethnologists, the attitude toward the tree ranges all the way from friendly feeling, such as might be inspired by another sentient being, to gratitude to it as a source of benefits, and worship as the body of a spirit with great power to help or harm man. Nearly always, the motive for revering and protecting the tree is religious rather than practical; only rarely, as in the case of the Wanikas' coconut palms, is the economic aspect prominent. The deliberate practice of conservation, as we now conceive it, is rarely apparent in the primitive man's treatment of trees. But whatever the explicit motivation, the practical result is obvious. Men who regard trees with awe or reverence, who must enlist the assistance of their priest or medicine man in order to fell them without dire consequences to themselves, who must make elaborate preparations for the accommodation of spirits evicted from their natural abodes, who perform expiatory sacrifices, or who at least approach the victim of their axe in an apologetic mood—such men are not likely to destroy trees wantonly or without great need. These religious practices and quasi-religious sentiments result in the preservation of the woodlands so essential to the continued prosperity of any society, whether of primitive hunters and food-gatherers or modern city-dwellers dependent for their food upon large-scale, mechanized agriculture supported by an elaborate technology. And as to the beliefs upon which these practices are founded, should we not respect and even honour them as representing an earnest attempt to apprehend truths to which we, in the smug materialism of our age, are too often insensitive and blind? Whatever the faults and errors of our remote ancestors, there was one at least into which they did not fall: they did not, like so many of our contemporaries, suppose that all values are human values, and that no other of the multitudinous goals toward which life tends is worthy of our consideration.

The animism which led primitive men to posit spirits in vegetables operated even more strongly in the case of animals, which move, see, hear, utter sounds, and eat, much as we do. This recognition of the essential similarity, in nature and in needs, of man and other animate creatures placed a restraint upon the wanton slaughter of the latter. In his summary of the religious beliefs of the South American Indians, Alfred Métraux stated:

> Among the spirits that tend toward a greater individualization are the supernatural protectors of the animal species usually called the 'Father or Mother of such-and-such kind of game or fish'. In the myths these spirits are represented as particularly large specimens of the species, and, as a rule, they may take on human form at will.... These custodians of the species freely permit the use of their protégés as food, but they do not tolerate their wanton destruction by man, and they punish severely hunters who kill more than they actually need to survive. In some cases, these guardians could be propitiated by prayer and small gifts, but the exercise of moderation and self-restraint was the best way to gain their favour. The notion of a protector of the species was strong in ancient Perú, where the supernatural custodians were identified with constellations to which prayers were addressed. Even in modern times the Indians of the Puna de Atacama believed that the wild herds of the vicuña were led by Coquena, a troll who punished men who hunted the vicuña out of greediness.[1]

The modern city-dweller or farmer who, taking his high-powered gun, sallies forth to kill animals he does not need for food, often imagines that he emulates his vigorous, self-sufficient ancestors of a remote epoch. He believes that he is giving free and salutary play to a deep-rooted human 'instinct' which centuries of civilized life has been unable to eradicate, and that by so-doing he demonstrates his essential hardihood and manliness. In equating this killing for 'sport', without danger to himself (except from the carelessness of other hunters) and without jeopardizing his means of subsistence, to the indispensable hunting of his distant forebears, he does a profound injustice to the latter. Our available evidence indicates that primitive man rarely went out to hunt in this offhand manner, for mere diversion. To him, the killing of wild animals was a serious business, to be undertaken only in response to pressing vital needs and to be approached, in many instances, only after fasting or

[1] Steward, *op. cit.*, p. 565–6.

laborious ceremonial preparations which would ensure the success of the solemn venture, ward off perils from the hunter, and prevent consequences of the slaughter that might be disastrous to the tribe. Doubtless in the excitement of the chase, when he pitted his strength, endurance, and skill against some powerful or wily animal, the primitive hunter experienced that exhilaration which comes from the exercise of well-practised faculties at their highest pitch. Yet the thrill that might be felt in the heat of the pursuit was rarely the motive for undertaking this pursuit. The savage huntsman as a rule required more valid reasons for killing his victims.

Australia was, until recently, occupied by some of the most primitive races of mankind, for some of which the kangaroo was the mainstay of life. A kangaroo hunt was not to be lightly undertaken, without due thought and adequate ritual preparation. The kangaroo men went first to a certain sacred spot which from ancient times had been the scene of this important ceremony. Upon a ledge of rock they traced with white gypsum and red ochre designs that represented the white bones and red fur of the kangaroo. Then, to the accompaniment of solemn chants calling for the future increase of the kangaroos, some of the men opened their veins and let their warm blood flow over the sacred ledge with its painted symbols of the kangaroo. Then followed the chase; and if one of the animals was killed, its flesh provided a meal shared by the whole group. Even such primitive savages are not wholly 'children of nature', thoughtless of the future. They believe that the maintenance of their means of subsistence depends upon their active endeavour, and do not hesitate to pour out their blood to ensure a continuance of natural bounty. It is not the ineffectiveness of the means but the greatness of the intention and the soundness of the underlying thought which should, in this instance, arrest our attention and command our respect. A substantial part of man's religious practices, from the Egyptian cult of Osiris and the Brahmanical kindling of the altar fire to the rain dances of the Arizona Indians, stemmed from this same pervasive belief that the maintenance of the providential order is dependent upon the ritualistic and symbolic cooperation of mankind.

'The savage', wrote Frazer, 'makes it a rule to spare the life of those animals which he has no pressing motive for killing.' His care to avoid the needless slaughter of other creatures had various motives, some of which appear sound to modern man, whereas others fail to impress us as valid. In the case of large and dangerous animals, like the elephant, the bear, the crocodile, or the whale, there was the genuine danger that some of the tribesmen would be maimed or killed by their powerful adversary. There was the apprehension that hunting would diminish the abundance of a species indispensable for the clan's subsistence, either through the natural diminution of the population by the removal of some of its members capable of reproducing, or because animals of this kind might be offended and henceforth avoid the hunters. There was the misgiving that the dead animal's ghost or spirit might pursue and take vengeance upon the man who killed it, or that its surviving relatives might take up a blood feud and exact retaliation, as, in similar circumstances, the tribesman himself felt bound to do. There was sometimes evidence of genuine sympathy for the creature about to lose its life, or perhaps for its bereaved mother. Each of these perils and misgivings gave rise to rites appropriate for the propitiation of the prospective victim, for the appeasement of its ghost, or for the multiplication of its kind.

When the inhabitants of the Isle of Saint Mary, to the north of Madagascar, went whaling, they singled out a young whale for attack and humbly begged the mother's pardon, stating the necessity that drove them to deprive her of her offspring, and entreating her to retire beneath the water so that her maternal feelings would not be outraged by the sight of her child's suffering and death. When men of the bear clan in the Ottawa tribe had killed a bear, they offered him his own flesh to eat, addressing him with these words: 'Cherish us no grudge because we have killed you. You have sense; you see that our children are hungry. They love you and wish to take you into their bodies. Is it not glorious to be eaten by the children of a chief?'

Many explanations have been advanced for the cult of totemism so widespread among primitive races, and anthropologists have been unable to reach general agreement as to its significance. This is not surprising, for even among the members of a single totemic tribe different views on this subject prevailed. Among the Winnebago Indians of Wisconsin, Radin was given at least four different explanations of the relationship of a man to his totem animal:

1. He was descended from that animal.

2. The animal had been changed into the human being from whom his clan was sprung.

3. His totemic clan name was taken from the animal, although it was not an actual ancestor.

4. The clan was called after the animal because his ancestors had imitated it.

There were, moreover, two different conceptions of the original clan animal. According to one, it was a real animal; according to the other, it was a generalized spirit-animal who had assumed a real and specific animal form when it appeared on earth.[1] Confusion is increased by the fact that the totem acquired different meanings, and was associated with diverse rites, among different peoples. It is clear, however, that in many instances the totem was the animal or plant upon which the clan chiefly depended for food, and that the ceremonies associated with this totem were for the purpose of assuring its continued abundance.

Professor Murphy has traced a curious inversion of the relation of a clan to its totem animal. In the most primitive type of totemism, the totem represents the creature which is chiefly used for food. Although eaten freely, its death and the meal which follows are attended by certain ceremonies, designed to propitiate its spirit and ensure the propagation of its kind; as in the rites which accompany the feasts of bear flesh among the Ainus of Japan. Such ritual gradually increases the aura of sacredness surrounding the food animal. There also arise sentiments of brotherhood between the tribesmen and the animal upon which they subsist; eater and eaten become in a sense one in flesh and blood. The notion that a sacred bond exists between the victim of the sacrificial meal and those who partake of its flesh is widespread among mankind, and is echoed in the symbolism of the Eucharist. Thus there comes a time when the animal which once formed the habitual diet of a clan can be eaten only on certain solemn occasions attended by elaborate ritual; as in the yearly meal of buffalo flesh among the Todas of southern India, who otherwise abstain from eating this animal so important in their pastoral economy. Finally, the animal becomes too sacred ever to

---

[1] Paul Radin, *Primitive Religion: Its Nature and Origin*, Dover Publications, New York, 1957, p. 205.

be eaten, as among the Bataks of Sumatra, of which one clan strictly abstained from the flesh of the ape, another from that of the dog, another from that of the dove, and so forth.[1]

It is obvious that when the animal which was once the chief support of life becomes too sacred to be eaten, the people among whom this occurs must have discovered alternative means of subsistence. The chief factor operative in this change of attitude toward animal life was the domestication of plants and the development of an adequate agriculture. It was earlier mentioned that primitive man often felt uneasy about taking life, especially that of certain animals and trees, yet was constrained by life's cruel predicament to kill in order to remain alive; and that this conflict of motives led in many instances to behaviour which has all the marks of an unsatisfactory compromise. With the development of agriculture, the necessity for such compromise diminished or ceased. Men could now at least refrain from taking the life of inoffensive animals, yet continue to live. This occurred in some of the most ancient civilizations, especially in the fertile river valleys in the vast region stretching from the Mediterranean to China, with momentous consequences for animal life.

As frequently happens when two conflicting motives which had been held together by force of circumstances are made independent of each other by altered conditions, it was uncertain which would become dominant to the virtual exclusion of the other. It was possible for the development of agriculture to have quite different consequences. When men no longer depended upon wild animals as their primary support, they were free to adopt a more casual attitude toward them. The religious restraints upon their slaughter, the rites intended to ensure their multiplication and continued abundance, died away. Religion, which in its earlier stages was never indifferent to the primary vital needs of mankind, now had its eyes turned in other directions—to fertility cults to ensure the vernal awakening of the vegetation and the continued productivity of the grain fields, and finally to the salvation of man's immortal soul.

With his waxing economic competence, his greater power, his growing luxury, his increasing distance from wild Nature, the soaring range and widening scope of his thought, man began to feel

[1] Modified from Murphy, *op. cit.*, p. 93–6.

far superior to animals with which he had earlier been almost on a footing of equality. There grew up, alike among Hellenic philosophers and Hebrew prophets, a teleologic view of the world which held that all other living things had been expressly created for the service of mankind. (Indeed, Aristotle went beyond this by teaching that 'inferior' races of man had been made to serve their betters.) Since Greek philosophy and Hebrew theology have dominated all subsequent thought in the Western world, this is the attitude that has remained with us through all our changes in cosmic outlook and coloured all our views. With religion finally devoting itself largely to man's welfare in another world, with philosophy all but submerged in problems of epistemology and the validity of knowledge, the economic motive has controlled man's relations with other forms of life, with little restraint from either.

It often happens that the too-intensive cultivation of a single motive defeats its own purpose. It is at last becoming apparent to thoughtful men that in giving free rein to the economic motive in our relations with the natural world, with none of the restraints and controls that religion once imposed, we have come within an ace of killing the goose that lays the golden egg. Of course, a far-sighted application of the economic motive in dealing with nature might have had different consequences; but we are rarely far-seeing when we are greedy. Men have, as a rule, cultivated longer thoughts under the influence of religious feeling than under that of their acquisitive instincts. Paradoxically, those peoples who, after becoming proficient in agriculture, allowed stronger weight to the religious motive in their dealings with other living things, chose also the way which was soundest from the point of view of a far-seeing economy. Although from different motives, they advanced the cause of the conservation of nature centuries before the West gave much thought to this pressing need.

Persian dualism gave to man's treatment of living things a most curious twist, without parallel in any other religion known to me. Each of the two rival Gods, Ormuzd the Righteous and Ahriman the Wicked, not only created lesser deities but also various species of animals and plants. Ormuzd's creatures are serviceable, or at least favourable, to man; Ahriman's, the reverse; although the reasons for including certain animals in one class or the other are not always evident to one unfamiliar with Iranian life. To mistreat or kill an animal of the good creation was a heinous offence, to be expiated by tortures in hell; but to destroy Ahriman's creatures was a meritorious act. To the good creation belonged cattle, sheep, dogs, birds, hedgehogs, and otters; to the evil, ants, frogs, snakes, scorpions, and water-rats. The sin of killing an otter could be expiated by (among other things) killing ten thousand land-frogs.

In *The Book of Arda Viraf*, a Parsee equivalent of Dante's *Divine Comedy*, the composition of which is attributed to the Sassanid Dynasty, we glimpse many curious consequences of men's treatment of the various creatures. In the highest heaven, Arda Viraf found the souls of those who had killed many noxious animals while in the world. Agriculturists, shepherds, and those who constructed irrigation systems and fountains for the improvement of tillage or the benefit of creatures, also fared splendidly in heaven. But those who unlawfully slaughtered cattle, sheep, and other quadrupeds, as likewise those who killed, beat, or starved the dogs of householders and shepherds, suffered Promethean tortures in hell. The souls of men who muzzled plough-oxen, or forced them to work while hungry or thirsty, were constantly gored, torn, and trampled by cattle. While in hell, Arda Viraf also saw an adulterer whose whole body was ever cooked in a brazen cauldron, with the exception of his right foot, which remained outside, because while in the world it had often crushed frogs, ants, snakes, and scorpions. The Zoroastrians believed that at the final judgment at the Cinvat Bridge—the bridge on the road to paradise which for the righteous was a broad avenue but for the wicked as narrow as a razor's edge, so that they fell from it into the flaming pit below—the souls of the deceased had to give an account of what they had done on earth, not only to their fellow men, but also to cattle, sheep, earth, trees, fire, and water. This is a true expression of a morality that grew up close to nature; only a city-bred morality judges us solely by our treatment of other men.

Of all the religions that have survived into modern times, Jainism and Buddhism have most consistently taught the sacredness of all living things. Both are closely allied to Hinduism, some sects of which are equally insistent upon the sanctity of life in all its forms. Thus the duties enjoined in the ancient Hindu *Brahmanas* include: 1. those to the gods, 2. those to seers, 3. those to ancestors, 4. those to men, and 5. those to the lower creation. No devout man would touch his daily meal without offering parts of it to gods, fathers, men, and animals, and saying his daily prayers.[1]

The great teachers of the Jains and the Buddhists, Mahavira and Gautama, were contemporaries in northern India in the sixth century before Christ. In Chapter 8 we shall consider the very stringent Jaina prohibitions against destroying animals of every kind, and even plants. Buddhism, the younger religion which has exerted a far wider direct influence upon men's thoughts and conduct, is somewhat more lenient, for, in at least some of its sects, it permits its adherents to eat the flesh of animals, although, inconsistently, they may not kill those which they devour. The Buddhist faith had only a small following until, about the year 261 B.C., it was embraced by Asoka Maurya, grandson of the monarch who had so effectively resisted the efforts of Alexander's successor, Seleukos Nikator, to control northern India. With Asoka's conversion, Buddhism became the court religion of a great empire, although other faiths were not only tolerated but even supported by the emperor. One of the first effects of Buddhist teaching was to cause Asoka to put a total stop to the wars of conquest which, during three generations, had given the Mauryas dominion over a vast territory extending from southern India to the Hindu Kush mountains. This was the immense field in which Asoka strove to make effective some of the more concrete consequences of Buddhist doctrines.

Asoka's decrees were carved in stone on magnificent pillars set up in the more central districts of his domains, or in more remote regions cut into great boulders and the exposed faces of outcropping rocks. The imperial order known to antiquarians as Pillar Edict V is, for the student of the history of man's relations with the natural world, a document of outstanding interest. It contains one of the most comprehensive lists of protected animals ever issued by any government, ancient or modern. Asoka prohibited the killing of parrots, starlings, geese, doves, and other birds; of bats, tortoises, river skates, boneless fish, and queen ants; of porcupines, tree-squirrels, barasingha stags, monkeys, rhinoceros, and all quadrupeds which are neither utilized nor eaten. For the kinds of fish whose capture and eating was permitted, closed seasons were established;

[1] S. Radhakrishnan, *Indian Philosophy*, George Allen & Unwin Ltd., London, 1948, vol. I, p. 131.

on certain specified days, fish could be neither caught nor sold. And on these same days, the destruction of animals of any kind in elephant forests and fish ponds was strictly prohibited. Forests were not to be set on fire either wantonly or to drive out animals for slaughter. The chaff from threshing floors could not be burned, because of the small living creatures which lurked in it. Likewise, restrictions were set upon the castration and branding of domestic animals. Female goats, ewes, and sows were exempted from slaughter so long as they were with young or in milk, as well as their offspring up to six months of age.[1]

The primary purpose of Asoka's comprehensive laws was not, as with modern legislation of a similar nature, to preserve forests as sources of lumber and protectors of watersheds, or to ensure an abundance of game to be hunted at appropriate seasons. Asoka, who in his unregenerate youth had been addicted to the chase, had after his conversion abandoned this practice and henceforth took his outings in the form of royal pilgrimages to places of religious interest. There was no ulterior motive behind the protection of any of these multifarious creatures listed in the edict; they were exempted from destruction simply because they are living beings like ourselves. But the practical results of some of the measures contained in Asoka's edicts would be difficult to distinguish from those of modern conservation laws whose motivation is economic. We lack information about the strictness of their enforcement; but from all we know of Asoka's conscientious personal attention to the details of government and the efficiency of his administration, we may infer that it compared favourably with the best present-day enforcement of similar measures.

After the passing of the able Maurya dynasty, Buddhism declined, and finally died away, in the country where it had been born. In the Middle Ages, India was overrun by Moslem invaders whose attitude toward nature was quite different from that of Hinduism and its associated religions. It is of interest, however, to observe the influence of religious belief on the treatment of animals in the reign of the Mogul emperor Akbar, the most famous of the Mohammedan rulers of India. Intensely interested in religious and philosophical questions, this remarkable man, unable to read or write, invited to

[1] Vincent A. Smith, *Asoka : The Buddhist Emperor of India*, Clarendon Press, Oxford, 3rd edn. 1920, Ch. 5.

his court a succession of learned doctors of the most diverse faiths, to expound their views to him. According to V. A. Smith, the Emperor was for a while greatly influenced by the doctrines of the Jaina teacher Hiravijaya, who from 1582 to 1584 resided at the imperial court, and is credited by his co-religionists with having converted the great Mogul to the faith of Mahavira. Although Akbar was, in his youth (as also at a later period), an enthusiastic devotee of the chase, while under Jaina influence he renounced his much-loved hunting and restricted the practice of fishing. He ordered the release of prisoners and caged birds, and later he prohibited the slaughter of animals during periods amounting collectively to half of each year. He himself abstained almost wholly from eating flesh. The edicts which, under the influence of Jainism, Akbar issued for the protection of animal life resemble in many respects those which Asoka, almost two thousand years earlier, had decreed after he became a devout Buddhist.[1]

The effect, over a period of many years, of a people's attitude toward nature depends upon many factors, among which are the consistency with which the dominant concepts are honoured, the understanding of natural cycles and how they may be affected by man's activities, and, above all, by the magnitude of the pressure which the human population exerts upon the natural environment that surrounds and sustains it. India was too long dominated by aliens whose religions take a very different attitude toward living beings, too long torn by internal dissensions, to permit us to form a picture of how the doctrines of Hinduism, if consistently carried out, might have affected the natural world on this great sub-continent. Certainly she has not always cherished her soils, her waters, her forests, and the multitudinous life which they support, as well as she might have done. But doubtless the present situation would be far more deplorable if this ancient, densely populated country had, millennia ago, adopted the policy of unrestricted exploitation of living things which was until recently characteristic of the West. Late in the nineteenth century, John Lockwood Kipling noticed among the people of India an attitude highly favourable for the survival of free animals of all sorts, along with amazing tolerance of their depredations on grain fields, orchards, and even merchandise

[1] Vincent A. Smith, *Akbar the Great Mogul*, Clarendon Press, Oxford, 2nd edn. 1919, p. 166-8.

in shops. At the same time, the lower classes exhibited a lamentable lack of kindness and consideration for domestic animals.[1]

In Burma, Buddhism fared better than in India. The interior of the country remained relatively free of European influences until the British invasion of Upper Burma in the 1880s. H. Fielding, an Englishman who resided in the country during the early days of British occupation and wrote a delightful book on his observations, attested the tenderness and respect which the Burmese felt for all classes of living things, their reluctance to destroy the fauna or to fell the great trees, which they believed to be the abode of tutelary spirits. Their attitude was in part determined by animistic beliefs far older than Buddhism but which had been found not incompatible with adherence to Buddhist doctrines.[2] In appraising this point of view, we may well ask whether animism diverges farther in one direction from the elusive truth than our modern materialism does in another direction. But however we may assess the beliefs which lead men to treat with some degree of sympathy and restraint the living world around them, the practical results are those which scientists have of late been loudly proclaiming to be essential to our continued survival.

For another Buddhist country, Tibet, we have the testimony of an ornithologist who resided there before the recent Chinese invasion. He wrote that

> shooting in Lhasa is forbidden and so it was quite impossible to make a collection. . . . One of the most delightful attributes of the birds of Lhasa is their amazing tameness. Even migrants, such as the various species of duck, seem to realize that they are inviolate in the neighbourhood of the Holy City. Brahminy Duck breed regularly in holes in the basement of the Dalai Lama's palace, and on a winter's morning I have seen flocks of Bar-headed Geese waddle across the road within a dozen yards of my pony, and barely condescend to notice me.[3]

[1] John Lockwood Kipling, *Beast and Man in India*, Macmillan & Co., London, 1892.

[2] H. Fielding, *The Soul of a People*, Macmillan & Co., London, 1898.

[3] F. Ludlow, 'The Birds of Lhasa', *The Ibis*, vol. 92, p. 34–36, 1950. For additional recent testimony on the respect for life in Buddhist countries, see Norman Lewis, *A Dragon Apparent: Travels in Indo-China*, Jonathan Cape, London, 1951, *passim*, but especially Ch. 17.

One wonders how this idyllic situation has resisted the dissolving acid of Communism and Dialectic Materialism as practised by the Chinese. Yet the ancient culture of China is not lacking in a tradition of loving care for all living things such as any country might envy. This is especially marked in Taoism, whose great sage, Laotse, declared that the best of men is like water, benefitting all things and competing with nothing. The Taoist *T'ai-Shang Kan-Ying P'ien*, the Treatise of the Exalted One on Response and Retribution, admonishes us to turn toward all creatures with a compassionate heart. Not only the higher animals, but even the multifarious insects, herbs, and trees, must not be wantonly injured. Setting fire to the woods to drive out hunted animals is condemned. Virtuous actions include liberating captive birds and refraining from killing animals, no less than abstinence from pleasures of sense and the avoidance of harmful speech. In a way, the Taoist's tender care for all creatures is an expression of a purer, more disinterested compassion than that of the Indian religions, or of Pythagoreanism in the ancient West. These point out that in harming an animal one may be causing pain to a soul that formerly inhabited a human body, perhaps that of a close relative or friend; whereas Taoism does not stress this motive for restraint.

When we recall the annual clamour in North America by those who wish to amuse themselves by shooting more and more of the diminishing wildfowl which conservation agencies are valiantly striving to preserve, it is refreshing to know that there are, or until quite recently were, parts of the earth where free creatures are protected by the religious feeling of the people rather than by wardens appointed by the government to restrain hordes of men impatient to kill. The wanton, reckless slaughter which in North America led to the irreparable extinction of whole species of living things once abundant, to the reduction of other species almost to the vanishing point, sprang from a lack of religious feeling, from the failure of the dominant Western faiths to provide that comprehensive guidance along life's perplexing path which many of the older religions undertook to give.

7

The Great Revolution
in Religion

Like all things great, religion began humbly. It grew out of the universal need of living beings to adjust their lives to surrounding conditions. Among plants and the simplest animals, this is effected largely by immediate response to directive stimuli; as when a green shoot bends toward the light, or a protozoön swims into some nutrient substance diffusing through the water. In more highly endowed animals, there is a more active search for the conditions necessary to sustain life, undertaken in response to inner urges rather than to immediate external directives; as when an animal returns, after a long interval, to some distant, remembered source of food. There is often an attempt to anticipate future needs, as by the storage of foodstuffs for the season of scarcity; or to improve the environment, as when beavers build a dam. With the increasing sharpness of their sensory organs and the correlated advance in intelligence, animals strive to ensure their prosperity by taking account of events ever more distant in time as in space.

At what evolutionary stage religious feeling began it seems unprofitable to speculate; possibly it is implicit in all sentient creatures. But religion as an overt activity was born when imagination and reflective thought grew up, along with foresight, in minds preoccupied with the struggle for existence. It then became apparent that the effective environment, upon which the prosperity of the individual and his family depends, is not wholly revealed by the eyes, the ears, or the other senses. A creature's welfare is affected by many things of which its senses give no direct information. Not only is the little familiar sphere of action surrounded by a vast uncharted realm hidden from our gaze, our lives are penetrated through and through by influences emanating from this region of

93

darkness and mystery. Life begins in a manner of which the primitive mind can give no adequate account; its termination poses questions equally perplexing. Each evening the sun, sinking in the west, passes wholly beyond the savage's ken; he has no knowledge of what befalls it until, next morning, it somehow reappears from the opposite side of the sky. The surging life of nature floods and ebbs with the passage of the seasons in a manner that defies explanation. The savage huntsman draws his bow and lets his carefully aimed arrow dart toward its target. The moment he releases his grip, it passes beyond his control; whether it strikes or misses the mark depends upon circumstances he cannot foresee. Not only in the grandest processes of the natural world, but even in the simplest acts of his daily life, there is an element of uncertainty, an intrusion of the mysterious beyond into the familiar course of his existence.

At a certain stage in their intellectual development, it became evident to our ancestors that success in living depends upon the unseen no less than upon the seen, upon events over which men have no control no less than upon those which obey their will. As a vital necessity, every creature strives with all the means at its disposal to attain harmonious equilibrium with its environment; it was in response to this need that its bodily and mental powers developed. A feeling of helplessness and frustration might overpower the intelligent being who had begun to realize that, for all its pains and exhausting efforts, it could regulate only a small and minor part of the processes that most intimately affect its welfare. It would be irrational to take great pains to regulate certain segments of the environment, while leaving out of account other aspects of equal importance.

To man's dawning intelligence, such a restriction of his efforts to control the conditions pertinent to his welfare appeared intolerably unsatisfactory. Many of the problems of his life he saw concretely and met with practical expedients, as when he entered a cave and kindled a fire to escape the rain and cold. But of that vast, dim region hidden from his senses yet so important to his prosperity he could think only imaginatively, because his imagination had developed more rapidly than his capacity for abstract thought— a field in which he was hampered by lack of adequate words. What more natural than that imagination should suggest procedures for controlling this unseen realm and making it favourable to his vital needs. Practical expedients for dealing with concrete situations where human will and muscular effort avail; fanciful or symbolic recourses for dealing with those unseen factors in life which could only be imagined or symbolized—this was early man's solution of the most pressing problem of his existence, that of finding and preserving external conditions favourable to human life. Thus were born magic and religion, which in primitive cultures can hardly be sharply separated.

Whether, as Frazer contended, magic is older than religion is a question that need not detain us here. More recent ethnologists find in mana—the mysterious complex of life-will-power which the primitive mind detects in any object that by unusual behaviour or outstanding qualities strongly engages its attention—the common point of departure of both religion and magic. For Frazer, the chief distinction between magic and religion was that in the latter men attempt to obtain desired results by appealing to superior powers which, like themselves, can be swayed by praise, gifts, or supplications; whereas magical practices compel results by setting in motion impersonal causal sequences in which the same means inevitably bring about the same effects. But he recognized that in the most ancient religions, as well as in many of recent date, the priest was also a magician, and magical practices were inextricably combined with rites properly religious. Magic, he showed, was the precursor of science.

In the earlier stages of human culture, it is hardly possible to draw a boundary between church and state, religion and government, ethics and economics, magic and science. All that will finally emerge sharply and distinctly is at the beginning implicit in a single confused mass. Whether we regard magic and primitive religion as the same or different, it is certain that they had the same objective: to bring about those events or conditions necessary for man's welfare but which he could not adequately control by his muscular exertions. We shall see in the course of this chapter how, as religion became more spiritual and gave increasing attention to our inner life and future happiness, it tended to abandon the endeavour to control the material conditions necessary for human prosperity. It no longer attempted to ensure the succession of the seasons, regulate weather, guarantee the fertility of the fields, avert pestilence, or bring success in battle. As religion gradually withdrew from the practical field, magic and science were free to move in; the latter still strives to take possession of important regions long ago evacuated by the higher religions.

It is difficult to draw up a definition that will sharply delimit magic from applied science. To take a single example, many of the sorcerers' schemes for causing rain to fall seem, on a superficial view, more likely to bring success, and less 'magical', than recent experiments that have given positive results. The principal difference between magic and science is in their methodology. Science owes many of its triumphs to mathematics, in which the magician was rarely proficient. The scientist controls his experiments and keeps careful written records, so that he can tell at the end how many times his procedures yielded the expected results and how many times they failed. The magician neither uses 'controls' nor keeps records; he forgets his failures and is always hopeful. Science does not differ from sorcery so much in its procedures as in its attitude of mind, which values truth above practical results, hence is as eager to recognize its failures as its successes. Science is more powerful than magic because it is better able to learn by its errors. The earlier religions would have found in modern science an ally far more efficient than primitive magic. The more spiritual religions are concerned with matters that science hardly touches, so that they neither depend upon nor compete with it. Science and religion complement each other in covering the whole range of human life.

Many philosophers and ethnologists have tackled the knotty problem of the origin of religion, but most have become enamoured of some plausible explanation which blinded them to other important aspects of the matter. The more deeply we delve into any subject, the more suspicious we become of neat single-factor explanations, and we shall do well to preserve the same mental attitude when examining religion. Why should not the impulses and emotions which gave birth to religion be as varied as those which suffuse life as a whole? If religion, as seems to be true, springs from the whole experience of living, we should expect it to be tinctured with all our desires and emotions. Fear, it has been alleged, made the gods; and greed has been a strong motive in religious rites. But love, and gratitude, and wonder also had a share in the genesis of religion.

A strong influence in the development of ritual and myth was the mystic yearning for identification with those forces which made us and sustain our life. We wish to feel less strange in our cosmic setting, to assimilate it to ourselves and ourselves to it, and as far as possible to take part in those processes which support us. Our bodies are inescapably involved in natural processes, participating in them by intimate reciprocal relations. But our minds, which we feel to be more truly ourselves, seem to stand apart, not entering freely into the activities of the external world save by deliberate effort. The philosopher and the scientist develop a feeling of intimacy with the universe by delving deeply into some of its myriad aspects. For them, knowledge and insight break down the barrier between the mind and the environing world. When we can explain why rain falls and lightning flashes, why summer alternates with winter and day with night, we in a sense enter into these processes which regulate and preserve our lives. And by means of this intellectual participation, we acquire confidence in their continued operation, so necessary for the continuation of our own experience.

For primitive man, this purely intellectual identification with, or participation in, the processes which sustain his life is impossible. He has not developed the techniques for studying them; his language is inadequate to deal with these complexities; his mind is baffled by broad generalities. So for the ideal representation of the philosopher or the scientist he substitutes visible, tangible symbols. Better still, he dramatizes these natural processes; with his own hands and body he symbolizes the sequence of events which culminates in the falling rain and the return of fertility to the earth. Thereby he feels that he shares in these momentous occasions, helps them along, and ensures their perpetuation from year to year. By identifying himself through symbolic ritual with cosmic processes, he imagines that somehow, in some obscure way, they depend upon his will; he expects their continued renewal with some of the confidence that he feels in his ability to move his own limbs.

Much of the ritual of primitive peoples seems to be performed in the spirit of the child eager to participate in the occupations of its parents. The little girl, patting out a mud pie while her mother kneads the bread, fancies that she is helping to prepare the family meal. Placing his hands on the steering wheel beside those of his

4   97

father, the little boy imagines that he is guiding the automobile. So, in their dances, the Zuñi Indians believed that they were helping the rain clouds to gather in the desert sky; and in building the altar and laying the sacrificial fire in the prescribed fashion with the traditional hymns, the Brahmin symbolically renewed the world.

The religions of mankind fall naturally into two main groups: religions of preservation and religions of emancipation or salvation. The former are the earlier, and from them by gradual transition the religions of emancipation evolved. Religions of preservation have as their primary objective the maintenance of a society—a tribe, a city-state, or a nation—and the environment which supports it. Their objectives are earthly, immediate, and material rather than heavenly, distant, and intangible. Although the welfare of the individual is not forgotten, it is at every stage subordinated to that of the community. Religions of preservation are of the mana type, or animistic, or polytheistic. They are scarcely ever monotheistic or monistic, although these more advanced religions may at times be so perverted by intense, selfish nationalism that they acquire some of the characteristics of religions of preservation. This class includes tribal cults in general, the state religions of Greece, Rome, and other ancient communities, and Judaism until after the Babylonian exile. Confucianism, if it can properly be classed as a religion, is one of preservation.

Religions of preservation belong predominantly to that stage of human development characterized by internal amity and external enmity. At the period when they arose, man's outlook was still pathetically narrow, and the concept of universal brotherhood in the distant future. Far from viewing the whole world as a single community of interrelated interests, primitive man looked with hostility upon surrounding groups of men. This constant tension and threat of destruction by neighbouring peoples served to emphasize the importance of cohesion within each small society, which in times of plague, famine, or other troubles could rarely turn to its neighbours for sympathy or succour. The very absence of external concord made internal concord more imperative. Primitive man strove to achieve a harmony that embraced the members of his own tribe, the visible aspects of the natural world which supported the communal life, and those invisible forces which, in his view, so powerfully influenced his welfare. His gods belonged to his tribe alone, and were unfriendly to the deities of neighbouring peoples to which he himself was hostile.

The main concerns of primitive men are personal safety, an adequate supply of food, and the propagation of their kind. These preoccupations account for almost the whole content of religions of preservation. Spells, incantations, and magical practices to avert disease and cure the sick are prominent features of primitive cults. In many of the earlier human societies, children were considered necessary not only to enhance the prestige of the parents and to support them in advanced age, but also to ensure their welfare in a future life. Hence marriage and birth rites are prominent features of early religions. In the incessant wars with neighbouring peoples which claimed so much time and thought, the aid of the tribal or civic gods, without which victory could hardly be expected, was enlisted by supplication, ceremony, and sacrifice, sometimes with human victims. In all the emergencies of life, no less than in the daily routine of preparing food, eating, washing, and sleeping, men sought to propitiate and win the support of those unseen powers upon which their welfare depended.

At every stage of culture, men fall sick, desire offspring, and, unfortunately, go to war; and in all these situations they are likely to remember that the fulfilment of their desires depends on powers over which they have no direct control, and to seek to enlist the good offices of these unseen beings by means which differ greatly with the cultural background, yet betray the same tragic conviction of our dependence. Even in countries where men no longer sacrifice to the gods for health, or offspring, or victory in battle, they still pray for these advantages. But methods of obtaining food have altered greatly with the passage of the centuries; the advance of civilization has followed these changes; and religious practices have been profoundly modified by them. While still hunters and food-gatherers, men invented many ceremonies, charms, and magic practices to ensure success in the chase. Often fasting, abstention from sexual intercourse, and ritual purification preceded the hunt. When this was successful, elaborate ceremonies might attend the eating of the animal's flesh; for it was necessary to appease its spirit, lest it warn others of its kind to avoid the people who had slain it, or perhaps wreak vengeance upon its murderers. Primitive man rarely hunted wantonly, but to satisfy his pressing needs, and with a thought for the continuing supply of his essential food. To cultivate favourable relations with the animals that supported his life, to eat without upsetting the delicate balance of nature, primitive man looked to his religion for guidance and support.

The rise of agriculture brought tremendous changes in the content of religions of preservation without altering their spirit. Now not the free animals, which could maintain their own numbers if not too hard-pressed by those who preyed on them, but the cultivated plants and domestic animals which at every stage of their life cycle must be closely watched and controlled, became the centre of human interest. The alternation of the seasons, the advent of the rains, the preservation or renewal of the earth's fertility, were matters too momentous to be left to hazard, or to the blind regularity of natural laws of which the primitive mind could scarcely conceive. The modern farmer feels that he does his part when he sows and tills and reaps at the proper seasons, leaving it to the impersonal operations of nature to provide the conditions of temperature, humidity, and the like, without which sowing and tilling are vain. The primitive agriculturist would think that his modern successor does things by halves. He believed it necessary to put forth his active efforts not only in preparing the land and sowing the seed, but in controlling those natural conditions without whose cooperation agriculture yields only aching backs and calloused hands. Hence those ancient fertility cults which the researches of ethnologists have revealed in nearly all lands where agriculture was practised, those mystic rites of Osiris and Isis, Attis and Cybele, Venus and Adonis, those periodic sacrifices of man and beast, which to the modern mind are so amazing and incomprehensible, so futile and so cruel.

For religions of preservation, the happiness of the individual is a minor consideration. The Kantian concept of each man as an end in himself, of society as a community of such ends, is foreign to the primitive mentality. To the tribesman, it appears, the individual is important only as a member of the tribe, apart from which he is of no account. Primitive man does not hesitate to starve and mutilate himself, to endure privations and self-inflicted tortures utterly repugnant to his modern descendants, all for advantages more often imaginary than real. How can one with so little regard for his own feelings be very considerate of the sensibilities of others?

Tribal taboos, which safeguard the community from dangers actual or fanciful, are enforced by the tribal leaders, who punish offenders or condemn them to an exile that is usually the equivalent of a death sentence. But to injure or kill one's neighbour is often merely a private misdemeanour, to be requited by the injured party or his relatives rather than by the community as a whole. Yet, since blood feuds weaken the tribe and diminish its ability to confront its enemies, society at last found itself obliged to interfere in such private quarrels, to preserve its own strength if not to shield individuals from sorrow.

Religions of preservation commonly recognize a future life, and often make elaborate provisions for the dead person's journey to the region of the shades. Although affection for the deceased relative and an unselfish wish for his happiness might have been sufficient motives for the laborious and costly funeral rites, a less altruistic consideration was seldom absent. If the dead man's needs were not adequately met, if the spirit were not coaxed into repose with the appropriate ritual, it might return to terrify and harass those who had been negligent in the fulfilment of filial obligations. Religions of this class view the soul's destiny quite differently from the more spiritual religions which superseded them. There is, at this stage, little evidence of yearning to behold the source of our being, to reach the fountainhead of righteousness, beauty and truth, or to attain mystic union with the One. The future life is seen as merely a less substantial replica of this earthly existence, with the same activities, the same pleasures, the same perils, and requiring material supports of the same nature. Hence food, clothing, weapons, wives, slaves, and animals were often placed in the tomb or upon the funeral pyre of the deceased, to serve his needs in the shadowy land beyond.

Whether deliberately or through the blind gropings of vital impulse and instinct, all living things seek the security they need to complete their little cycle of birth, growth, and reproductive maturity, without rude disruption by external forces. By attempting to enlist the support of unseen powers in safeguarding his vital needs, man adopted an expedient which, so far as we know, was unprecedented on this planet. It was an audacious venture, perhaps deserving of success. But the problem he set for himself was radically insoluble. Security, peace, and happiness can at best be fleeting and imperfect on a planet where a potentially unlimited number of living things compete for a strictly limited quantity of space and materials. Moreover, the solution to which primitive man was led by his whole past experience tended to aggravate rather than to ease the situation. By supposing that his tutelary spirits were different from, and hostile to, those which guarded the interests of neighbouring peoples, he prepared for himself strife and frustration on a scale hitherto unknown among the animate creatures of this planet. The pluralism of primitive religions could provide no adequate solution for the perplexities of an essentially unitary world.

Not only did the religions of preservation, however valuable they may have been in promoting the unity of a tribe or city-state, fail to solve the problem of bringing security and felicity to men; the very goal which they set for themselves could no longer satisfy the kind of man who began to appear as civilization marched forward. As agriculture and the arts advanced, as the unification of many tribes under a powerful ruler brought a measure of security, a few at least among the teeming multitudes in the agricultural valleys found leisure to cultivate their minds and think long thoughts. Their interests and speculations soared far beyond the material preoccupations of daily life. Men began to regard themselves as individuals, each with a unique personality, rather than as tribesmen who could have no life and interests apart from the collective activities of their tribe. This new experience of the free life of the mind gave rise to the concept of a soul or spirit that is no mere bloodless shadow of the body, but a being of a different order, enjoying prerogatives of its own independent of, and superior to, the animal functions of the physical organism. Thus there grew up the ideal of a future life which would be something more than the continuance, in the land beyond the grave, of the same old occupations of hunting, feasting, fighting, and mating—an existence in which the spirit would find release from these animal necessities and enjoy perfect freedom in its own pure sphere.

Yet despite these advances in the size of kingdoms, in the ease and security of living, in the range of knowledge, in the height and breadth of men's thoughts, the old shackles still bound, the old afflictions still assailed the flesh and the mind. Men still toiled and sweated for their daily bread, they were still led astray by their own unruly passions, still quarrelled and hated, fell ill, suffered, and died.

The savage, too, had fought and bled, hungered and sickened, perhaps far more frequently than the civilized man who succeeded him; but his nascent intellect could picture no existence greatly different from the only one he intimately knew. More abundant food, quicker victory in battle, longer life, better hunting in the realm beyond the grave—these were the only improvements to his actual condition that his mind was capable of conceiving; these were the boons he asked of the gods to whom he prayed and sacrificed. But to the civilized man who now began to emerge and to develop the capacity for abstract thought, who could think of himself as a duality of body and spirit, a new solution presented itself. In the second millennium before the Christian era there may be detected, among the civilized peoples of the eastern Mediterranean and southern Asia, the first vague glimmerings of a new type of religion which during the next thousand years or so took definite form. Religions of emancipation slowly grew out of the religions of preservation that had temporarily satisfied primitive man. The great revolution in religion began.

The first point to be noticed about this new type of religion is the complete shift in emphasis. In religions of preservation, the tribe took precedence over the individual; there was little thought of saving a man apart from his society. In religions of emancipation, interest centres on the individual, who is promised freedom from pain and sorrow, everlasting bliss, if he will faithfully follow their precepts. Nations may rise and fall, societies grow and decay; but each man's destiny depends upon his own intrinsic worth, on his own thoughts, words, and deeds. This altered outlook corresponds to a new conception of man's nature. As long as the animal body was the centre of interest, a man was wholly vulnerable to external forces and unlikely to escape whatever misfortune overtook his community. But when the soul acquired the dignity of an independent entity, distinct from the body which temporarily housed it and capable of a free life of its own, it was not necessarily involved in all the unhappy predicaments of its dwelling of clay. Victory or defeat in battle, abundance or scarcity of provisions, made tremendous differences to the prosperity of the society and every one of its individuals; but these vicissitudes in the external world need not affect the ultimate welfare of the indwelling spirit, whose destiny is determined by events on a different plane.

As men became spiritual, the deities they adored were transformed in the same direction. The earliest individualized gods were mere magnified images of the undisciplined men who conceived them, feasting, loving, and quarrelling exactly as their earthly worshippers did. Gradually there arose the concept of a Deity spiritual and moral, without body or passions, pervading the whole universe, which was at best an imperfect manifestation of the divine Being who made and supported it. Since the idea that men could form of this supernal Being was conditioned by their own spiritual maturity, metaphysical acumen, and cultural background, it varied greatly with the time and place. Sometimes God was conceived as a spiritual person tenderly loving those who served him devotedly; or the Supreme Being became an unconditioned Absolute, an eternal Reality beyond all attributes and distinctions, unthinkable by the mind of man: again, as in Jainism and early Buddhism, the supreme Reality took the form of an impersonal Law, an inexorable principle of justice, changeless from age to age, with mechanical precision bringing back to the doer the moral consequences of his every deed. In the religions of preservation, God or the gods were primarily Providence—the providers of man's physical necessities. In religions of salvation, God became the upholder of a moral order and the giver of immortal life.

It is evident that a personal God is not essential to a spiritual religion, nor is belief in the immortality of the individual conscious of his own ego. The basic requirement of a higher religion seems to be the conviction that the universe contains some principle or power that works for righteousness and order, and that if we attune ourselves to this moral force, all will ultimately be well with us. Pantheism, in its simplest form, is incompatible with this belief, for if God and the universe are one and the same, all that happens, good or evil, are equally effects of this world-God or God-world and, one would suppose, equally acceptable to it. A Spinoza may be filled with love for a pantheistic God who is indifferent to his worshippers and their values, but this attitude of extreme detachment from personal interests is exceedingly difficult for the ordinary mortal to cultivate.

In whatever guise the Supreme was conceived, the new religions and religious philosophies that now grew up adopted the same attitude toward him or it: External conditions were of minor importance; what really counted was the relation between the individual human spirit and the spiritual Being who pervaded the universe. Men had prayed and sacrificed to their gods for peace and health and enduring happiness without obtaining much satisfaction. The world was still a house of strife and sorrow. Well, let it be so, if so it must be. It is, after all, only the external man who sweats, hungers, sickens, and bleeds. Behind this mask of skin and flesh resides the true man, the spiritual being who needs neither food nor riches, neither bleeds nor dies. Behind the ceaseless flux and change of the world stands an eternal Being who remains unaffected by all this play of fleeting images. Let us bring the eternal in man into harmony with the Eternal in the universe; then, happen what may, all will be well with us. This new attitude, which had been lurking vaguely in men's minds, found definite expression during the millennium preceding the death of Christ. In Greece and Palestine, India and China, the doctrine was taught in different languages, clothed in different images, supported by different arguments. Yet in their central core, the new religions were everywhere much the same.

While religions of preservation try to alter the world, making it more propitious to human interests, religions of emancipation emphasize the need to alter the inner self, bringing all one's thoughts and desires into harmony and cultivating submission to the divine will. The primitive man, indeed, is not unwilling to change his own state, by fasting, ablutions, lustrations, and often self-mutilation of the most drastic sort; but nearly always he does so in the belief that by such means he will the better attain certain material objectives, such as success in the chase, endurance on the march, victory in battle, or healthy offspring. The hard conditions of primitive life teach submission to the inevitable in a way which civilized man, with his greater control over his environment, finds it difficult to achieve. But to the savage, as to the wild animal, silent, uncomplaining endurance of pain and adversity is a practical necessity rather than a religious virtue. He is always eager to enjoy material advantages when he can. The religions of emancipation tended to make of submission a mark of holiness. Not to change external conditions to our advantage, but to regenerate the inner self, is their highest goal. Often, as in Christianity, this spiritual awakening is referred to as rebirth.

The great revolution in religion was, above all, a shift in allegiance from the tangible to the intangible, from the seen to the unseen, from the familiar to the remote. Primitive man, like the natural or carnal man of every age, prefers corporeal to spiritual satisfactions, his familiar life in the land of his ancestors to the shadowy existence of the hereafter. Convinced that unseen powers control visible events, he propitiates these powers as a means of safeguarding his earthly prosperity rather than because he loves them; he is capable of blaspheming them if they thwart him. In the new religions, the spirit takes precedence over the flesh; the life of the released soul is infinitely more desirable than earthly life; Deity becomes a goal to be reached for its own sake, rather than an agent to be wooed for the material benefits it can give.

Although this spiritualization of religion was, on the whole, a great gain, it was not achieved without a deplorable loss. The experiences of earthly life were too often grossly undervalued. The sceptical and incredulous could well ask whether the votaries of these new faiths were not turning their backs on the only solid satisfactions they knew, in order to chase will-o'-the-wisps they might never catch. But the greatest tragedy was that the new religions, in varying degrees but especially in the West, ceased to care about the natural foundation of human life, the earth with its waters and soils and the vegetation and animals they support, leaving them exposed to ruthless exploitation by greedy, destructive men undeterred by religious restraints.

8

Caring for the Soul—I

William James distinguished four constituents of the Self: the material Self, the social Self, the spiritual Self, and the pure Ego. In Chapter 3 we considered some of the religious or magico-religious beliefs and practices concerned with the care of the external aspects of the Self, the material and the social. Such beliefs and practices arose, and are most prevalent, in religions of preservation; but many have been carried over, in more or less modified form, into the higher religions. We have now to consider the care of the two remaining constituents of the Self, the spiritual Self and the pure Ego. These comprise that more recondite part of the Self which is often called the soul. This word has been employed with the most various meanings by different religions and philosophies: some have held that there is a substantial soul that survives the body's decay; whereas others maintain that the soul has no existence apart from a living organism, so that there is, strictly speaking, no soul, but only certain dispositions of the body which we so designate. In the following discussion, except when dealing with the view of the soul maintained by some particular religion or philosophy, we shall mean by this term the conscious or spiritual aspect of a human being, which is directly known to himself alone—that part of himself which survives his body's dissolution, if any part does.

The quality of a man's inner self is known directly to him alone. Those around him can only conjecture this quality, or reconstruct it imaginatively, from his words, facial expression, gestures, and acts. From such outward indications of his inner life as he vouchsafes to us, we form an impression of him, which we call his character. Our estimate of a person's character is based largely on his attitude toward, and treatment of, the beings around him, especially other people. As seems inevitable in a social animal, our appraisal of a soul's worth, and view of its future prospects, is so bound up with its relations to other creatures that, in all the higher religions, caring for the soul consists in large measure in refraining from acts injurious to others. Although such overt conduct is undeniably an important indication of a soul's quality, it has other, more private, aspects which seem to have an important bearing on its ultimate destiny. Such intrinsic qualities as cheerfulness, serenity, love, benevolence, the consistency of desires, and the quality of memories, may be far from adequately revealed by behaviour. And some religions have held that the soul's ultimate destiny depends upon right faith or right knowledge, especially a correct understanding of its own nature, more than upon conduct.

To value men and women for their character rather than their outward circumstances is a sign of spiritual maturity, whether in an individual or a society. On the whole, savages have little appreciation of character, or they judge it by standards quite different from those which people of higher culture apply. (The Arapesh of New Guinea, whom we earlier considered, seem to be an exception.) Likewise, the lower social strata of more advanced societies have a deficient regard for character, as is evident to anyone who examines some of the popular heroes, such as the dictators and demagogues of the present day. With all such people, savages and underdeveloped members of higher civilizations, the accidental circumstances of a person's life count far more than his character. The successful warrior, the loud-mouthed braggart, the clever cheat, are too often admired more than the quiet, unassuming person of sterling character; to suffer a misfortune, such as an accident or a disease, is regarded as a personal blemish more serious than a moral defect.

In conformity with this lack of appreciation of character among primitive peoples, their eschatology disregards the moral quality of the deceased. In the earlier conceptions of the afterworld, there are no special torments for the wicked nor special delights for the good. When any classification or segregation of souls is contemplated, it is based on accidental circumstances rather than inner worth. Thus, in the belief of the northern Ostyaks of Siberia, the assassinated, the drowned, and the suicides must go together along a special road to the land of the dead in the far north: the concentration of attention on externals causes one who lays violent hands upon himself to be classed with the victim of another man's violence or of the superior power of nature. In the same vein, the Kol of India believe that all those who have been mutilated, devoured by a tiger, or killed in an accident, become evil spirits unable to enter the land of the dead. Similar views are widespread among savages.[1]

In Chapter 5, we examined another aspect of the failure to regard the soul's destiny as determined by its own volitions alone: in the more primitive religions, the ghost's welfare depended above all on whether the body had been interred with all due rites and whether the descendants of the deceased maintained the cult of the dead, offering food and drink at daily or longer intervals. Not the least advance, from the moral point of view, of the newer religions of emancipation was their recognition that the soul's destiny depends wholly on its own quality, as revealed by its conduct while incarnated, or in other ways. Now the soul was assured its merited reward or punishment whether the body was interred with magnificent obsequies, or sunk in the sea, or lay neglected in the wilderness torn by vultures; whether the deceased was lovingly remembered or wholly forgotten by survivors. Yet practices now, or until recently, persisting in the higher religions, such as praying for the dead, burning candles, or buying indulgences for them, prove how stubbornly the belief that the living can influence the destiny of the dead man's soul has lingered in men's minds, encouraged, in some cases, by a venal priesthood.

It will simplify our survey of the different systems for ensuring the soul's ultimate welfare if we carry a little further the classification of religions begun in the preceding chapter. There, it will be recalled, we divided religions into two great classes, the earlier religions of preservation and the more recent religions of emancipation or salvation. Of the latter, two main types may be distinguished by the importance they attribute to the flow of events in the phenomenal world—to evolution, human history, the birth and development of individuals, and similar phenomena, which collectively are conveniently designated as the 'world process'. Is something of ultimate value, something new and precious which might not otherwise be achieved, emerging from the flux and strife of the phenomenal world; or is the world a meaningless interplay of forces, signifying nothing, and leading to nothing of permanent

[1] Arnold van Gennep, *The Rites of Passage*, Routledge & Kegan Paul, London, 1960, p. 150–2.

value? Is Being striving to accomplish or realize something through the world process; or is this process all a mistake, a cosmic error difficult to explain or to rectify? According to which of these contrasting views they adopt, the religions of emancipation may be classified as religions of regress and religions of progress. The whole scheme of classification then becomes:

A *Religions of Preservation*
1 Mana religions
2 Animistic religions
3 Theistic religions (primitive polytheisms in general, including the civic religions of Greece and Rome; the monotheism of Biblical Judaism)

B *Religions of Emancipation or Salvation*
1 Religions of regress (Advaita Vedanta of Samkara, primitive Buddhism)
2 Religions of progress (Jainism, Visistadvaita Vedanta of Rama-nuja, Stoicism, Christianity and Islam—in part)

It is questionable whether religions of regress should not, in our scheme of classification, be placed after rather than before religions of progress, as a later, and possibly more advanced, development of metaphysical thought. Western philosophy began in Ionic Greece with the recognition of substances and only after long ages reached the Idealistic or Phenomenological outlook of the Advaita Vedanta and Buddhist metaphysics. Nevertheless, the Vedantic viewpoint is very old, being derived from the *Upanishads*, which are generally attributed to the first millennium B.C.; and the Buddha himself lived before Socrates. Moreover, we must remember that in the more primitive religions, that which survived the body was a ghost or shade dependent upon the offerings of living descendants, and it took men a very long while to develop the concept of a soul or spiritual substance capable of enjoying an independent existence. This concept is just as far removed from primitive modes of thought as the seemingly more sophisticated metaphysic of religions of regress. Although it might be going too far to say that these latter religions are incompatible with our modern notions of evolution, they certainly deprive evolution of much significance. Religions of progress, however, fit in well with the view of evolution as a true advance, lifting creation to ever higher levels of awareness. They give meaning to organic life and its often painful struggle to perfect itself, as religions of regress do not.

The central idea of a religion of regress is that salvation is to be achieved by extricating from its tragic involvement in the phenomenal world a self that was originally pure and serene. Through what pathetic miscalculation spirit became enmeshed in matter, or in the illusion of a material world, is never made quite clear, nor is it of great moment in the logical development of the doctrine. But somehow the spirit in each living thing, which is everywhere the same universal spirit, forgets its true nature, suffers the delusion of individuality, and identifies itself with the body in which it is entangled. The essential self of every man is the same, for it is not other than the universal Self. The illusion of separate identity arises from ignorance and the false identification of the conscious self with an animal body. We pay with pain and misery for the blindness that attaches us to the perishable body, subject to a thousand ills.

The first step toward salvation consists in dispelling the mist of ignorance and understanding the essential nature of the self, its sameness with the universal Self, the transitory and accidental character of its association with the flesh. If by means of long and severe mental discipline we achieve this supreme realization, we are released from the wheel of existence with all its toils and pains and enter into eternal, changeless bliss in the Absolute. But all sense of individuality, all personality, is necessarily lost. Everyone's bliss is the same bliss, since by absorption into the One the distinction between you and me is irretrievably extinguished. Nothing is ultimately gained by individual experience and strenuous effort to perfect oneself, since the most that we can accomplish is our extrication from the tragic predicament in which we inexplicably found ourselves. At the end of the whole cosmic play, if there be an end, there will remain only the single, timeless, blissful Being, without distinction of persons. There is no such thing as personal immortality.

Such, in essence, is the teaching of the *Upanishads* and of the Advaita Vedanta, a religious philosophy which is the logical development of the germinal idea advanced by the ancient Indian sages. The absolute Being is Brahman, timeless and changeless, whose attributes are *sat-cit-ananda*—being-consciousness-bliss. The individual soul is the atman, which is not ultimately distinct from Brahman. The world, an emanation from Brahman, has at most relative reality; it is not self-subsistent. Its relation to Brahman is inexplicable, beyond the fact that it is an expression of his *maya* or power. The atman suffers because it is ignorant of its identity with Brahman and ascribes reality to the world process. By the practice of meditation and contemplation, which are most systematically and efficaciously carried out in accordance with yogic discipline, the atman becomes aware of its true nature and, after it has freed itself from karmic deposits, attains release and reabsorption in Brahman.

Like all very old religions which have become naturalized in many countries among people of different races and temperaments, Buddhism has split into a number of sects, each of which interprets in its own fashion the teachings ascribed to the Buddha, whose reluctance to dwell upon the metaphysical foundations of religion left his followers unparalleled freedom to indulge their own propensity for speculation in these fields. Among the metaphysical questions which Gautama banned as unprofitable and leading to discord is that of the condition of a released person after death, whether he exists or does not exist. The Buddha was also silent about the existence of God. The southern or Hinayana school of Buddhism gave a negative interpretation to the master's silence on these transcendental questions. It recognizes no deity. The soul is not a substance or entity but a mere complex of transitory psychic events, whose character is in large measure determined by past events in the same series. So long as the individual is chained to the wheel of *samsara*, this causal sequence persists through his death and rebirth, his destiny in each incarnation depending on the karma stored up by his activities in previous existences. When, by means of enlightenment and right conduct, the individual's karma is exhausted, he attains Nirvana or release. Then when he dies the causal sequence comes to an end, the psychic complex is dissolved. Since the 'soul' was nothing more than this sequence, nothing remains of it. There is final and complete extinction. The flame expires because the fuel has all been consumed, and that is the end of it. All that one can hope to accomplish by right thought, right speech, and right conduct is his extraction from an unfortunate involvement and reduction to non-entity. Hinayana Buddhism is thus a religion of regress which views the world process as a purposeless show causing much suffering but leading to naught. The northern or Mahayana branch of Buddhism has developed in a different direction.

Views of this nature are foreign to the spirit of Christianity and Islam; yet there have not been lacking mystics of these faiths who practised a religion of regress, attempting by austere living and rigorous spiritual discipline to divest themselves of everything individual and particular, so that they might become indistinguishably one with a timeless Absolute. Whenever mysticism follows the *via negativa*, it becomes in effect a religion of regress, no matter with what church it is associated.

To a religion of progress, the world is a creative process of fundamental importance. However grim and tragic it may at times appear to the sentient beings caught up in it, it leads somewhere; it is purposeful or rational. Salvation is something more than the complete loss of individuality and reabsorption into the Absolute by dispelling the illusion of separateness. It consists in attaining harmony with God without the sacrifice of personality. The righteous liberated soul abides forever in God, or in sight of God, enjoying the ineffable bliss of being enveloped in God's love and sharing his knowledge. As a result of the world process, Being is enriched by the formation of individual souls or spirits. There is disagreement among the several religions and philosophies of this group as to whether individual souls have always existed, or arise anew as each organism is conceived or born. But they agree that, once it enters the flesh, every soul forges its own destiny by its conduct, and that it can never be destroyed.

An imperfectly developed religion of progress was the Osirian faith of ancient Egypt, which provides an interesting example of transition from the amoral view of the afterworld typical of primitive peoples to the strictly moral view of all the higher religions. According to the *Book of the Dead*, the dead person enters the subterranean hall of judgment, boldly hailing his judges and proclaiming his righteousness. The chief judge, Osiris, is assisted by forty-two gods, hideous demons with terrifying names, to each of whom the deceased declares his innocence of some particular sin. Most of the transgressions of which he must prove that he is guiltless are genuine moral faults, such as murder, theft, lying, stirring up discord, covetousness, anger, adultery, and blaspheming the gods. In so long a list of sins, there are subtle distinctions no longer evident to the modern reader, as well as several verbal repetitions. The number of assessors was apparently made large to include one from each nome or administrative district of Egypt, so that every dead person would confront a judge from his own neighbourhood, too familiar with the character he had borne in his lifetime to be deceived by false statements.

The next step in the awful judgment is the weighing of the dead person's heart against the feather of Truth, in the balances of Re, the sun-god. This is carried out in the presence of Osiris who, in the wrappings of a mummy in which he is customarily depicted, is seated on a throne, with the goddess Isis and her sister Nephthys standing behind him. The nine gods of the Heliopolitan Ennead, headed by Re himself, witness the weighing. Jackal-headed Anubis, the ancient mortuary god, operates the balances; while Thoth, scribe of the gods, stands by with pen and tablet, ready to record the result. At the critical moment, the deceased cries out to his heart on the weighing pan, adjuring it not to betray him. If the heart weighs true, Osiris's son, Horus, takes the dead person's hand and presents him to Osiris, who admits him to all the blessings that await the justified dead. If the heart proves false, the cowering soul is delivered up to a grotesque chimera, with a crocodile's head and a body part lion and part hippopotamus, which has been waiting close by, ready to spring upon and devour the wicked.

Except for the bewildering size of the tribunal, the judgment of the Egyptian's soul before Osiris is rather similar to that of the Christian or Mohammedan before his God. The most important difference is that the Egyptian proclaims his own innocence and pleads with his heart, or conscience, not to bear witness against him; whereas the omniscient Judge of later religions already knows how each mortal has lived and sees right through his heart, so that any declaration of innocence by him would be superfluous. Nevertheless, the Egyptian who believed in the competence of his judges and hoped to dwell blissfully in the subterranean realm of the dead would, while on earth, be careful never to sully his soul by evil words or deeds.

Although the elements of a moral eschatology were already present in Egypt 3,500 years ago, the Egyptians failed to develop a truly ethical doctrine of the life after death. It has been said that the spiritual development of the Egyptians was hampered by their bondage to the concrete and their inability to forget a distant past whose monuments and relics were so marvellously preserved by the dryness of their climate. The persistence of primitive magic and a materialistic view of the afterworld worked strongly against an ethical conception of the soul's fate. Venal priests and scribes distorted the Osirian faith for their own pecuniary gain, grotesquely multiplying the fears which naturally assail a mind contemplating death, then selling protective charms. Such charms make up the bulk of the *Book of the Dead*, which in ancient Egypt never existed as such but is a collection of mortuary texts copied on rolls of papyrus and placed in coffins. No single scroll contained the whole of the collection, although the longer and more sumptuous of them bore the majority of the two hundred or so extant texts. In addition to incantations that assured the deceased person's admission to the afterworld, there were charms which prevented the loss of his mouth, head, or heart, charms that protected him from the attack of serpents or monsters, charms which prevented his drinking water from turning to flame, and numerous others against contingencies equally fantastic. Moreover, the deceased was equipped with a stone image of the sacred scarabaeus or beetle, inscribed with a potent command to his heart not to betray his true character at the moment when it was weighed in the balance against the feather of Truth. By such devices, designed to enrich unscrupulous priests, the lofty moral conception of a final assessment of a man's life was turned into a farce that must have been devastating to any conscience not vigorous enough to resist such childish impositions.[1]

In sharp contrast to the situation in Egypt, the sages of ancient India conceived a system of retributive justice which allowed no room for deceit and chicanery but operated as impersonally, as immune to human interference, as gravitation. This is the law of karma, which cannot be understood without its indispensable accompaniment, reincarnation or the transmigration of souls. According to this dogma, which has been held by various races scattered over the globe but nowhere more firmly than in India, each soul is an entity which may occupy a succession of bodies, now with a human form, now that of some other animal. Between incarnations, it may sojourn for a while in a temporary heaven or

[1] Breasted, *op. cit.*, Ch. XIV.

hell, enjoying the rewards, or suffering the punishments, it has merited by its conduct in its last preceding life on earth.

The whole object of the religions and religious philosophies of India is to liberate the soul from this tedious round of incarnations, known as the wheel of existence, so that it may enjoy everlasting bliss in its pure, bodiless state. So firmly rooted in the Indian mind is this belief in metempsychosis or rebirth that some of the most acute metaphysicians that the world has produced, including the Buddha and Samkara, retained it in their doctrines, although it seems incompatible with Buddhism or the Advaita Vedanta, which do not recognize a substantial, individual soul. Only if the soul is a substance or self-subsisting entity does it seem capable of preserving its identity while passing from one body to another. The early Buddhists were not unaware of the difficulty; with great subtlety they distinguished between the transmigration of a substantial soul and the transmission from body to body of psychic traits in the absence of such a soul. They compared the latter to lighting one torch from another, or to learning a poem which another person recites. In such cases nothing substantial passes from body to body, yet in each instance the second receives an impress from the first.[1]

According to the doctrine of karma, what happens to us in one embodied existence is determined by the moral quality of our conduct in previous embodied existences, all quite automatically, without the intervention of any God or supernatural being. A well-born man of high caste who lives wickedly may be reborn in a lower caste, perhaps as a cripple or imbecile, or he may even be reincarnated in some irrational animal. Moreover, many hardships and much suffering will afflict his days. But the person who lives righteously will be reincarnated in more auspicious circumstances, with a good mind in a sound body, so that he may advance rapidly along the stony road to final release.

As an example of a religion built upon the foundation of karma and reincarnation, let us take Jainism, which claims to be the world's oldest living religion and is certainly very ancient; for indications of its existence, in the form of figurines standing in the posture characteristic of Jaina yogis, have been unearthed by the excavators

[1] This doctrine is well presented in an ancient, entertaining work, *The Questions of King Milinda*, The Sacred Books of the East, Oxford University Press, 1890, reprinted 1925.

of the old Indus cities of Harappa and Mohenjo-daro. Its metaphysic, if less subtle than that of certain Indian doctrines of later development, is more logically consistent, for in viewing each *jiva* or individual soul as an eternal, indestructible substance it provides a firm foundation for metempsychosis. Karma it regards as a sort of material deposit, consisting of very subtle particles, which cling to the soul and prevent the free play of its faculties. In its pure, unalloyed state, every individual soul is endowed with infinite apprehension, infinite comprehension, infinite bliss, and infinite power. However, the pure state of the *jiva* is not its original state, for every soul, which being eternal had no beginning, entered the time process with its karmic incrustation. Nevertheless, by right living the soul can be freed from this dross and at long last come into full possession of its superb powers. Thus there is progress from the soul's original bondage to its karmic deposit to its final freedom. As the world marches forward, there is steady increase in the number of purified souls that have realized their own nature.

To a devout Jain, to care for the soul is to lead such a life that the influx of karma is prevented and the already existing incrustation falls away, so that at last the *jiva* may exist in perfect purity, enjoying the knowledge, power, and bliss proper to it. To this end, one must cherish the *triratna* or three jewels of Right Knowledge, Right Faith, and Right Conduct. Right Knowledge evidently means knowledge of Jaina doctrine; Right Faith is faith in the course of salvation that it teaches. Right Conduct is strict obedience to the five points of the moral code that are binding on both layman and ascetic, but more stringently on the latter.

The basic principle of Jaina morality, the bedrock on which its whole ethic rests, is *ahimsa*, which is variously translated as harmlessness or non-violence. Although Jainism shares this inclusive moral rule with other Indian religions, by no other religion is it so broadly applied and so scrupulously followed. For the *sadhu* or monk the rule against taking life is absolute; to destroy even the smallest living thing is a violation of his vows. He walks only on beaten paths, carefully watching where he sets his feet, even sweeping the ground before him, so as not to crush some tiny creeping creature, as he could hardly avoid doing if he passed over grassy fields, He wears a cloth over his mouth to prevent harming with his breath the invisible *jivas* that inhabit the air. He is careful where he sits; he avoids sudden violent movements. If he does not go quite naked (as is the rule of some Jaina sects) he periodically searches his garments to remove insects with gentle care not to hurt them. He drinks only water that has been boiled and strained to remove sentient beings; he cannot prepare his own food, but is dependent on that freely given to him by the lay community. He lives with constant vigilance to harm no living things, not even the least of them, for killing causes the influx of karma upon the soul.

For the Jaina householder or layman, the law of *ahimsa* is somewhat more leniently interpreted. Since neither he nor the monks dependent on his generosity could live without vegetable food, he may, when necessary, take the life of plants endowed with the single sense of touch; but he, no less than the ascetic, must carefully avoid killing animals with two or more senses. By this rule, Jains are excluded not only from occupations in which killing animals is essential, but even from those in which it is accidental. It is difficult for a Jain to be a farmer, because agriculture, even when restricted to vegetable crops, can hardly be carried on without much incidental destruction of insects and other small creatures. A strict Jain would not be a blacksmith, a limeburner, or a potter, nor engage in any other occupation in which a furnace is used, for many insects are destroyed in a fire. He would not make a cart or a railway carriage, for such wheeled vehicles run over insects and other animals, and railroad trains sometimes kill people.

If these restrictions seem extreme to Westerners, every humane person will approve of five rules, subsidiary to the law of harmlessness, which the Jain must follow in his treatment of domestic animals: he must not tie an animal up too tightly; beat it unmercifully; mutilate it; overload or overwork it; nor neglect to feed it properly. More questionable, from the humanitarian standpoint, is the prohibition of killing an incurable animal to terminate horrible suffering. The Jains defend this seemingly callous indifference by pointing out that the creature's pains are caused by the karma it accumulated in an earlier incarnation, when perhaps its soul inhabited a human body, and that only by such suffering can it work off the karmic deposit. Aside from doctrinal considerations, one who is not in the habit of killing is most reluctant to do so, even when compassion recommends such a course—as I can attest from personal experience. Animal sacrifice is, of course, wholly alien to

Jainism, not only because it violates the law of *ahimsa*, but because this religion recognizes no God.

Broadly interpreted, the rule never to harm any creature includes every moral prohibition that can be rationally defended; for all acts forbidden by a reasonable morality can be demonstrated to be, directly or indirectly, injurious to self or others. Moreover, for the Jains, the practice of *ahimsa* involves far more than overt activity; its spiritual value depends largely on the careful control of one's passions and attitudes. To wish harm to another is an act of *himsa*, even if nothing comes of the desire; whereas accidental injury to some other creature, for which one is sorry, is not sinful—provided, of course, that one lives with all due caution to avoid hurting any sentient being. Thus to cleanse the soul of hatred, anger, envy, greed, lust, and every other disturbing passion is the one sure road to holiness, as in every other advanced religion.

Although the whole of morality can be deduced from the first principle of avoiding injury to any sentient being, including oneself, not everyone has the time, or the insight, to make the deduction. Accordingly, accessory rules, and commentaries on these rules, are indispensable for the average person. In addition to vowing to follow the law of *ahimsa*, every devout Jain, ascetic or layman, pledges himself to abide by four other rules of conduct: to avoid falsehood, not to steal, to be chaste, and to refrain from excesses. Strictly applied, these rules would prevent any form of dishonest conduct, rash speech, or evil thoughts; and they also forbid instigating others to do wrong. Chastity includes not only absolute faithfulness to one's own husband or wife but likewise the avoidance of lascivious imaginings. The injunctions against falsehood, theft, and unchastity are common to the higher religions, but the final vow appears to be peculiar to Jainism. This vow of limitation, called *Parigraha viramana vrata*, is the product of deep psychological insight and a fine appreciation of the motives for transgression. In taking it, the Jain voluntarily sets an upper limit to the amount of property of various sorts that he will accumulate. When a successful merchant or professional man has earned all that he has allowed himself, he may give the excess to the building of temples, hospitals for people or animals, or other charitable undertakings. By accessory vows, a Jain may limit the extent of his travels, the number of personal articles he will use, the kinds of food he will eat, or the extent of his indulgence in luxuries. It is obvious how these vows, by placing restraints upon that inordinate greed which so often incites us to do wrong, make it easier to be faithful to the primary rules of conduct.

Implicit in Jaina ethics is the belief that in the moral world, as in the mechanical, action and reaction are equal and opposite. Just as, when I push against this table, it pushes as hard against my hand; so, I cannot harm other things without injuring my own soul. Even more, I cannot hate them, or wish evil to befall them, without spiritual deterioration. One aware of this reciprocity will follow the same rules of conduct whether his primary motive is egoistic or altruistic, whether he is more concerned to preserve his own soul from harm or to avoid giving pain to other creatures. Yet there is a vast spiritual difference between these two motives; the soul filled with love for others is vaster, more luminous, than that concerned only for its own ultimate good. These contrasting points of departure may be reconciled by universal love, which embraces all creatures, including oneself. In the Jaina texts, however, we hear little about love, which along with other affections seems not quite proper for the stern ascetic traversing the last stage of the long road that brings him to *moksa* or final liberation. It was left for Jesus to recognize the full power of love as a moral motive; the older religions and philosophies stressed rather the rigorous rational adherence to rules conducive to an intellectually approved goal.

Be that as it may, no other religion has ever quite equalled Jainism in the care it takes of the soul by scrupulously avoiding the infliction on other beings of injuries which would react unfavourably upon itself. The ethics of the Jains is deduced from their metaphysics with strict logic and a passion for minute classification such as, in the West, one finds only among biologists. If the Jains are correct in their primary assumption that the soul is omniscient, all-powerful, and blissful, that it needs only the removal of its karmic incrustation to realize these inherent capacities, then the steadfast practice of their exacting moral code should bring a priceless reward. If, on the contrary, the soul in its pristine state is not so generously endowed as not only the Jains but Plato and others have supposed; if it requires not only catharsis but also furnishing; if it is necessary not only to restrain and extirpate evil passions but likewise to nourish generous affections by means of fruitful interactions with the surrounding world—if all this be true, then the Jaina ascetic who lives subjected to a thousand restraints is being far kinder to the creatures around him than to himself.[1]

To review even briefly the various systems of caring for the soul and ensuring its final liberation which developed in ancient India would require many pages. Despite contrasting metaphysical pre-suppositions, all have much in common, for all of them view spiritual advance not as a matter of enriching the soul by means of its experiences in the familiar world, but as one of isolating the soul from this world and the body which is part of it, so that it may enjoy full possession of those incomparable attributes which are its own inherent possession. The practice of austerities, meditation, and yogic concentration are widely recommended; good works help only if done as a sacrifice with no thought of reward.

[1] The most comprehensive exposition of Jainism in English seems to be Mrs Sinclair Stevenson, *The Heart of Jainism*, Oxford University Press, 1915, a scholarly but not quite sympathetic work. The Tamil *Tirukkural*, of which several English translations with commentaries are available, well expresses the spirit of Jainism.

9

Caring for the Soul—II

Turning now to the westward-flowing stream of thought, we find that Judaism was, throughout the Biblical period, a religion of preservation rather than of emancipation. Although Biblical references to Sheol and ghostly apparitions, as when Saul induced the witch of En-dor to raise the shade of the recently deceased Samuel, show that it did not flatly deny the survival of the soul or at least of the ghost, it lacked a doctrine of immortality, and accordingly it failed to develop a spiritual discipline for the attainment of eternal blessedness. The righteousness which the Law prescribed and the prophets demanded consisted, in addition to endless ritual minutiae, in the worship of one God and the practice of such social virtues as justice and mercy. The reward which the ancient Hebrew expected for righteous living was not heavenly bliss but earthly prosperity, which included the begetting of descendants who would for many generations benefit from the merit of their godly ancestor. The Psalms show us clearly the kind of recompense that the godly man would win: 'He shall be like a tree planted by the rivers of water, that bringeth forth his fruit in his season; his leaf also shall not wither; and whatsoever he doeth shall prosper.' 'Thou preparest a table before me in the presence of mine enemies; thou anointest my head with oil; my cup runneth over. Surely goodness and mercy shall follow me all the days of my life, and I will dwell in the house of the Lord forever.'

The Messianic hope to which the Jews clung through all their dreadful misfortunes was a vision of a purified and pacified earth rather than of a far-off heaven. In the post-Biblical period, at about the time of Christ, the Essenes, as Josephus recorded, held that the soul is immortal, and that if righteous it would, when set free from the body by death, mount upward to a paradise which he compared to the Elysium of the Greeks. More than the other Jewish sects of the period, the Essenes led ascetic lives, with strict spiritual discipline, that won the admiration of Gentile contemporaries. Yet even the Essenes, as appears from the literary remains of the Qumran community, were more concerned with preparing the way for the Messiah than with preparing their souls for immortal life. In having neither a cult of deified ancestors nor a developed doctrine of personal salvation, the Judaism of the canonical Bible occupies a peculiar position among the religions of the world.

Without sacred scriptures or an organized, influential priesthood, the civic cults of ancient Greece long remained archaic religions of preservation, concerned with sacrifices, purifications, and the prosperity of the several city-states. Those Greeks who yearned for immortal life sought admission to the Orphic or Eleusinian mysteries, while those who felt the need for intellectual illumination and ethical guidance turned to the great schools of philosophy that grew up in the fourth and third centuries before Christ. Since for their adherents they were a substitute for a popular religion, these philosophies were necessarily much concerned with the development of character, the care of the soul.

Plato recognized a three-fold division of the soul: the rational soul, resident in the head; the spirited soul, located in the chest; and the appetitive soul, situated lower in the body. To each of these divisions corresponds a particular virtue, wisdom to the intellect, courage to the spirited element, and temperance to the appetitive. A fourth virtue is necessary to mediate between these three and ensure that each plays its appropriate role in the life of man; and from the laborious investigation in the *Republic* it became evident that this virtue is justice.

The true philosopher is ever vigilant to preserve the several parts of his soul in a healthy state, and above all to maintain the supremacy of the rational part, which alone is immortal. The spirited element, when properly disciplined, helps the rational element to hold the rebellious appetitive principle in due subjection. Plato's analysis of the soul and its appropriate virtues has had great influence on subsequent thought. The four cardinal virtues recognized by the Catholic Church to this day—prudence (practical wisdom), fortitude, temperance, and justice—came into Christianity from Greek philosophy rather than from Hebrew religion, which was notable for its lack of philosophy. The three theological virtues—faith, hope, and charity—are peculiarly Christian.

Plato failed to transmit his religious fervour and moral zeal to his successors at the Academy which he founded at Athens, and his school presently became politely sceptical. Aristotle's greatest contributions to the culture of the soul were, first, his insistence that virtue, and the happiness that springs from its exercise, is an active rather than a passive state; and, second, his doctrine that virtue is a mean between extremes.[1] Although we may agree that courage is intermediate between cowardice and rash exposure to danger, and that temperance stands between gluttony and starving oneself; veracity seems to lie at the opposite pole from falsehood rather than between mendacity and something else. Despite the limitations of Aristotle's doctrine of the mean—so characteristically Greek!— it could provide a wholesome corrective for religious enthusiasts who so frequently run to pernicious extremes in their zeal to purify and save their souls.

Epicurus taught that men could be happy by living temperately and cultivating earnest friendships. Although he developed his philosophy with the laudable intention of freeing people from superstitious terrors and bringing them peace of mind in a troubled world, his advocacy of aloofness from civic affairs and family responsibilities encouraged moral relaxation.[2] A contrasting philosophy of life was developed by Zeno of Citium, founder of the Stoic school, which became the foremost proponent of the strenuous moral life in the ancient world. In its reliance upon rational demonstration rather than revelation, its interest in physics and logic and grammar, its lack of temples and priesthood and ritual, Stoicism was a philosophy; but in its view of the universe as governed by absolute Providence, its moral fervour, its proselyting zeal, its attitude of uncomplaining submission to a higher Power, it was a religion—one of the noblest that the world has known. Unfortunately, it was too unemotional, it demanded too much from its adherents and promised them too little, to appeal to the masses, which preferred the mystic cults, with their often orgiastic rites, that were creeping westward through the Roman empire. But among the cultured and educated classes of the ancient world, Stoicism was

---

[1] Aristotle, *Nicomachean Ethics.*

[2] The long account of Epicurus in Diogenes Laertius, *Lives of Eminent Philosophers*, Book X, is one of the best sources for his views. Lucretius, *On the Nature of Things*, is a comprehensive exposition of Epicurean philosophy.

a beneficent power, making men steadfast to their civic duties in trying circumstances and teaching kings to rule with a benevolence, clemency, and dedication to the public weal that has too often been lacking in the monarchs of all countries and ages. The most illustrious of these Stoic rulers was Marcus Aurelius, who reigned in Rome from A.D. 161 to 180 and was one of the most interesting and lovable men who ever bore a sceptre.

The Stoics were among the most uncompromising moral perfectionists that the world has known. For them, as for Kant many centuries later, nothing but the virtuous will can be called good without qualification; all the various ends which men so feverishly seek—wealth, power, family, fame, pleasure, even health—are not properly goods, only 'things preferred'. To strive with all one's strength to play well one's appointed part in the community of gods and men which they held the universe to be, to do one's duty as one sees it regardless of consequences to self, to avoid sensual pleasures, to treat all men with justice, benevolence, and clemency— this is the course which the true Stoic must uncompromisingly follow. And in this stern struggle for moral perfection, no partial victory is recognized; there is either total victory or defeat. Although many of us believe that a man may possess one virtue but lack another —he may be generous but imprudent, truthful but intemperate— such indulgent acceptance of our human frailties was foreign to the Stoic. To him, virtue was one and indivisible, so that we must seize it whole or lack it entirely. Like other philosophers, he found it convenient to talk about the several virtues, but to him they were only aspects of a single entity, like the variously painted sides of a wooden block; or better, they were related to each other like the vital organs of an animal, so that if any one is absent none can live. To the critic who argued that virtue has degrees, that one man may be more virtuous than another and a venial moral failure does not place a man in the ranks of the wicked, the Stoic would reply: If you say five times five is twenty-four, you are wrong, no less than if you say it is a hundred; if a shipwrecked sailor's nose remains an inch below the surface of the sea, he will drown, just as surely as though it were ten fathoms deep. If you wish to live morally, get your nose quite above the water of weakness and sin, otherwise you are lost!

What are the rewards for the few strong enough to win in this strenuous campaign for moral perfection? Virtue is its own reward, infinitely superior to any other that you can name. Moreover, there is friendship; all good men everywhere, of whatever race or nationality, are friends, who will never injure each other but can count on each other for unfailing help in time of need. Even more, the reward of perfect virtue is perfect happiness. It was widely held by ancient philosophers that virtue alone is sufficient for happiness, so that amid the most adverse external circumstances— hungry, cold, friendless, sick, shot through with bodily pains— the perfected sage could be serenely happy. Even Epicurus went so far as to declare that the philosopher, by concentrating his thought on pleasant things, could remain happy while his limbs were being torn apart on the rack!

To preserve the unruffled serenity which was the goal of the Stoic sage, he must avoid becoming too strongly attached to external things, including his own body. Epictetus was constantly warning his students against indulging their paltry bodies. To marry and rear children who might continue to carry on man's part in this community of gods and men was regarded as not only a civic but, one might almost say, a cosmic duty, which the Stoic teachers exhorted their students to discharge. Nevertheless, they warned against becoming too strongly attached to wife or children, for at any moment the inscrutable will that governs human affairs may snatch them from us, leaving disconsolate the man unable to restrain his affections. Yet, as centuries passed, Stoicism, like many another religion, lost much of its primitive rigour. It would be difficult to find in any language a correspondence that reveals a warmer friendship or more tender affections than the letters which passed between Marcus Aurelius and his old teacher Marcus Cornelius Fronto, often giving little intimate details of the Stoic emperor's family life. Although many of us live today in such luxury and self-indulgence as the Stoics of old would hardly approve, our more superficial and reserved personal relations rarely encourage such free expression of mutual affection and regard between master and former pupil.

Although the Stoic philosophy demanded firmness of character, it did not expect men to march unaided along the steep and stony road to perfect virtue, did not refuse them succour when they faltered. When Cicero, smarting from the failure of his second marriage and the death of his beloved daughter Tullia, barred from public office by the triumph of the enemies of the Republic that he had so devotedly served, turned for solace to philosophy, he compiled, largely from Stoic works, a treatise on the diseases of the soul, which has come down to us under the title of *Tusculan Disputations*. 'Assuredly', he wrote, 'there is an art of healing the soul—I mean philosophy, whose aid must be sought not, as in bodily diseases, outside ourselves, and we must use our utmost endeavour, with all our resources and strength, to have the power to be ourselves our own physicians.'[1]

From Cicero and other sources we learn that the four diseases, or sinful conditions, which the soul must guard against are:

1. Fear, in which a future disadvantage, such as death, is mistaken for a future evil.

2. Greed, in which a future advantage, such as an opportunity to gain great wealth, is regarded as a future good.

3. Grief, in which a present disadvantage, such as the loss of a loved one, is mistaken for a present evil.

4. Hilarity, in which a present advantage, such as some intense pleasure, is mistaken for a present good.

Since these diseased conditions of the soul are due wholly to wrong opinion or, as we might say today, false value-judgments, they can be overcome by freeing our mind from delusions. Virtue, as Socrates had maintained long before, can be taught. Dread of pain, for example, may be conquered by reflecting that, if intense, it cannot last long. Fear of death may be overcome by the realization that, since it comes inevitably to the good man no less than to the wicked, it cannot be evil; for it was axiomatic that no evil could befall the perfected sage. Indeed, insisted Epictetus, the whole notion that evil exists is just another example of wrong opinion: the good God who made this magnificent cosmos could not have gone so far astray as to permit it to contain evil.[2]

At first sight, Stoicism, the product of a distinct philosophical tradition, has little in common with such Indian religious philosophies as Jainism, Buddhism, and the more advanced sects of Hinduism. But, if we look more deeply, making allowance for their different idioms, we detect important similarities. To win perfect

[1] Cicero, *Tusculan Disputations*, III, iii, 6.
[2] A comprehensive account of Stoicism is E. Vernon Arnold, *Roman Stoicism*, Routledge & Kegan Paul, London, 1911.

unruffled bliss, declares the Jain, you must, by right knowledge, right faith, and right conduct, work off the karmic matter that cloys the *jiva* or soul and reduce it at last to its naked purity. If you can accomplish this, nothing in heaven or earth can destroy your felicity. To be perfectly happy, affirmed the Stoic, you must free your soul of all evil and establish it in perfect virtue. If you succeed in this, the cruellest blows of outrageous fortune cannot diminish your joy, because virtue alone is sufficient for happiness. Stoicism, preaching active service to the community, never developed a monastic order; whereas the Indians believed that the soul's final liberation was most readily achieved by withdrawing from the world, in a monastery or in anchoritic solitude, to live austerely while meditating undisturbed on the eternal verities. However, a number of Indian faiths taught that work performed for a good cause, without thought of personal reward but rather as a sacrifice to God, did not produce karmic involvement to retard the winning of Nirvana— a view that is developed at length in the sacred *Bhagavad-Gita*.

Thus Stoicism, no less than Jainism or Hinduism, may be regarded as a spiritual discipline to release the soul from bondage to the flesh and bring it perfect happiness. There is, however, one profound difference. Jainism, as we have seen, teaches that the soul is eternal, and that, even before winning final release, it may, if righteous, enjoy intervals of purest happiness in temporary heavens between incarnations. Stoicism holds forth no such alluring prospects. As a free philosophy, it had no canonical scripture from which one can readily learn the orthodox view; but the opinion most widely held among the later Stoics seems to have been that after death the soul mounts into the heavens, where, like the stars, it is nourished by exhalations from the earth. Marcus Aurelius feared that if all souls endured for ever, they would so fill the upper spaces that presently there would be room for no more. Some Stoics believed that the souls of the righteous survived much longer than those of the wicked, finding a quiet and peaceful home in the clear bright ether, enjoying the company of the great ones of the past, gazing upon the earth far below and the sublime company of the stars all around. In any case, a soul could not be expected to survive the periodic destruction of the universe, when, after a long age, the whole cosmos would dissolve in the creative fire that had made it, to be born anew from its primal source.

Since this creative fire was regarded as divine, the soul's ultimate destiny was union with God, with the total loss of individuality. Here Stoicism reached a conclusion rather similar to that of the Advaita Vedanta, which teaches that the released soul becomes one with Brahman. Why, then, should we classify the latter as a religion of regress, while Stoicism is included among the religions of progress? For the Vedanta of Samkara, this ultimate loss of personal identity in God is the supreme goal of religious endeavour, to which the development of a virtuous character is at best incidental. For Stoicism, on the contrary, the highest goal is to perfect the individual character, so that one behaves with unblemished rectitude as a neighbour and a citizen of the cosmos, enjoying the happiness which virtue brings. Since the course of evolution is the differentiation and perfecting of individuals, Stoicism maintains the direct line of evolutionary advance. That the soul is finally absorbed in the Divine is, for the Stoics, a deduction from their cosmology, not, as in the Advaita Vedanta, an aspiration.

An eternal reward is cheaply bought with any finite price that may be exacted from us. It is not too difficult to understand the attitude which leads the Christian martyr to welcome the flames on which, he believes, his soul will mount to heaven, or that which impels the ascetic, Christian or Mohammedan or Hindu, to submit to long years of deprivation and hardship for the sake of everlasting bliss. But the Stoic could look forward to no such infinite recompense for a life of strenuous effort to perfect his character. He was, indeed, promised impregnable happiness as the guerdon of perfect virtue, but he had no assurance that he could preserve this felicity indefinitely. If he calculated, he might conclude that the prize was not worth the race. To overcome this difficulty, the Stoics had recourse to another of those famous paradoxes, like that which maintained the equality of sins, about which their philosophical rivals in the ancient world never ceased to tweak them. They held that happiness does not depend upon duration but only on intensity, so that two men who are equally virtuous are equally happy, no matter how much longer one lives than the other. 'In a single instant', exclaimed Seneca, 'virtue completes an eternity of good!'[1] Elsewhere he asserts that, whether one dies late or soon, the measure of the Supreme Good is unvaried in spite of the difference in years.[2] This

---

[1] Seneca, *Moral Epistles*, XCII, 25.   [2] Seneca, *op. cit.* LXXIV, 26.

contention rests upon an ambiguous use of the word 'equal'. Two hundred-watt electric bulbs emit equal amounts of light; but if one is broken at the end of a minute and the other burns for many hours, the amounts of light they give are most unequal.

Yet, despite the absurdity to common sense of the contention that our happiness is independent of its duration, this paradox raises a problem of great philosophic interest. In mathematics it might be maintained that one divided by infinity equals one million divided by infinity, for infinity is so vast that the value of both fractions is infinitesimal. In the long view of eternity, whether one is happy for a day or for fifty years seems to make little difference. Consider two forgotten Stoics of ancient Greece or Rome, one of whom was virtuous and happy through a long manhood, while the other was a promising young disciple who died, as too often happened in antiquity, before the adolescent down had stiffened on his cheeks. If there was any difference in the amount of happiness each enjoyed, where now is it registered? When, as the astronomers assure us will occur ages hence, life has been extinguished on this earth by either the cooling or the fiery explosion of the sun, what difference will it make in the universe that during millions of years untold billions of sentient beings joyed and suffered on our planet? Unless, somehow and somewhere, at least some earthly events are preserved in memory, it would seem to make no difference at all.

Only with reservations can we admit Christianity and Islam into the class of religions of progress. According to these faiths, for many souls mundane existence is a progress leading from the infant's nescience to spiritual perfection and everlasting blessedness; but for many others earthly life leads only to the pit of excruciating torments from which there is no release. No living being can be absolutely evil, nor can organic life be a state of endless pain; yet in the view of certain Christian sects, such a state is the destiny of the majority of men. As the world marches on, there is a steady increase in the number of those who have advanced to blessedness, but likewise of those who have fallen by means of the relative evil of earthly sin to absolute perdition. There is progress on one side, but irretrievable loss on the other; and to judge by the number of individuals involved in it, the latter seems to outweigh the former.

If, instead of condemning as heretical Origen's opinion, that all men and even devils will be saved at the last, Christianity had adopted this liberal view, it would have become perhaps the most perfect example of a religion of progress that the world has thus far known; for it does not, like Indian religions, recognize the pre-existence of souls, but starts each one off from a fresh beginning on a career which may, in favourable circumstances, culminate in spiritual perfection and eternal felicity. Actually, the religion whose founder taught us to forgive our enemies developed into the most implacably unforgiving of all religions. Its attitude contrasts unpleasantly with that of Eastern religions which hold that, given sufficient time and effort, every last soul may be saved. Exceptional among Hindu theo-logians was Madhva, who maintained that some souls are destined to final damnation and others are irretrievably caught in the round of reincarnations, with no prospect of release. Since he lived in the thirteenth century, the possibility that his grim doctrine was influenced by Christianity or Islam cannot be excluded.[1]

It is above all the religious attitude toward life that has inspired men to take such devoted care of their souls as no secular or purely utilitarian ethic can ever persuade them to do. Although belief in the soul's indestructibility has been a powerful incentive for guard-ing it zealously from sin and corruption, even without this comfort-ing faith people of strong religious feeling are mindful of their soul's perfection. Just as Jainism provides an example of a philosophical religion which encourages care for a soul deemed eternal, so Stoicism is an example of a religious philosophy which emphasized the importance of guarding the purity of a soul deemed perishable.

In spite of the most diverse metaphysical views, every system of spiritual culture that has had an enduring influence on mankind has insisted on the necessity of catharsis, of subduing, or sub-limating, or somehow getting rid of, many of the attitudes and emotions which so strongly agitate the ordinary unchastened mind—an historical fact too often overlooked by contemporaries who adopt the 'permissive' attitude toward life. To the evolutionist who reflects on the psychic consequences of the long, severely competi-tive struggle through which our ancestors, prehuman and human, have passed on their aeonian march toward civilization, the defects of character which must be pruned away—the 'innate wickedness' of man—present no mystery. Such psychic traits as anger, hatred,

---

[1] S. Radhakrishnan, *op. cit.*, vol. II, p. 737–51.

malice, jealousy, envy, greed, and lust developed inevitably in animals which, in order to survive and reproduce, needed to contend fiercely with others of their own or different species; indeed, these traits were in many instances an actual aid to survival, for the animal which fights passionately, spurred on by appropriate emotions, fights more effectively.[1]

Yet these same passions, useful though they have been, are not only incompatible with a peaceful, cooperative society; they perturb the spirit, destroying that inner calm which the sage calls liberation. Whether, as in the ancient pluralistic realism of the Jains, these ugly blemishes on the unchastened soul are viewed as a material karmic deposit, or whether, as in the phenomenalism of the Buddhists, they are regarded simply as psychic modifications, matters little from the practical standpoint, so long as we recognize the urgent need to remove them.

It is common experience that this catharsis, this eradication of violent and disruptive attitudes, does not leave a psychic vacuum. In the measure that these ugly traits are removed, a contrary set of attitudes gradually takes possession of the soul, making it loving, friendly, benevolent. And the feeling of peace, of having cast off a heavy burden, which accompanies this change of attitude, is designated by the religious as self-realization, liberation, or *moksa*. The soul seems at last to have shed something foreign to itself and to have realized its own true nature.

Although the necessity for spiritual catharsis has been widely recognized by religions and religious philosophies, the value of furnishing or enriching the mind, as by experiences that leave treasured memories, has been almost as widely neglected by them. Doubtless one reason for this is that these systems of thought were mostly developed long before Locke published his searching, if too drastic, criticism of the innate content of our minds. If one believes, as in Jainism, that the soul is inherently omniscient; or if one agrees with Plato that learning eternal truths, such as those of geometry, is simply a question of anamnesis or recollecting what was forgotten; then it follows that all we need do to perfect the mind or soul is to brush away foreign accretions, to stir to activity its slumbering

---

[1] This matter is treated more fully in my *The Quest of the Divine*, Meador Publishing Co., Boston, 1956, especially Ch. VIII.

depths. If, on the contrary, we agree with Locke that the mind is originally a blank sheet of paper—although, as we now recognize, a sheet with a complex structure that powerfully affects the shape of the figures which experience draws upon it—then not only purification but likewise furnishing seems necessary for its perfection.

Even for the purpose of catharsis, the value of an active interest in things has been too often overlooked by the religious. As the history of St Anthony, the first Christian eremite, attests, the ascetic who shuts himself up in a monastic cell or a cavern in the wilderness, along with the appetites and passions that he hopes to subdue, has frequently made of them intimate companions that stubbornly intrude upon his solitude. Carried out into the open, in a life of strenuous intellectual or practical endeavour directed toward some worthy end, these same disturbing passions lose much of their force; yet perhaps only in the most fortunate do they dwindle to the point where they can be effortlessly controlled. Although we owe much to the wisdom of the ancients, to the wisdom of the moderns must be credited a fuller recognition of the value of sublimating, rather than of trying vainly to extirpate, those Dionysian energies of the soul which when ungoverned plunge us into lamentable excesses, but which when harnessed and bridled may give us an almost godlike strength—a truth recognized by the mystic who wrote: 'Not only is man more than an animal because there is the god in him, but he is more than a god because there is the animal in him.'[1]

On the whole, the ancient philosophies which encouraged free inquiry seem to have been more successful in sublimating human energies than the religions whose doctrines congeal into dogmas. Already in the dawn of Greek philosophy Pythagoras realized the value of combining the pursuit of knowledge with the cultivation of holiness. His followers banded together in a sort of religious brotherhood, holding their possessions in common, living simply and abstemiously, and obeying rules intended to promote purity and virtue, while they diligently applied themselves to the study of mathematics, which they believed to be the key to all the secrets of the universe.[2]

[1] 'M. C.', *Through the Gates of Gold: A Fragment of Thought*, Theosophy Company, London & Bombay, 1948, p. 81.
[2] Diogenes Laertius, *op. cit.*, Book VIII, Ch. 1.

10

Caring for Humanity
and the Universe

For long ages, human tribes lived in fear and hatred of neighbouring tribes, with which they were continually at war. Even when tribes were joined, by confederation or conquest, into populous nations, the old situation of internal amity and external enmity persisted, with the difference that the opposing groups had become larger. Throughout history, nations have been far readier to fight than to help neighbouring nations; and their gods have shared their animosities. When a friendlier spirit prevailed, it was often because one country needed another as an ally against some threatening power. This situation has hardly changed in the modern world. Although today we see highly industrialized countries, such as the United States of America, annually giving billions of dollars to less prosperous countries to help improve their economy, such enormous donations can hardly be regarded as an expression of pure philanthropy. This practice did not arise until after the Second World War, when the democratic nations, headed by the United States, began to contend for global dominion with the Communist nations, led by Russia. Since poverty breeds Communism, it was to the interest of the United States to help less developed countries to raise their standard of living, thereby making them more resistant to Marxist propaganda. Whether, in the absence of the threat from Communism, the United States would have given such huge sums to other countries, or anything at all, is questionable.

Although international almsgiving, on a vast scale and as a regular practice, is something new in the world, it has occurred sporadically since ancient times. We read in Plutarch's biography of Pericles that the pharaoh of Egypt sent as a gift to Athens forty thousand bushels of wheat, to be distributed among the citizens.

Incited by greed, many Athenians brought suit to deprive their neighbours of citizenship, under a law which restricted this privilege to men both of whose parents were Athenians. Many people whose status had not hitherto been questioned were now denounced, some falsely. Nearly five thousand were convicted and sold into slavery, so that each of the remaining fourteen thousand citizens might receive less than one more bushel of wheat. Such were the tragic consequences of one of the earliest recorded instances of international almsgiving! One wonders to what extent the greater international donations of the present era also bring unfortunate consequences, such as inciting graft among public officials and propping up inefficient or unpopular governments which would fall without this support from outside. Material benefits without spiritual enlightenment or a change of heart often do more harm than good, whether given to individuals or to nations. All too often the recipients, far from being grateful, are greedy for more.

Although since prehistoric times men acting as tribes or nations have been more ready to fight than to aid people beyond their borders, and when help has been given it has frequently been with an ulterior motive, the advanced religions have encouraged a friendlier and more generous attitude. Men who believe they have a fresh spiritual insight or a more certain method of salvation are eager to broadcast the joyous news, among aliens no less than their neighbours. The cynic may assert that such generosity is cheap, because we can share spiritual goods with many others yet keep them whole, so that in giving we deprive ourselves of nothing while we win renown. This is certainly not the whole explanation, for the diffusion of a creed has rarely been accomplished without hardships, perils, and an expenditure of wealth and energy which, applied in commercial enterprises, might make one wealthy.

Missionary effort has not, of course, always been wholly unselfish, for frequently the propagation of the faith, and especially martyrdom incurred in the endeavour, has been regarded as a certain means of gaining merit and winning an eternal reward, beside which the greatest earthly treasure, which at best we may enjoy for a few score years, shrinks to insignificance. Yet we can hardly doubt that in many instances a more purely altruistic motive has predominated. Religions of emancipation have rather consistently taught that salvation is unattainable so long as the soul is infected by hatred, anger, envy, greed, and similar disruptive passions. In the measure that these wither away, the contrary affections of friendliness, love, sympathy, and generosity suffuse the soul from its subconscious foundation, making it eager to promote the welfare of other beings. And what more precious gift can one man give to another than the secret of eternal life, or at least of release from endless suffering? Moreover, one who intensely loves God, or the inspired teacher who showed the way to salvation, longs to do 'God's work', or to spread the teacher's message, undertaking arduous service with a joy that overcomes all trials and disappointments.

Probably no religion, including the most primitive, has become established without some proselytizing. Radin believed that even tribal religions do not spring up spontaneously in a communal mind but owe much to the few thoughtful individuals who in primitive communities, as in those more advanced, take an interest in religious and philosophical questions.[1] Doubtless these innovators found it necessary to persuade their fellow tribesmen to accept their new rituals or beliefs, often at the risk of being killed as sorcerers or violators of taboos. All the historical founders of religions were teachers who laboured strenuously to spread their insights or revelations among their fellows. The Buddha, after winning enlightenment beneath the Bodhi-tree, devoted forty patient years to showing others the way to Nirvana. The religion that he founded seems to have been the first to carry its message to alien races on a large scale.

Gautama was well aware of the risks that those who spread his gospel would incur. In the Sanskrit scriptures we find him examining a certain Purna, who early in the course of his religious life decided to go as a missionary to a savage border tribe called the Sronaparantakas. The Buddha reminded his disciple that these were evil, violent people, who would abuse the stranger with harsh speech, strike him with hands and clods, if not with sharper weapons. To each more terrifying prospect that the master held before the disciple, Purna replied that he would regard the savages as good and kind for not treating him still more harshly. Even if they killed him, he said, he would be grateful to them for releasing him from his body: did not some disciples, weary of the ills of the flesh, resort

[1] Paul Radin, *op. cit.*

136

to suicide to gain the same end? Seeing that the would-be missionary was equipped with the necessary fortitude and patience, the master sent him on his way, exhorting him to console others, as he had been himself consoled, to help them win Nirvana as he had won it.

So, taking his begging bowl and robe, Purna travelled to the land of the Sronaparantakas, where the first man he met was a hunter. The savage set an arrow in his bow and drew it back to his ear, aiming it at the stranger. Purna met this threat by baring his breast to the weapon. Such calm submission pacified the savage huntsman, who not only permitted the missionary to continue on his way, but became the first of many converts that he made.[1] Even if the story of the Buddha and Purna is not factual, it well illustrates the spirit in which all true missionary work is undertaken.

It is doubtful whether the Buddha sent forth many missionaries; for two centuries after his death his doctrine was hardly known beyond the small area in northern India where he had lived, taught, and died. Only after Buddhism, about the year 260 B.C., made a royal convert in the person of the Indian emperor Asoka, did the religion begin to expand widely. A man of great energy, tenacity of purpose, and religious zeal tempered by tolerance, this able ruler was eager to promote the welfare of every sentient being. According to his biographer, Vincent A. Smith, to him belongs 'the honour of having personally organized, with the aid of his enormous imperial power, the most comprehensive scheme of religious missionary enterprise recorded in the history of the world'. Not only were his proselytizing monks sent through much of India, in and beyond his dominions, including the wild forest tribes; they travelled, doubtless afoot, to the distant realms of Alexander's successors in Syria, Macedonia, Epirus, Egypt, and at least as far as Cyrene in northern Africa. In the Hellenistic kingdoms to the west, the teaching of Gautama's 'Law of Piety' seems to have failed to establish lasting Buddhist communities. Northward, eastward, and southward, Buddhism continued to diffuse until it became well rooted in China, Japan, Central Asia, Burma, Siam, Indo-China, Indonesia, and Ceylon.[2] In contrast to the expansion of Christianity

[1] E. G. Thomas, *The Quest of Enlightenment: A Selection of the Buddhist Scriptures Translated from the Sanskrit*, John Murray, London, 1950, p. 40–43.
[2] Vincent A. Smith, *Asoka, op. cit.*, p. 41–50.

and Islam, that of Buddhism owes little to military conquest but was almost wholly the work of peaceful persuasion.

No other religion has ever equalled Buddhism in the scope of its caring. Others, especially Christianity, have no doubt laboured with as much strenuous heroism to carry their saving doctrines to all mankind. The Jains, as we have learned, are careful to harm no living thing; but aside from establishing a few animal hospitals, they seem on the whole to believe that every non-human soul should be permitted to work out its own destiny in its own way. Buddhist saints, however, especially those of the northern or Mahayana division of the faith, have felt responsible for the salvation of every living thing. Their ideal is the *bodhisattva*, the perfectly enlightened soul who has won his way to Nirvana but pauses on the threshold, delaying his final release in order to remain in the world and guide other beings along the difficult path that he has victoriously trodden. The spirit of the religion is epitomized in the resolution of Avaloki-tesvara, who vowed that he would not accept salvation until the last particle of sentient dust had attained this desired goal before him. Evidently even the most inspired teacher can do little for any soul until it has been incarnated in a human body, with a mind capable of understanding and benefiting by his instruction. This must finally occur, for no soul, however deeply it may be sunk in ignorance or sin, is irretrievably lost; all may ultimately win Nirvana, even if this requires a long series of incarnations. Purifica-tion is attained by gaining true knowledge, thinking right thoughts, and doing good deeds. In the view of the Mahayana, all sentient beings are marching through the trials and sorrows of the world toward a blessed existence, which can be won by personal effort under the guidance of the Buddha and other magnanimous teachers, who postpone their own emancipation in order to help less fortunate ones along the way.

In the expansion of Western Europe since the end of the fifteenth century, the emissaries of Christianity, both Catholic and Protestant, have played a major role, not only as bearers of the Gospel but also as explorers and intelligent describers of the cultures that were about to crumble under the impact of a too-aggressive civilization. The tale of their hardships and sufferings, their struggles to learn languages with grammatical constructions as strange as their vocabularies, the hideous tortures and martyrdoms they endured,

fills countless volumes. Their heroism exceeded that of the Con-
quistadores, whom they closely followed and sometimes preceded,
for when true to their faith they did not resist the attacks of savages
who misunderstood or resented their intrusion; whereas the
conquering warrior invariably confronted aborigines with inferior
weapons and a less advanced military technique.

It has been the task of the dedicated missionary everywhere to
soften the impact on the natives of an alien culture which otherwise
first contacted them, in all too many instances, in the form of its
least admirable products, human and material. The Spanish Crown
had benevolent intentions toward its newly conquered subjects in
the Americas and depended on the several monastic orders to
educate, Christianize, and protect the Indians. But at the great
distance from the central authority at which the friars were obliged
to operate, they were often powerless to shield their charges from
the rapacity of European colonists and adventurers. Similarly in
North America, the frontiersman, restless and undisciplined,
greedy for wealth or adventure, rarely half so admirable as nostalgic
romance depicts him, stirred up trouble between the colonists and
the aboriginal tribes and thwarted the intention of the home
governments and missionaries to treat them more justly.

Missionaries and their work have too often been undervalued by
the irreligious. Perhaps the missionary's most frequent fault is a
cocksureness that ill befits fallible man in the face of the greatest
mysteries and is incompatible with the humility that becomes a
religious spirit. Yet a man must be very sure of his doctrines and his
purposes to go for years into voluntary exile, facing deprivations
and perils, as an intimate of savages whose habits are often revolting.
The indigenous religion which the missionary intends to displace
is an outgrowth of the whole ancestral experience of the tribe which
developed it, adapted to its mental habits and its economy as no
imported article is likely to be. Ignoring the value of tribal customs
for which he offers no substitute, such as the whole body of beliefs
and practices that adjust the tribe's population to the productivity
of its territory, the missionary has too often swept aside good and
bad alike in his zeal to introduce alien thoughts and ways. Besides,
it seems an impudence for a civilization so imperfect as our own,
falling so far short of its professed ideals, to try by force or persuasion to bring some different culture into its fold, however

savage that culture may be. On the other side of the account, missionaries have combated many cruel and barbarous customs, including human sacrifices, cannibalism, slavery, and mutilation of the body. When all is said, it must be admitted that the better of them have loved their God and cared about their fellow man, whatever the colour of his skin, with an intensity that overruled all considerations of personal safety and comfort—and this is no small commendation.

Sometimes, viewing the harassed and fearful world of the mid-twentieth century, we mistrust the accomplishments of civilization and doubt the value of the religions and religious philosophies that have shaped its ideals. In such a mood, it is reassuring to contrast the spiritual outlook of the missionary and that of the primitive he has gone to serve. Albert Schweitzer, who relinquished a brilliant career in Europe to spend long years as a medical missionary among negroes in the trying climate of equatorial Africa, wrote: 'If I ask an ambulatory patient to undertake some small service for a patient who must stay in bed, he will do it only if the bedridden patient belongs to his tribe. If that is not the case, he will answer me with wide-eyed innocence: "This man is not brother of me." Neither rewards nor threats will induce him to perform a service for such a stranger.'[1] And this in the presence of a man who has given his whole life to strangers, not of a neighbouring tribe, but of an alien race!

Christianity, emphasizing the fatherhood of God, exhorts us to love all men as brothers. Buddhism, recognizing no Supreme God, teaches us to care about all sentient beings, united in the brotherhood of sufferers. The outlook of Stoicism was still wider, for it regarded the whole divine cosmos as one ordered community, in which everyone must play his appointed part for the welfare of the Whole. If this cosmos, whose rhythmic movements won the reverent admiration of the ancient philosophers, was far narrower than the universe that modern astronomy reveals to us, it was as wide as astronomers without telescopes could make it.

In ancient times, before the rise of far-flung empires, the *polis* or city-state was the little world of its citizens, a microcosm existing precariously amid jealous or hostile neighbours. This city was

[1] Albert Schweitzer, *The Teaching of Reverence for Life*, Holt, Rinehart & Winston, New York, 1965, p. 9.

under the protection of its own gods, whose rites must be duly performed by every citizen, lest in anger they withdraw their patronage. Even if the citizens were not all descended from a common ancestor, they found it helpful to believe that they were. As the citizen received from his city everything that made life precious to him, so he owed to the city everything that it might ask of him, his allegiance, his services, his life itself in case of need. And this need often arose, for enemies not infrequently invaded its territory, forcing the country-dwellers to take refuge within the walled city, which closed its gates and prepared for a long siege. Even when provisions and hope fell low, when pestilence raged within the congested town, the defenders held out with the stubbornness of despair; for the inrushing enemy would convert the doomed city into a hell of rapine and massacre. The survivors would be carried off as slaves, separating families; the sacred citadel would be burnt; houses and walls might be levelled. No wonder the ancient citizen clung to his city as he clung to his life!

Although Plato was disgusted with the Athenian city which had sentenced to death his master Socrates and had been humiliated by Spartan arms, all his political thinking centred on the city-state; his two longest works, the *Republic* and the *Laws*, were delineations of utopian cities, differently conceived. Aristotle had seen his pupil, Alexander the Great, unite cities and nations into one vast polyglot empire, which before his untimely death he had evidently intended to weld together on the principle of racial equality. The master disapproved, as he held Hellenes to be a superior race, fitted by nature to rule, as others were made to obey. Aristotle, too, pinned his faith on the city-state, which should not become too large; if its population exceeded one hundred thousand, it would be a city no longer.[1]

Yet, in an earlier generation, Socrates and Diogenes the Cynic had been in the habit of replying, when asked of what city they were, that they were 'citizens of the universe'. This did not prevent Socrates from being so loyal a citizen of Athens that he chose to die rather than evade its decree. It remained for Zeno of Citium, a foreigner who declined the honour of Athenian citizenship, to make the cosmopolis, the city of the world, a fundamental principle of his philosophy. In this world-wide city all men are, or are at least

[1] Aristotle, *Nicomachean Ethics*, IX, 10.

capable of becoming, citizens of equal rank, without distinction of Hellene or barbarian, freeman or slave. And not only men, but likewise women; for at least in its later development Stoicism taught the equality of the sexes. There was no point on which it more uniformly insisted than that all good people, of whatever race or sex or social status, are friends and equals. And this cosmopolis, this universal city, included not only humans but all rational beings, gods as well as men. To the class of gods belonged the stars, which among the ancient philosophers were widely held to be intelligent beings, endowed with immortal life. The cosmopolis, then, stretched from the earth to the stars, forming one great community of which every member, when virtuous, uncomplainingly played the part assigned by the *Logos* or Cosmic Intelligence, for the benefit of the Whole.

Probably no Stoic was more mindful of his relation to the cosmic Whole than Marcus Aurelius, the philosopher-king burdened with the care of the vast empire stretching from Mesopotamia to Mauritania and Scotland. As he wrote in his intimate journal:

'Everything harmonizes with me, which is harmonious to thee, O Universe. Nothing for me is too early nor too late, which is in due time for thee. Everything is fruit to me which thy seasons bring, O Nature: from thee are all things, in thee are all things, to thee all things return.'

Later:

'In the morning when thou risest unwillingly, let this thought be present—I am rising to the work of a human being. Why then am I dissatisfied if I am going to do the things for which I exist and for which I was brought into this world? Or have I been made for this, to lie in the bed-clothes and keep myself warm?—But this is more pleasant.—Dost thou exist then to take thy pleasure, and not at all for action or exertion? Dost thou not see the little plants, the little birds, the ants, the spiders, the bees working together to put in order their several parts of the universe? And art thou unwilling to do the work of a human being, and dost thou not make haste to do that which is according to thy nature?'[1]

[1] Marcus Aurelius Antoninus, *Meditations*, George Long's translation, IV, 25; V, 1.

In this remarkable passage, we have the conception of man cooperating with other creatures to preserve something greater than humanity, the cosmic order itself, on which the welfare of man and every other living thing depends. The plants, the little birds, and the insects seem almost to be admitted to citizenship of the cosmopolis, along with gods and men. The motive for their exclusion was doubtless that we cannot reason, plan, and compromise differences with them, as we can with other rational beings endowed with speech. Yet, when we understand their nature, we can often cooperate with them for the benefit of the whole of which we and they are parts. Unless the rational, the non-rational living, and the lifeless components of nature work together, our planet cannot support life; and for the prosperity of the whole, intelligent beings must often make the adjustments which those governed by instinct, or by the laws of physics, cannot make.

The universe is no longer so small and neat as the Stoics supposed it to be; and it is difficult for us to believe that all its components, including such things as wicked men, ferocious animals, venomous snakes, parasites of many kinds, and pathogenic bacteria, contribute to its perfection or play an indispensable rôle in its maintenance. Yet if the discoveries and inventions of the last five centuries have expanded the world in one sense, they have shrunken it in another sense; for we can now fly to the antipodes in less time than it took a Roman emperor to cross Italy. And our biological studies have demonstrated that the various components of the natural world are interdependent to a degree that the ancients could scarcely conceive. Unless we can rise to the grandeur of the Stoic emperor's conception of caring for a world order that transcends not only cities and states but humanity itself, this world seems to be doomed to destruction by man's growing technical competence.

11

Conflicts of Caring

Scarcely anything is more gratifying than to see in a flourishing state that for which one has lovingly cared. Whether we have nursed a flower garden into profuse bloom, or planted and attended a tree until it yields abundant fruit, or finished to our satisfaction a work of art or a scientific investigation, or guided a loved child to the completion of his studies, we greet with triumphant joy the success of our efforts.

Yet, as everyone with a large capacity for caring knows to his cost, this is a source of perplexities and sorrows no less than of joys. Too often we lavish care upon something that fails to respond; too often that which responds brilliantly to our attention is overcome by some unforeseen disaster. The more widely our care extends, the more difficulties we encounter. Distressing conflicts arise when our cherishing labours compete with each other for our limited time and strength, or when the things for which we care prove to be incompatible. Emerson found it difficult to cultivate both his mind and his garden. Many a man has been forced to neglect his intellectual development in order to provide for wife and children. The farmer who protects the birds and other free animals on his land is sometimes faced with the bitter alternative of warring against them or losing the crop on which he depends to feed his family. It is no accident that the word 'care' has acquired a double meaning, that it signifies not only painstaking attention but likewise heavy anxiety and a burdensome sense of responsibility. Whenever, by choice or necessity, we undertake to care for more than we well can, whenever our devoted service yields only failures and disappointments, caring may become a source of grief rather than of joy.

This brings us to the most serious conflict of caring, that between caring for external things and caring for one's own soul. There is scarcely any point on which the chief religions and religious philosophies that arose in the ancient world are in closer accord than on the need to preserve the spirit calm and untroubled, neither agitated by strong passions and desires nor clouded by sorrow, grief, or regret. Unshakeable serenity is indeed the distinguishing characteristic of the emancipated spirit, whether in a body or liberated from it. For the Epicureans no less than for the Stoics, for Buddhists and Jains and Hindus and Taoists, the aim of all strenuous discipline, of yogic exercises and philosophic discourse, was to free the soul of disturbing thoughts and passions and establish it firmly in untroubled peace. From the most diverse points of departure, their doctrines converged upon this goal.

No religion or philosophy that taught men to care only for themselves could long survive; indeed, to propagate such a creed would be logically inconsistent. The best religions are those which give the greatest encouragement to our capacity for caring widely and deeply. Yet, as we have seen, to care for anything external to ourselves, over which we have imperfect control, is all too frequently to expose ourselves to disappointment and sorrow, which is considered to be deleterious to that which above all we should cherish— our own soul. Hence a dilemma, which different creeds resolved in different ways.

The Epicureans chose the easiest way; by following their master's example of refraining from marriage and involvement in civic affairs, many of them avoided fertile sources of troubles and disappointments. For the Stoics, the problem was more serious, for their ideal wise man must not only do his part in carrying on the world's work but preserve perfect serenity while so engaged. Stoicism taught that what really matters is our moral determinations, the conscientious fulfilment of our obligations; the results of our devoted efforts, which to a large degree depend upon circumstances beyond our control, are of only secondary importance, hence we should not be downcast when our efforts fail. Epictetus exhorted his disciples to marry and beget offspring as a social obligation, yet to beware of becoming too fond of wife and children, lest they be prostrated by grief if, as might at any moment happen, death snatch them away. The proper attitude was exemplified by the philosopher Anaxagoras, of whom it is related that, upon receiving news that his son had died, he calmly remarked: 'I knew that my children were born to die.'

The same problem is considered at length in the *Bhagavad-Gita*, one of the most esteemed of the sacred scriptures of the Hindus. Arjuna, hesitating to engage in battle, even in a righteous cause, with relatives and friends arrayed before him on the field of the Kurus, raises the question whether such activity will not, through karma, bind the soul to the cycle of births and deaths, delaying its ultimate release. Krishna, the incarnate God who drives the warrior's chariot, persuades him that the karmic effects of work of any kind depend wholly on the spirit in which it is performed. Work done by one eager to enjoy its fruits does indeed bind the soul to the flesh, delaying its liberation. But one who, labouring in a worthy cause, renounces the fruits of his efforts, preserves his soul's freedom. The wise man offers his work as a sacrifice to God. Just as the Supreme Deity, who has all things and needs nothing, works to preserve the world-order; so should every righteous man, within the limits of his strength, labour selflessly to preserve society. 'Therefore, without attachment, perform always the work that has to be done, for man attains to the highest by doing work without attachment.'[1] Despite the very different idiom, this conclusion is surprisingly similar to that reached in the West by the Stoics.

In this connection, it will be enlightening to consider briefly the ancient sage's attitude toward pity or compassion, which has been often misunderstood, especially by Nietzsche, who declared that until modern times philosophers were absolutely unanimous as to the worthlessness of pity. Aristotle believed that the function of Greek tragedy was to purify the soul of pity and fear. To pity is to be distressed by the sight of another creature's misfortunes or suffering. Pity may, to be sure, be tinged with contempt for the sufferer whose woes seem to be the result of his own folly or ineptitude. The word 'compassion' suggests a more brotherly and sympathetic attitude, which spares the victim of an intended blow and raises up the fallen; but literally it means to share, or participate in, the passion or suffering of some other sentient being. But a principal object of the ancient philosophies, as of the ancient religions of India, was to free the soul from passion in all its forms. No matter what terrible sufferings afflict the body, the soul must remain serene and cheerful.

[1] *The Bhagavad-Gita*, S. Radhakrishnan's translation, George Allen & Unwin, London, 1948, Ch. III, 19.

Would it not be most irrational to take great pains to school the mind to remain calmly indifferent to all the mishaps that might befall one's body or one's property, while permitting it to be distressed by another's misfortunes? The old philosophers would not be guilty of such a glaring inconsistency.

The ancient sages' condemnation of pity as an irrational contraction of the mind does not, however, prove that they were heartless monsters, careless of humanity's manifold woes. The Stoics, who censured pity as a weakness, were indeed the chief humanitarians of the Graeco-Roman world, eloquent advocates of beneficence and clemency. But they held that it is reason, not pity, which prompts the wise man to treat his fellows humanely and help them in distress. No one has expressed the philosophic attitude toward pity more clearly and concisely than Spinoza, who wrote: 'Pity, in a man who lives under the guidance of reason, is in itself bad and useless.' In the proof of this proposition, he explained: 'Pity is a pain, and therefore is in itself bad. The good effect which follows, namely, our endeavour to free the object of our pity from misery, is an action which we desire to do solely at the dictation of reason; only at the dictation of reason are we able to perform any action, which we know for certain to be good.' This analysis seems to fail to do justice to the non-rational springs of our actions, but it is not the utterance of a callous man.[1]

For Christianity the problem, whether we can care lovingly for external things without exposing ourselves to suffering that is injurious to the soul, can hardly be said to exist. Christians, whose Saviour cared so greatly that for humanity's sake he accepted the most acute suffering—the spiritual agony of Gethsemane no less than the excruciating torture of Calvary—have commonly seen positive value in suffering, not only in the body but likewise in the mind. The Christian has traditionally believed that through suffering he not only purifies himself of carnal faults but identifies himself with his crucified saviour, thereby preparing himself for final union with Christ. The Christian attitude is well expressed by a remarkable passage in the autobiography of the mediaeval ascetic Henry Suso:

[1] Spinoza, *Ethics*, Pt. IV, Prop. L. I have treated the matter of the two preceding paragraphs more fully in an essay on 'Compasión', *Revista de Filosofía de la Universidad de Costa Rica*, vol. II, no. 6, p. 43–54, 1959.

Lord, hitherto I have praised Thee in my writings by praising everything that is joyful or lovely in all Thy creatures. Ah, now I must cheerfully begin a new and strange song of praise that I have never known before, since it has now been revealed to me by suffering. It is this: I wish, from the boundless abyss of my heart, that all the pain and suffering that I ever knew, and all the painful grief of all hearts, the pain of all wounds, the groans of all the sick, the piteous sighs of all sad souls, the tears of all weeping eyes, the wrongs suffered by all oppressed persons . . . : that all this may become one song of eternal praise, heavenly Father, an everlasting glory to Thy only-begotten Son, from eternity to eternity. And I, Thy poor Servant, ask to-day on behalf of all suffering men, who perchance by reason of their sufferings are unable to give patient thankful praise to God, that I may be their advocate, that I may on their behalf offer up their sufferings this day by my praise, in whatever manner they have suffered, and offer it up to Thee in their stead, as if I myself had suffered it altogether right gladly.[1]

Before attempting to reach a conclusion, we must examine a matter of fact: is it possible, as both the *Bhagavad-Gita* and Stoicism seem to recommend, to care deeply for any person or thing, or to serve devotedly some institution or cause, the while remaining so detached that if the person dies or disappoints our hopes for him, the thing is destroyed, or the cause fails, we can preserve perfect equanimity, untouched by grief or despair? Or, to view the question from the other side, can we put forth our best effort in the service of some person dependent on us, or some noble cause, if we so withhold our affection from him or it that the death of the person, or the failure of the cause, hardly ruffles our serenity? I believe that only a most exceptional man or woman, well fortified by religion or philosophy, can answer either of these questions in the affirmative.

Yet, as we grow older, we may, without ceasing to care, approach a little closer to the philosophical ideal of detachment. Youth is often cast into the abyss of despondency by the loss or failure of that which it has served with all the passion of a first enthusiasm. As the years pass, to care devotedly for something or other becomes

[1] Henry Suso, *The Life of the Servant*, translated by James M. Clark, James Clarke & Co., London, 1952, p. 92.

a spiritual necessity, the confirmed habit of an earnest nature. But unless one has been extraordinarily fortunate, before he has lived fifty years he has seen so many of his most cherished projects fail, so many of the things he loved slip away, that he has become somewhat inured to such losses and can bear them with a measure of serenity. They do not deter him from continuing to seek that which is worthy of his devoted service.

Yet, despite the counsels of philosophy and the harsh discipline of the years, we rarely view with perfect equanimity the loss of things we have lovingly cared for. Devoted care and detachment are antithetic, and all the teaching of Krishna or the Stoa will hardly serve to reconcile them, except in a most exceptional nature. Few of us can detach ourselves spiritually from the things we have devotedly served as readily as the fighter pilot, by pressing a lever, ejects himself from his falling aircraft, to which he has stuck tenaciously as long as it would fly. For nearly all of us, to care lovingly for something is to expose ourselves, not only to troubles and annoyances, but to the pain of loss and failure. Whether we can care deeply for things outside ourselves without detriment to that which it most behoves us to cherish, our own soul, depends, in the final analysis, upon how suffering affects us.

Pain and suffering have not lacked advocates, who have contended, for example, that the contrast with pain heightens our pleasures; and that our satisfaction in great achievements is enhanced by the toils and hardships they have cost us. While we concede the value of active, voluntarily accepted suffering in an heroic endeavour, such as that of a mountain climber or an explorer in the wilderness, it is difficult to discover any saving grace in the purely passive, involuntary suffering which is infinitely more prevalent in the world —the physical suffering from diseases and accidents and hunger and extremes of heat and cold; the spiritual anguish from disappointed hope, loneliness, frustration, crippling doubt, and the loss of loved ones. It is this vast amount of useless suffering which, more than all else, makes us doubt that a benevolent Providence governs the world.

Since suffering is so widespread, one who had never suffered at all would have a most inadequate comprehension of reality; for pain and anguish cannot, like some mathematical or logical demonstration, be apprehended intellectually without any actual experience of them. To know what pain is, we must feel it; to understand suffering, we must suffer. If we had never felt any hurt, we would necessarily be quite callous to the pangs of others, for they could not by any means make us appreciate their plight. In a world like this, suffering is an indispensable part of our spiritual and moral education, which without it would be defective.

How much, then, is it desirable to suffer? I should say, just enough to make us careful never avoidably to hurt any creature. The amount of pain, bodily and spiritual, that is necessary to make us compassionate varies immensely from person to person. For those highly endowed with imaginative sympathy, very little suffices. For less sensitive natures, more is necessary. There may, indeed, be people so stupid and self-centred that no amount of pain will make them careful not to inflict pain. The world would certainly be better without such people.

Although at least a modicum of suffering is necessary for our spiritual and moral education, it should not be permitted to reside permanently in the soul. The suffering spirit is not the best or most desirable spirit; joy, not sorrow, brings salvation, in the figurative if not in the theological sense. We should regard suffering as a medicine, whose function is to remove careless, irresponsible, and selfish attitudes from our minds, until we never wantonly harm any sentient being. But just as a sick person does not fully recover his health until the medicine which cured him has itself been eliminated from his body; so the spirit chastened and enlarged by suffering is not perfected until it has risen above its sorrows and become joyously serene.

Although sympathy, to be perfect, should include participation in the joys no less than the sorrows of other beings, it is more often a source of pain than of delight. Those about us often find their pleasures in ways that are alien to us, even beyond our comprehension. But suffering we can always understand; it is the common bond that joins all sentient creatures in universal fellowship; so that to be sympathetic is largely to suffer. How, then, can the sympathetic spirit alleviate the pain it must inevitably feel when it takes a wide view of the surrounding world? Certainly not by merely *caring about* the whole realm of life, or the whole of humanity; for to care about ills that we are unable to alleviate brings only increase of sorrow. The fruitful procedure is to *care for* that which is within our reach and susceptible to improvement by our cherishing efforts. By such active endeavour and absorption in a beneficent undertaking, one casts off the gloom which overcomes him when he sits passively brooding over the world's woes. Doubtless everyone who has dressed the wounds of man or animal has noticed how this activity relieves the distress that he felt while he stood looking at them. The principle here involved is of wide application.

If our power were limitless, so also should be our care, so that we might make all beings perfect and joyous. But our power is tragically limited, so that our concern for things, our attachment, readily outruns it. When this occurs, our failure to perfect, or even to preserve, the things for which we care causes worry, frustration, and anguish of spirit. Thereby we harm that for which above all we should care, our own soul, which is the source of our caring for everything else. Hence it becomes imperative to find the golden mean between attachment and detachment; either in excess is injurious. Excessive caring consumes the soul in a frenzy of ineffective zeal; excessive detachment narrows and hardens it. The problem of attachment is scarcely different from the problem of pity. Excessive pity torments the self with no commensurate benefit to other creatures; callousness is hardening of the soul. Our pity should be adjusted to our ability to relieve suffering.

12

Aspirations

Man's burning desire for a longer and happier conscious existence gave birth to religion. It prompted him to devise magical practices to ward off perils and ensure the fulfilment of his wishes. It led him to care for himself, his family and tribe, his deceased ancestors who might help or harm him and whom he must some day join, his gods who maintained the world order yet depended on him for nourishment. As man's concept of righteousness and character developed, it made him cherish the purity of that spiritual part of himself which alone seemed able to survive his body's decay. When his expanding thought made him realize that the creatures around him cling to life even as he does, and his maturing moral sentiments made him rise to the challenge which this realization presented, he became careful of the welfare of living things the most diverse. At his highest, he wished to do his part, however small, in maintaining the cosmos to which he belonged. He developed ideals of personal conduct and achievement.

Yet, care as diligently as we can for all things precious to us, we cannot create the world of our desire—even after desire has been purified of the inordinate craving prompted by uncontrolled imagination. Despite the triumphs of modern science, we cannot control the great powers of nature—hurricanes and floods and earthquakes and volcanic eruptions—which destroy our proudest creations and bring sudden death. We cannot achieve harmony with all creatures, or even with all men. We can prolong life but we cannot defeat death, and we are uncertain what lies beyond. Most tragic of all, the power to subdue or control those disruptive passions forced upon animals by the long, fierce struggle to survive —passions which are the source of half our woes—is given to only the best of men. So that, when we have exerted ourselves strenuously and taken the best possible care of those aspects of existence over which we can exercise some control, we are still far from the realization of our longing for a happy existence indefinitely continued. When we have reached the limit of our power, we can only hope. The devoted care that we have taken of the things within our reach gives substance to aspirations that stretch beyond our reach. Our strenuous exertions fortify our hope.

Our present understanding of geology, organic evolution, and cultural development provides no foundation for the belief that man, since he attained approximately his present form, has ever lived more happily than he has done within the historic period. Indeed, it might be argued that mankind as a whole enjoys better conditions today than ever before; although never before has humanity faced menaces so terrible as those presented by thermonuclear bombs and a too-rapidly expanding global population. Nevertheless, harassed by present difficulties, men have always yearned nostalgically for the better times their ancestors enjoyed. The mythology of various races tells of a pristine age of blissful innocence, as in the Biblical Eden or in the Golden Age of the Greeks, when gentle men lived without care or sickness, nourishing themselves on fruits and nuts or by licking the rich exudation of their mother earth, expiring at last as though they fell peacefully asleep.

Despite the widespread belief that the world was formerly far better than we now find it, only a few of the advanced religions have looked hopefully forward to the transformation of this earth into such a place as would satisfy our highest aspirations. The Persian sage Zarathustra, founder of the Zoroastrian religion, evidently expected the renovation of the world, when right would prevail over wickedness and men would dwell happily on a new earth beneath a purer sky. Unfortunately, the most definite account of the messianic hopes of the early Zoroastrians that has come down to us is from a foreign source, in which Zoroastrian and Magian doctrines have been confused. In Plutarch's essay on Isis and Osiris, we recognize the familiar Persian dualism in 'Horomazes (Ormuzd) born from the purest light, and Areimanios (Ahriman) born from the gloom'. According to Plutarch, these two deities contend stubbornly for mastery of the world, but at the end of a long age the wicked Ahriman will be utterly destroyed by the good Ormuzd. Then the earth will be made level; men will be united into a single commonwealth in which they will live in blessed felicity, speaking one language, needing no food, and casting no shadows. It is impossible to tell how seriously the Zoroastrians believed in the renovation of the earth. More firmly established in their religion was the dogma of a final judgment, when the good and the wicked would be separated at the Cinvat Bridge, the former to enjoy everlasting rewards, the latter to endure endless torments.

Probably no people has ever clung so tenaciously to the hope of a redeemed world as the Jews, whose canonical Bible contains only scattered, brief references to immortality or resurrection.[1] Isaiah (53:3) proclaimed the character of the Messiah, the 'suffering servant', sprung from the house of David, who would take the sins of his compatriots upon himself and reconcile the nation to its God. 'He is despised and rejected of men; a man of sorrows, and acquainted with grief: and we hid as it were our faces from him; he was despised, and we esteemed him not.' In the post-Biblical period, when the Jews lived sullenly under Egyptian, Syrio-Macedonian and then Roman hegemony, their thoughts turned with ever greater longing to the advent of the righteous king who would liberate Jerusalem and usher in a new era of peace. Then the ghosts of the righteous dead would emerge from Sheol to be reincarnated in their former bodies and dwell joyously with the living on a renovated earth under a new sky; and their feeling of well-being would be heightened by the sight of the wicked suffering unending torture in Gehenna. One of the most pleasing of the apocalyptic visions which abound in the post-Biblical writings is found in the fifty-first chapter of the *Book of Enoch*:

> And in those days shall the earth also give back that which has been
>   entrusted to it,
> And Sheol also shall give back that which it has received,
> And hell shall give back that which it owes.
> For in those days the Elect One shall arise,
> And he shall choose the righteous and holy from among them:
> For the day has drawn nigh that they should be saved.
> And the Elect One shall in those days sit on My throne,
> And his mouth shall pour forth all the secrets of wisdom and counsel:
> For the Lord of Spirits hath given (them) to him and hath glorified him.
> And in those days shall the mountains leap like rams,
> And the hills also shall skip like lambs satisfied with milk,

[1] Daniel, 12, contains a definite promise of immortal life.

And the faces of [all] the angels in heaven shall be lighted up with joy.
And the earth shall rejoice,
And the righteous shall dwell upon it,
And the elect shall walk thereon.

The several apocalyptic writers differed as to the fate of the Gentiles when the Messiah arrived to renew the earth. The prevailing view was that only righteous Israelites would arise from the grave to participate in Messianic beatitude; but some thought that all Israelites would be resurrected. A more liberal attitude is found in the *Testaments of the Twelve Patriarchs*, in which Benjamin declared to his children that the Lord would reveal his Salvation to all Gentiles, and all who were righteous and accepted the Law would be saved.[1]

Although all the advanced religions have, by their moral precepts, tried to improve the relations between men, few have looked hopefully to a time when the earth will become a place where our aspirations for a blessed everlasting existence could be realized. For most of them, freedom from our present ills can be won only by escaping from the flesh into some higher realm. True emancipation involves either the soul's reabsorption into the Absolute Spirit of which it is an emanation, as in the Advaita Vedanta, or its immortality. We so often hear it argued whether the soul is immortal or whether death is the total extinction of consciousness, that we seldom stop to consider how difficult both of these alternatives have been for the human mind to grasp. Simple as these concepts seem to cultivated people today, they are so foreign to the untrained mind that they appear to have been reached independently only by the most philosophic nations of antiquity, especially the Indians and the Greeks. According to W. H. R. Rivers, among the primitive Melanesians the 'ghost eats and drinks, cultivates and fishes; he goes to war and takes the heads of his enemies and, most striking fact of all, he dies; the life after death is not to be confounded with immortality, which is a far later and more developed concept'.[2]

Primitive man was evidently unable to grasp either the notion of the complete extinction of consciousness or that of spiritual immortality. To him, the deceased person became a ghost, a pitiful

[1] *The Testament of Benjamin*, 10, 4–10.
[2] W. H. R. Rivers, *Psychology and Ethnology*, Kegan Paul, Trench, Trubner & Co., London, 1926, p. 48.

shadow of its former self, depending upon the food offerings and other ministrations of the living for whatever satisfactions it might enjoy. To a developed doctrine of immortality, the soul is indestructible and, if it has been righteous, enters upon a mode of existence infinitely superior to that of living men, from whom it needs nothing. This concept of immortality rests upon the distinction between matter and mind or spirit, as two substances with contrasting attributes that are conjoined in the living person but separate after he dies. The concept of the complete extinction of consciousness follows logically from a materialistic ontology, such as the atomism that was developed by Leucippus and Democritus and popularized by Epicurus and Lucretius; and this theory, crude as it may appear to some of us today, was the product of some profound thinking, beyond the reach of an untrained mind.

The ancient Egyptians, for all their concern for personal survival, never reached the concept of spiritual immortality, as is evident from their great care to preserve the corpse and to equip it with whatever it would need for an afterlife quite similar to that on this earth. The Jews also found immortality difficult to conceive. The unknown author of the apocryphal *Wisdom of Solomon*, probably an Alexandrian Jew who lived in the first century before Christ, adopted from the Greeks the concept of the immortality of the soul but failed to use it consistently, wavering between this idea and the quite different notion of the resurrection of the body.[1]

The Catholic Church borrowed from the Greeks the idea of the immortality of the soul and from the Jews that of the resurrection of the body. According to the official doctrine, each soul is judged shortly after its release by death and goes to purgatory, heaven, or hell, according to its merits. In addition to this particular judgment, there will be a general judgment at the world's end, when the body will rise from the grave to be reunited with its soul, and the reconstituted person will remain everlastingly in heaven or hell. To the difficulty of conceiving a disembodied soul, which some philosophers find insuperable, this doctrine adds that of the reconstruction of a disintegrated organic body, which to a biologist is a tremendous stumbling block. The reincarnation of a soul in a body

[1] See the Introduction to *The Wisdom of Solomon*, by Samuel Holmes, *in* R. H. Charles, editor, *The Apocrypha and Pseudepigrapha of the Old Testament*, Clarendon Press, Oxford, 1913, vol. I, p. 529.

generated by parents in the usual way of nature, as in Indian religions, presents less difficulty than its reincarnation in a body that had died, decomposed, and somehow been rebuilt, presumably from its scattered elements. To both the Indians and the Greeks, immortality, the desired goal, was the complete and final separation of the soul from the flesh, with all the ills to which it seems inevitably to be subject. Although Christendom argues endlessly over whether the soul is or is not immortal, its major religions are committed to the quite different doctrine of resurrection.

The human brain is an immensely complex structure, with many millions of neurones conjoined in intricate patterns. Through this maze run paths of heightened permeability, worn by repeated nervous discharges, which are held to be the neural basis of our mental habits, such as the association of ideas, and perhaps also of our memories. The only immortality that seems worth striving for is one which preserves something of our personality and the continuing strand of our experiences as a self-conscious being; if immortality means no more than reabsorption into some large, impersonal, undifferentiated, blissful consciousness underlying the universe, it would seem to make little difference to it, or to us, whether our little drop of self-conscious existence falls back into that infinite ocean, there to lose its identity, or is utterly extinguished. The difficulty is to conceive how our personality, with its laboriously cultivated spiritual attitudes, and cherished memories, and the pervasive love that alone seems to make it worth preserving, can persist without the complex organic structure with which it is now so closely associated.

One sunny morning I stood on a hilltop overlooking a wide verdant valley with a lofty mountain range rising above it. In the clear atmosphere, details of trees and craggy summits miles away could be plainly seen. It occurred to me that everything visible from my point of vantage was represented at a single instant by the light waves coursing through a space no larger than the pupil of my eye. To become aware of every detail of the wide landscape visible from this point would have taken me all day, if not several days. Present, too, in this little sphere of space were light waves from distant stars, which had travelled swiftly earthward for millions of years without losing their identity, and were invisible to me only because they were overwhelmed by the far stronger sunshine. Here, then, was immense complexity in an imponderable medium; since we may discount the presence of the air, which we know to be unnecessary for the propagation of luminous vibrations. And if 'empty' space can support a myriad light waves simultaneously coursing through a single point from all directions without losing their identity, why could it not support the vast complexity of our memories and spiritual attitudes, present perhaps in the form of standing waves, or as a 'field' analogous to a magnetic or electromagnetic field? We know too little about the mode of existence of mental contents in a living body to set limits to the possibility of their existence apart from a body.

Some may object that to find support for the soul's survival in physical phenomena is to bring the spiritual dangerously close to the physical, if not indeed to destroy the distinction between these two realms of being. Descartes, it will be recalled, took extension to be the fundamental attribute of matter, which distinguished it from unextended mind or thinking substance. This dualism, no less than the crude materialism of Democritan atomism and nineteenth-century science, is incompatible with our present understanding of the universe. No one has ever demonstrated the reality of the solid, indestructible atoms of Democritus and Lucretius; matter breaks down on analysis into something mysterious which physicists such as Eddington have not hesitated to characterize as 'mind-stuff'. Light is commonly treated as part of the physical universe; yet it is so imponderable, so etherial, the bringer of such blessings, that God himself has been called Light. In flying with inconceivable velocity from one part of the universe to others the most distant, it performs a spiritual ministry, overcoming spatial isolation and binding all things together.

Light is only one of the numerous emanations, such as ultra-violet, heat and radio waves and cosmic rays, of which space is full. Many of these have only recently been discovered, and the existence of most of them can be demonstrated only by special, complex apparatus. The room in which I write is full of voices and music and signals from all over the earth; but since a radio is too distracting to have in one's study, I cannot hear them. We still do not understand how gravitational influence is conveyed from body to body. Doubtless 'empty' space contains things we have not yet discovered, and it would not be surprising to find invisible spiritual beings among them. Arbitrarily to set limits to possibility is to neglect the grandest lesson that the rapid advance of modern science can teach us. To minds that are not omniscient, dogmatic negations are as unbecoming as dogmatic assertions.

If disembodied souls or spirits exist, why is communication with them so difficult that many of us never even imagine that we achieve it? Before trying to answer this question, we should ask another: Why is it so difficult to convince ourselves of the reality of direct, or telepathic, communication with the living people around us? Few of us doubt that they have thoughts and feelings rather like our own, yet they can convey them to us only by means of bodily movements —speaking, gesturing, writing—of which we become aware through our sensory organs, especially our eyes and ears. That men and animals, other than one's individual self, have any mental or spiritual life at all is for us a matter of inference or intuition rather than of direct perception.

The answer to this problem seems to be that without insulation we could not survive. Biologists are well aware of the supreme importance of physical insulation. If a minute aquatic organism, such as an amoeba or a paramoecium, were not enclosed in a semipermeable membrane that regulates the passage of solutes to and from its protoplasm, it could neither retain the soluble substances that it requires for life nor prevent the entry of undesirable substances from the surrounding water; it could not preserve that distinctness from the medium that is a prime requisite of life. When life, which arose in the water, invaded the land, each organism had to enclose itself in a more or less impermeable covering, such as the cuticle of plants and the skin of animals, to diminish the loss of the water of which it was chiefly composed. If it lived exposed to strong sunshine, it needed pigment to shield its delicate protoplasm from radiation. Not the least important aspect of evolutionary advance has been the development of ever more adequate insulation. With highly efficient insulation by fur, feathers, or blubber, warm-blooded animals can live and carry on their activities at environmental temperatures so low that all other organisms become torpid. Man's success in colonizing most parts of the earth is due to the fact that to natural insulation he has added artificial insulation, by enclosing his body in clothes and buildings, the temperature of which he learned long ago to regulate by heating, and recently by cooling too.

Although the importance of physical insulation has been long recognised by biologists, that of psychic insulation, especially in social animals, has been largely overlooked. And just as a higher grade of physiological organization is accompanied by improved physical insulation; so it may well be that more perfect psychic insulation is a concomitant of advancing mental life. When we watch a flock of birds or a herd of quadrupeds, at one moment all busily eating, a moment later all fleeing together in consequence of some alarm, we can hardly decide whether they move in response to sensory impressions or whether, a few of them having perceived the danger, these set up a wave of intelligence or emotion that passes directly from mind to mind through the whole group, without the intervention of sense organs.

To gregarious animals that engage simultaneously in the same bodily activities, the absence of psychic insulation might be advantageous. But consider the plight of the schoolchild who, trying to concentrate on his lessons, could not avoid becoming immediately aware of the wandering thoughts of all his classmates. Consider how impossible it would be for us to concentrate on a book in a public library, if the thoughts of all the surrounding readers intruded upon our consciousness. Consider how we should be driven to distraction in a crowded train or bus, if all the thoughts of the silent passengers around us registered in our mind along with the chatter of the loquacious ones. Consider, too, how often we should be embarrassed if others became aware of thoughts that surge up unbidden in our minds. Psychic insulation may well have evolved in man as an adaptation accessory to the growing complexity of his inner life. Indeed, without it could we properly be said to have an inner life?

The same insulation that screens from us the psychic states of the embodied souls around us might conceal from us the existence of purely spiritual beings, consisting of thoughts or psychic states alone—if, indeed, released souls remain close to us or have any desire to communicate with the living. Just as some people are less resistant to cold than others, so some may have less perfect psychic insulation, which would express itself in greater sensitivity to psychic influences. Such people should be able to communicate with disembodied spirits better than most of us; they would be natural 'mediums'. Such mediums, and their intercourse with the souls of the departed, have been taken seriously by men whose intellectual accomplishments and probity command respect. Some time ago, I read a book that almost convinced me that the spiritualistic medium was receiving communications from departed souls; but when, to prove its reality, a spirit brought a material object from a closed room in a distant building, my credulity snapped. It is easier to believe in the existence of charlatans than in such violations of the natural order!

Although it seemed desirable to call attention to certain considerations usually overlooked, it is far from the purpose of this book to review the voluminous arguments for and against spiritual survival. What I wish to do in the remainder of this chapter is to consider the relation of human immortality to the whole course of evolution that has made us what we are.

There was a time, a billion years or so ago, when the cooling earth was still without life. The surface of the land was covered with barren rock and doubtless also ash extruded from vents and fissures in the planet's shrinking crust. The seas, still tepid, were less briny than they have become during the long ages that countless rivers have washed down to them salts dissolved from disintegrating rocks. Probably they then contained simple carbohydrates formed by the action of sunlight on an atmosphere rich in carbon dioxide, most of which has since been removed by plants. The terrestrial sphere was less massive than the contributions of billions of large and small meteors, which we still see burning themselves to dust in our nocturnal skies, have made it through the ages. The expansion of the universe had not yet carried the stars so far away as we now find them, so that they shone more brightly upon the earth, although probably their refulgence was dimmed by a heavier, more vaporous atmosphere. That did not matter, for there were still no eyes to behold the splendour of the firmament, no minds to respond with wonder and awe to its vastitude.

Stirred by wind and waves, the solutes in warm coastal waters combined and recombined, until through endless permutations they happened to come together in the form of complex molecules capable of reproducing themselves. These seeds of life, self-sown, brought a new promise to the barren earth. The earliest progenitors of life were probably as far removed, in time and complexity, from those one-celled animals and plants that figure in our biological textbooks as the simplest living things, as these are from the most highly developed members of the vegetable and animal kingdoms. Doubtless, still lacking the complex catalysts essential for the synthesis of organic compounds, these precursors of life subsisted upon energy-yielding substances then present in the water, until the supply ran low.

The promise of life would never have been fulfilled, if some of these primitive organisms had not developed the capacity to employ the energy in sunlight for the synthesis of carbohydrates from carbon dioxide and water. These accomplished organisms were the forerunners of vegetation; while those that never developed—or lost—the capacity for photosynthesis took to eating the plants as their original sources of energy ran low, thereby becoming the progenitors of the animal kingdom. With richer sources of food, the primitive animals multiplied so rapidly that they were thrown into competition for space and nourishment and began to prey on each other. Thus began that fierce conflict to survive which on the one hand has accelerated the evolution of life into a myriad diverse forms, but on the other hand has been the source of most of the ills from which living things suffer. In this internecine strife, animals developed sense organs that became ever more acute and methods of locomotion that increased in efficiency, but at the heavy price of becoming infected with strong appetites and passions that would one day distress them.

From the seas, life crept forth upon the land. Probably the intertidal zone of the shore was the school in which organisms periodically exposed to desiccation at low tide learned how to conserve the water in their tissues, thereby solving the basic problem of terrestrial life. Seaweeds that needed only holdfasts to attach themselves to the rocks gradually evolved true roots that served not only for anchoring them in the soil but likewise for absorbing water and salts and passing them to the exposed shoots. Gradually, through the geologic ages, plants solved the many problems of subaerial life and spread a green mantle over the continents and islands, now covered with soil from disintegrating rocks. Animals followed the plants that provided food for them. Although at first animals exploited plants without making any return, at long last terrestrial plants discovered a use for animals, to carry their pollen from flower to flower and to transport their seeds. These services were procured only at a price, that of providing nectar for the pollinators and edible fruits for the disseminators of seeds.

It was to the mutual advantage of the plants and the animals which cooperated with them to make the nectar-yielding flowers and the edible fruits easily distinguishable from the green foliage by becoming differently coloured. The success of this innovation led to the evolution of brilliant blossoms and colourful fruits, and concomitantly to the development, or at least the great improvement, of the ability to distinguish colours in the animals that served the plants, principally insects and birds as pollinators, birds and certain arboreal mammals, especially the monkeys of warm forests, as carriers of seeds.

In the multiple interactions among living things, the possession of colour-vision inevitably reacted upon the animals themselves. They too developed bright colours, often in intricate patterns, as a means of attracting mates and of distinguishing individuals of their own species from those of related species. Now the earth, which in the epoch when ferns and their allies were the predominant vegetation had no lack of beautiful forms but was still monotonously green, was embellished by the colours of a myriad flowers, birds, and insects, especially the wide-winged butterflies. Since these animals needed to be mobile to serve and profit from the plants, as also to escape their enemies, swift, graceful movement was added to beautiful colours and shapely forms. The birds developed a vast repertory of melodious songs, that in times to come would sound jubilant or carefree or melancholy to attentive human ears.

Meanwhile, the vegetation had cleared the atmosphere of the heavier gases. By day, the sun shone brilliantly in an azure sky made lovelier by soft white clouds, illuminating all the varied colours of flowers and birds and insects, glinting in a myriad spears of light from glossy leaves. Showers fell to refresh the vegetation, and as they passed, a rainbow would often arch colourfully above the landscape. As the sun set, star after star opened its eye in the darkening heaven, until it was spangled with a glittering host, through which wandered the moon, ceaselessly changing its its shape. The earth, at first so grim and forbidding in its silent barrenness, had through the course of long ages become a place of marvellous beauty, teeming with sentient life. As more powerful telescopes have been turned upon the planets, as Mariner spaceships crammed with sensitive apparatus have scanned Venus and Mars at close range and radioed back reports and photographs, we have become increasingly convinced that no other member of the solar system is so well endowed as ours; the other planets seem either too hot, too cold, or too dry to support life. Possibly some among the billions of stars scattered through space have satellites which equal our earth in beauty or even exceed it immeasurably, but they are so vastly distant that we shall probably never know about them.

The earth had already become populated with the same types of plants and animals that we know today, and was certainly no less beautiful than we now find it, when, about a million years ago, man began to assume his present form. He was descended from an ape-like ancestor that had apparently been forced, by the deterioration of the forests in an era of increasing drought, to live upon the ground. From arboreal, largely vegetarian ancestors he had inherited two priceless endowments, the ability to manipulate objects with hands once used for climbing, and to distinguish colours. To him the earth must from the first have appeared lovelier than it does to most quadrupeds, which apparently see colours merely as grey in shades that vary with the intensity of the light more than with its wave-length.

Man early showed his appreciation of form and colour by his artistic efforts. Some of the earliest artistic productions that have survived to the present, such as the Paleolithic paintings of animals on the walls of caves in France and Spain, were evidently motivated by primitive man's incessant preoccupation with his precarious food supply. Yet the grace of some of these figures testifies to the artist's delight in form and movement for their own sake; many a cruder representation has served all the purposes of compulsive magic. Before long, we find men all over the world adorning their pottery and other artifacts with coloured forms, and even covering their bodies with designs made by tattooing, scarification, or painting—practices which horrify a civilized taste but doubtless delighted them. Tribes that live in savage squalour decorate their utensils, weapons, and ceremonial objects in ways that win the admiration of connoisseurs. Man's aesthetic faculty ran ahead of such civilized virtues as cleanliness, moderation, self-control, justice, and compassion. It seems incongruous to use a tastefully decorated war club to crack the skull of the poor victim of a cannibalistic orgy!

As men increased in culture, they made greater efforts to reproduce, in painting or sculpture, the exact proportions of each natural form, to catch the grace of each curve of stationary or even moving bodies. The Greeks attained an excellence in such naturalistic representations which has never been surpassed; their superb statues and reliefs, unlike modern sculptures, were brightly coloured. Poets delighted to describe in polished verse the quiet loveliness of natural scenes. In more recent times, travellers busily painted, sketched, or wrote detailed descriptions in their personal journals, to help preserve the precious memory of scenes that enchanted them. In this more hurried age, the photographic camera has replaced the sketchbook as a means of recording our impressions of the natural world. Peaceful cultivated landscapes once pleased men far more than wild forests and rugged mountains, full of real or imaginary perils. Now that the wilderness has been made safer and more readily accessible, those who delight in natural beauty seek the majesty of unspoiled forests and the grandeur of snow-capped peaks rising unsullied into the blue.

This earth, made a fit habitation for us by a billion years of slow evolution, is the scene set for our enjoyment of every value which life offers. Friendship, domestic affections, the pursuit of knowledge, social recognition, high adventure in pitting one's strength and resourcefulness against the sea or the mountains—all our joys and all our triumphs are enhanced, far more than many people are aware, by the background against which we experience them. The more sensitive and capable of enjoyment one is, the more he is depressed by ugly surroundings and gloomy skies, the more his spirit is lifted by sunshine and a smiling earth. One might suppose that the whole course of evolution on this planet has been directed toward converting it into a fit abode for beings ever more adequately equipped, by means of sensory organs and responsive minds and retentive memories, to appreciate their presence on it. Although evolution may be viewed from various angles, this is the only aspect of the process that has ultimate significance. A world devoid of sentient beings, capable of finding satisfaction in their own existence and delight in the things around them, is a world devoid of significance. Whether it evolves elaborate forms or remains for ever in primal chaos can make no difference to anyone or anything. Only in so far as it provides desirable experiences for its inhabitants does a world acquire value.

Unhappily, our world did not evolve in one direction only. While it became increasingly fitted to give joy and delight, it became also an abode of terror, pain, and sorrow. The strife that arose when crowding caused some primitive organisms to prey on others increased in intensity as animals became more complex and evolved more effective means of attacking each other. In the measure that man's developing mind became more sensitive to the earth's beauty and all the other values which human life provides, it likewise became more acutely aware of the perils which beset him. All animals suffer and die, but perhaps only man anticipates suffering and death and tries to fathom their meaning. And man rebelled against death; he refused to believe that it is the natural and inevitable end of a living being. Although the Hebrew Bible ascribed man's mortality to the disobedience of his first parents, primitive tribes have usually cast the blame on some wicked, envious deity, male or female. Moreover, doubtless because in primitive conditions people rarely survive long enough to fade peacefully away at an advanced age, they usually attributed a death to their enemies, which included wild beasts no less than hostile human neighbours. If the deceased had not been torn by fangs or assaulted with weapons, he must have died because malicious people or spirits cast a spell on him, causing him to fall sick, to be struck by lightning, or to drown while crossing a river. And even with the lifeless corpse before him, primitive man could not believe in the reality of death. The living person, the essential man, must simply have abandoned his body and gone elsewhere—a belief reflected in the mortuary rites that we glanced at in Chapter 5.

Man's revolt against death is more than that instinctive avoidance of lethal situations which is indispensable to the preservation of any species of animal. Men rebel against death because they foresee in it the deprivation of the pleasures which life affords them; even when they have persuaded themselves that the ghost will not lack similar satisfactions in the afterworld, the prospect has rarely been attractive or convincing—except to those minds thoroughly conditioned by a religion of emancipation. It is because we live in a beautiful world with multiple sources of delight that death is cruel and hateful to us. We can conceive a mode of existence so lacking in joy that we should welcome total extinction. It is true that countless men and women, under the spell of religions of emancipation, have regarded this as a base and wicked world, a vale of tears, from which they averted their eyes and other senses while preparing themselves, by means of ascetic rigours and penances, for the earliest possible escape to a better one. But their whole conception of a better world was based on their experiences in this one; they could imagine none that were radically different. The heaven for which they panted was simply a place where such satisfactions as they had already known were multiplied and intensified, while all the toils and pains of earthly existence were excluded. The heaven of which we dream is merely the finest moments we have known on earth, indefinitely prolonged. Even while he reviles and scorns the world, the ascetic preparing for eternal bliss is unwittingly commending it. Man's revolt against death, his yearning for everlasting life, is the most sincere compliment that the world process has ever received. It is proof that it has made conscious existence highly desirable.

Not only must each of us perish individually; all life will one day be extinguished on this planet. The belief in the destruction of the world was widely held in ancient times; but having no notion how long the earth had already existed, the ancients expected its dissolution far too soon. Modern scientists who place the age of the earth at a few billions of years give it a correspondingly long future; but those best qualified to form an opinion hold that eventually its life will be totally destroyed, either as a result of the cooling of the sun or else of its explosion, to flare up as a nova in the sky.

This is the most desolating prospect of all. In the measure that they succeed in passing on to loved descendants their wisdom, their values, their ideals and enthusiasms, to say nothing of their property, generous people can sometimes reconcile themselves to death. In a way, they live on in those to whom they have given life and its goods. But the longer this globe continues to exist, the more its cargo of precious things is augmented, the more appalling will eventual extinction become. Some optimists believe that humanity can avoid extermination by settling on another planet. To a biologist mindful of how closely every organic species is adapted to its actual environment, the notion that man could long survive on a planet physically so different from the earth as Mars or Venus seems fantastic, even if the difficulty of transport could be overcome. And although there are probably innumerable planets beyond our solar system, to discover which stars have them, then to reach them, appear to be insuperable problems.

If we rebel at the prospect of our individual extinction, how much more must we protest against the utter annihilation of everything of value that this planet has brought forth in the billion years of its existence, of humanity as a whole and everything that it has accomplished! Philosophers have sought an escape from this depressing conclusion. Christian theology has long maintained that an omniscient Deity knows all that has happened and will happen in his universe. This doctrine of divine foreknowledge raises perplexing problems about the freedom of creatures and (more importantly in my opinion) about the significance not only of their individual strivings and achievements but indeed of the whole world process. The only events in the world that have any ultimate—as opposed to instrumental—value are those registered in some creature's experience; and to experience fleetingly what God experiences eternally seems to be so slight an addition to the total sum of value in the universe that it might as well be omitted. Nothing new is ever achieved, for all events in time are but transient shadows of what is eternally present in the divine consciousness.

To overcome this and other difficulties of the classical theology, Professor Charles Hartshorne has elaborated the concept of a God who does not foreknow what will happen in a developing universe, but remembers everything that occurs. His perfect memory retains infallibly all our experiences, all our joys and all our sorrows, which in our imperfect memory become blurred and faint with the passage of the years—and so for every creature everywhere. Thus all the value that the universe produces is preserved for ever, along, unfortunately, with all the disvalue—all the unpleasant or horrible experiences that we should like to forget—but each is seen in true perspective as the good or evil it is and reconciled to the whole in God's all-embracing vision.[1]

Apparently the only other means of avoiding the eventual total loss of everything this planet has achieved is by preservation in the memory of the immortal minds or souls of its inhabitants, or some

[1] Charles Hartshorne, *The Divine Relativity: A Social Conception of God*, Yale University Press, 1948.

of them. Such preservation would not be nearly so complete as that in the supposedly infinite mind of God, for our experience is limited and our recollection imperfect; yet collectively, in all the souls of all the creatures of whatever kind that have developed conscious memory, a vast amount might be saved. And our latent memory is far more adequate than we commonly imagine it to be; sometimes it requires only a slight stimulus—a word, a melody, a scent—to bring back with almost painful poignancy some long-past experience that seemed forgotten. Hence there is wisdom in the ancient fancy, repeated in Dante's *Purgatorio*, that on its way to heaven the righteous soul drinks successively the water of Lethe, which washes away all painful recollections, and of Eunoë, which gives vividness and permanence to every precious memory.

Of these two methods by which something of value might survive the earth's dissolution, the second involves the smaller assumption. There is no convincing evidence for the existence of an infinite or cosmic mind; as we shall see in Chapter 16, the very conception, sublime though it be, is founded on an inadmissible extrapolation of experience. But no one can doubt the reality of his own mind; it is the one existence that the thorough sceptic must admit, because doubting is itself a mental act that confirms the existence of mind. The only question is whether one's own mind, or any mind, can exist apart from an organic body. The two methods are not mutually exclusive, and the incontrovertible proof of the existence of either a cosmic mind or a disembodied human mind would encourage belief in the possibility of the other.

It has become evident, I hope, that the question of the survival of the human soul or mind involves issues far vaster than just the everlasting preservation of each individual's awareness of his personal identity, which certain thinkers have viewed as an absurd or presumptuous obsession. The question resolves itself into whether the world process will achieve anything of permanent value, or whether all its accomplishments will be ultimately cancelled. We have seen it converting a huge sphere covered with lifeless water, barren rock, and ash into a beautiful world crowded with marvellous living things, and at the same time creating animals whose sensory apparatus and minds make them ever more capable of responding appreciatively to its beauty and wonder. In memory it has given these animals a means of preserving for many years, although imperfectly, the recollection of their cherished experiences; and with the aid of written records, pictures, and the like, some of them strive to keep their memories more vividly alive. The survival, after the body's dissolution, of minds stored with precious recollections would be consistent with all the preceding development, the prolongation of a long-continued line of advance. Far from being a supernatural event, it would be the culmination of a natural process.

Indeed, it is not life indefinitely continued but death that seems incongruous with the whole movement that made us, an abrupt reversal of the processes of development and growth. An observer from another world, who arrived here with no preconceptions and started to study life from its beginnings, might be amazed to discover that plants and animals die, otherwise than by violence. It seems that organisms grow old and die because evolution failed to develop a means for the continuous progressive modification of existing individuals to ever higher forms, so that it must work by modifying a succession of generations rather than continuing to improve an existing generation. Although the development of each organic body is limited by its genetic endowment at birth, this need not apply to a mind, provided that it can exist apart from a body.

Earlier in this chapter, I gave reasons for believing in the possibility of the soul's persistence. But even if it could be proved— as it cannot be proved—that no soul has ever survived its body's decay, that would be no reason for abandoning hope. We live in an evolving world, where things previously unknown come to be; this has happened since life began, but in no era so often as in our own. Just as an electric charge must reach a certain voltage before it can spark or leap from its conductor; just as a child must gain a certain strength before it can live without its mother; so it may be that the spirit must attain a certain intensity and coherence before it can exist apart from an organic body. Souls torn by conflicting passions might disintegrate when no longer bound to a solid organism. Those wholly engrossed in bodily sensations would have no motive for existing apart from an animal body. The sensual and the violent might simply cease to exist when they die, so that hell would be superfluous. The soul's survival may be above all a question of its quality, of the intensity of its desire to exist for ever and its effort to prepare itself for immortal life.

As was remarked in Chapter 9, all the higher religions agree on the necessity of catharsis or spiritual purification for the attainment of a blessed immortal life; but, influenced by views on the innate content of the mind that are no longer tenable, they have given too little attention to its furnishing. When, as in the present chapter, we consider spiritual survival in relation to the whole world process of which we are parts, we are led to take a different view of this matter. Not the soul reduced by mystic or yogic exercises to pure un-modified consciousness—if, indeed, such a state is possible—but a receptive soul richly furnished by means of an observant, apprecia-tive life in a marvellous but perishable world, seems to be the most valuable contribution that such a world could make to eternity. Accordingly, in addition to that spiritual chastening and purification which is indispensable to creatures with an ancestral history such as ours, we should lose no opportunity to enrich our minds with memories of beautiful forms, and noble deeds, and warm friend-ships, and such sound knowledge of the world as we can attain. Our opportunities for gaining such experiences may be confined to our embodied existence, while we are equipped with sense organs for perceiving material objects; so that the store of such memories that we shall carry with us through a long future may be limited to what we can gather here. Even if experiences that we can now hardly imagine await us then, lacking knowledge of this aspect of reality, our souls would be incomplete.

Of all human aspirations, that for immortal life has been the most widespread, persistent, and intensely cherished. There have been religions that recognized no God, but none which taught that the soul perishes with the body has ever won a wide following or endured for long. No religion has furnished proof generally acceptable to conscientious thinkers that a soul can exist apart from an organic body. Nevertheless, religion has no more sacred task than to encourage this aspiration, to keep it alive. The whole purpose of religion can be summarized in one sentence: To prepare us for eternal life; to teach us to live as though the best and most intimate part of ourselves will endure for ever. All our duties, all our obliga-tions to self and others, are comprised in this effort; for to be worthy of eternal life a man must make the best of his present existence, living as a good neighbour, a responsible citizen, a loving parent and true friend, losing no opportunity to enrich no less than to purify his soul.

No matter what destiny awaits us, to live as though our souls are immortal is to make the best possible use of our earthly span. Even though spiritual survival is an aspiration which must remain for ever unfulfilled because mind cannot exist apart from an animal body, let it at least be said that our planet produced beings so appreciative, so filled with love, that they were worthy of immortal life. If we must perish utterly, let it not be because we deserve to perish. Unless some of its inhabitants carry its memory into another realm of being, everything that this earth has produced through long ages of creative evolution seems destined finally to perish without leaving a trace; for the indestructible atoms into which it will dissolve bear no record of the higher formations to which they once contributed. A tragic end, surely, of such vast effort; an end against which love rebels, which hope and faith deny.

13

The Faults of Religion

The positive contributions of religions to humanity have been many
and great; they have taught us to respect and care for ourselves;
they have widened our sense of responsibility for our fellow
creatures; they have nourished our aspirations for a better life, on
this earth and beyond it. Now, in order to complete our appraisal of
religions and reach a true estimate of their worth, we must look at
the other side of the account, examining their shortcomings, their
failures, their perversions. These are so great that some of the best
of men, aghast at the crimes of religion, have believed that they
could perform no greater service to humanity than to destroy it
utterly. It is not the wicked and dissolute, but good men eager to
promote the welfare of their fellows, who have been the most
formidable enemies of religion, for they attacked it on the side where
it was weakest and most vulnerable. One of the most renowned of
these righteous enemies of religion was Epicurus, a man reviled
and misrepresented by his philosophical opponents, especially the
Stoics, but revered almost as a god by disciples whose minds he
freed of superstitious dread. The most famous of these disciples,
who did more than any other to preserve his master's doctrines for
posterity, was the Roman poet Lucretius, who wrote:

> Whilst human kind
> Throughout the lands lay miserably crushed
> Before all eyes beneath Religion—who
> Would show her head along the region skies,
> Glowering on mortals with her hideous face—
> A Greek it was who first opposing dared
> Raise mortal eyes that terror to withstand,
> Whom nor the fame of Gods nor lightning's stroke
> Nor threatening thunder of the ominous sky
> Abashed; but rather chafed to angry zest
> His dauntless heart to be the first to rend

The crossbars at the gates of Nature old.
And thus his will and hardy wisdom won;
And forward thus he fared afar, beyond
The flaming ramparts of the world, until
He wandered the unmeasurable All.[1]

Then, after telling about the sacrificial murder of Agamemnon's daughter Iphigenia at Aulis, to raise a wind for the becalmed Argive fleet, he concluded with the famous line:

Such are the crimes to which religion leads.

It is not the purpose of the present chapter to recount these crimes, which would fill volumes. The earlier religions were too often affairs of blood and terror. Even to read about them is frequently a painful task for the sensitive, compassionate person who rummages for the grain of gold buried beneath mountains of absurd superstition and barbarous ritual. One wonders what psychic aberrations ever led man into such murky mazes. The superstitions are not difficult to explain; they are the unavoidable results of the attempt to answer, with half-formed, undisciplined minds, questions which still perplex us who are the heirs of a long philosophic and scientific tradition. Primitive man was deficient in scepticism, that high virtue of the mind which alone can preserve it free and chaste. He was too prone to believe that his wishes could compel natural events. Superstition dies hard; and for all our science and all our critical philosophy, there seems to be as much of it alive in the modern world as there ever was.

What is more difficult to understand than their superstitions is how men could bring themselves to do some of the things their wandering thoughts suggested to them: mutilate themselves most horribly; hack living animals to pieces; immolate their children on the altar of a bloodthirsty god; tear the throbbing heart from the living breast of a sacrificial victim; burn men alive. Such cruel practices mystify as much as they shock us, until we recall that they were done by a predatory, warring animal. In descending to the ground from the trees, where fruits and foliage were their principal foods, as of other Primates, man's ancestors became carnivorous beasts, inured to striking down their fellow creatures and tearing them apart for food. Although many monkeys and apes settle their

[1] Lucretius, *On the Nature of Things*, W. E. Leonard's translation in Everyman's Library, Book I.

differences by shouting and gesticulating, and animals of the most diverse kinds contend with others of the same species only long enough to decide which will have precedence because of its superior strength or agility or endurance, man fights to kill. The most imperious thing in the world is the human will, which to attain its ends spares neither others nor self; every cruel tyrant and ruthless dictator that the world has known has been but an embodiment of this same domineering will. And when instead of an individual's will we have the collective will of the people, and when what they will is survival itself, they stop at no deed, however appalling, which their scheming priests or raving oracles propose as a means of overcoming the enemy, arresting the plague, or ending the famine that threatens to destroy the city or tribe. Not the least of the services of the higher religions is the chastening of the inordinate human will, the cause of so much suffering not only by man but by all the creatures that surround him.

Another charge often brought against religions is that they have invariably failed to make any considerable proportion of a population live in strict obedience to their precepts. The ancient Greek philosophers held that only youths who had been well brought up, trained in good habits from childhood, could profit by the study of ethics; they sometimes went so far as to drive away with blows importunate young men whom they did not regard as promising disciples, as Antisthenes did to Diogenes. But the great popular religions have tried to carry their message to everyone, often concentrating on just that backward, downtrodden section of the population that the philosophers regarded as too unpromising to bother with. No wonder their converts often failed to live according to the teaching they professed to accept, perhaps without half understanding it! The failure was often caused by men's stupidity and waywardness rather than defects in the religion itself.

Yet the wide gap between the precepts of a religion and the practices of its adherents is not always the fault of the latter alone. To serve as a guide and incentive to effort, our ideals should always be held beyond our reach, yet not so far as to discourage us. Sometimes religious teachers have been guilty of just this fault. Christ's beautiful teaching of non-resistance to evil, of not worrying about the morrow because God will take care of us as he does of the lilies, is understandable when we recall that he expected the speedy destruction of this world and its replacement by a better one. No society that took such a permissive attitude toward its criminals, or neglected its economy and its family obligations to the degree that Jesus sometimes seemed to recommend, could long survive. Similarly, Jainism's strict rule against the taking of life of even the humblest creatures tends to defeat its own purpose. By diverting Jains from occupations such as agriculture, in which the incidental destruction of insects and other small creatures is unavoidable, it leaves indispensable tasks to others who follow them with less care to avoid injuring living things than a devout Jain would take. One might go on to point out other instances of how religions, by regarding certain of their loftier precepts as rules to be undeviatingly followed rather than as unattainable ideals to be approached as closely as our human predicament will admit, have failed to serve these ideals as well as they might do.

The higher religions have happily been purified of the bloody practices that defiled the earlier ones and also of much, but by no means all, of the superstitions—although every religion maintains that it is free of superstitions such as it detects in the doctrines of its rivals. If religions hold their ideals too far beyond our reach, it is not altogether to their discredit. More serious are their failures in those aspects of religion which are its very heart—failures of appreciation, failures of caring, failures of aspiration. Most lamentable of all is the failure of appreciation that is so general in religions of emancipation. If living were not a precious experience that men desire intensely to prolong and to perfect, religion would never have arisen; for every rite in both primitive and advanced religions owes its origin to its supposed efficacy in preserving ourselves and the institutions by which we live in this world or else in preparing us for the next. And we wish to prolong our existence because the planet beneath our feet makes this present life—the only one we know— a desirable experience. As already pointed out, every heaven that men have ever imagined—every heaven that we can imagine—is created by the ideal intensification of the joys or values which this earthly life has provided for us, with the exclusion of all its disagreeable features. A religion true to its origins would use all its arts to heighten our appreciation of every beautiful and rewarding feature of this earth that produced us, supports us, and nourishes our aspirations. No religion that I know has done this to the extent that it should; and in religion after religion, we find the sterner sort of ascetics averting their gaze from outward things as though the very sight of earth and sky and creatures living joyously would pollute their souls.

An outstanding exception is St Francis of Assisi, whose *Canticle of the Creatures* reveals deep appreciation of every beneficent aspect of nature, from our father the Sun, glorious and resplendent, to our sister Water, humble, useful, precious, and pure. Such undisguised delight in the natural world, no less than his brotherly affection for birds and quadrupeds, were so little typical of medieval ascetics that they helped to win for this amiable friar the sobriquet of 'The Pagan Saint'. The nature mystics, who view the natural world as God's visible garment, manage by this conception to preserve a reverent attitude toward it. The religious poets, from the ancient psalmists onward, have necessarily helped us to appreciate the earth's beauty and the heaven's glory; for visual imagery is the life of poetry. But in modern times it has been above all the secular poets and prose writers who have sharpened our appreciation of the world in which we live.

Just as caring, which is the very substance of religion, follows from appreciation, so failure of appreciation results in failure of care. A most valuable feature of the old religions of preservation which has dropped out of religions of emancipation is concern for the conservation of nature (see Chapter 6). In Genesis it is written: 'And the Lord God took the man, and put him into the garden of Eden to dress it and to keep it.' The religions which accept the Pentateuch as God's word seem generally to have overlooked this most pregnant statement. Man has multiplied so greatly that the whole earth has become his garden; and if faithful to the charge that God laid upon him, he would dress it and keep it as a holy abode. Instead, what do we find him doing? Without piety or forethought, he ravishes whole continents, while the religions which revere the Bible as divine look on with hardly a word of protest. The recent effort to protect the natural world from spoliation has been made by naturalists, foresters, agriculturists, and men of similar interests, who were alarmed and distressed by the rapid shrinkage of the wilderness with all that it offers to a receptive spirit, no less than by the erosion of the soil and the pollution of the waters which are the foundations of any civilization. The few who heroically strive to save what the many thoughtlessly destroy have received all too little encouragement and support from the organized religions of the West. By their reluctance to deprive any creature of its life, Eastern religions have from ancient times exerted a beneficent restraint on man's destructive exploitation of the natural world.

Since our bodies belong to the natural world rather than to the realm of the soul, it is not surprising that the neglect of things natural so widespread in religions of emancipation should extend to them, too. I do not know who it was who first declared that cleanliness is next to godliness, but he was evidently not a religious ascetic. In both the East and the West, never to bathe, to have lice in one's clothes or beard, has been considered the mark of a saintly man. Likewise, to deprive oneself of needed food has been widely regarded as a holy practice; we even read, incredulously, of Indian saints who lived for years without eating. As though to neglect the body, inside and outside, were not enough, many an aspirant for salvation has tortured his 'mortal frame' most cruelly. The Buddha prescribed for his monks and nuns a 'middle path' between luxury and ascetic harshness; but the restriction of their possessions to eight articles, and the prohibition of eating after midday, seem too severe for most of us.

Not only have religions of emancipation encouraged neglect of the body, they have frequently taken the same negative attitude toward the mind. This follows logically from those Indian philosophies which regard the *manas*, or mind with its discriminatory and logical powers, as pertaining to the body rather than to the soul, whose essence is pure, unmodified consciousness. (Jainism, as we have seen, takes a different view.) It follows, too, from disdain of the natural world, in the contemplation and study of which our aesthetic sensibility, our sympathy, our powers of observation, discrimination, and interpretation are so immeasurably strengthened. Was there ever any perversion so great as that of imagining that to have an ignorant, uncultivated mind in a meagre, festering body clad in dirty rags is the surest way to the soul's salvation? To one who realizes the great power of habit not only over our muscular reactions but likewise over our psychic attitudes, it seems fantastic to suppose that by habituating ourselves to misery and mental impoverishment in one stage of our existence we prepare ourselves for joy in the next.

The more liberal religions of the present day no longer encourage neglect of body and mind, yet the old negative attitude toward the natural world is far from dead. Compassion for all creatures so deep and sincere that he shirked no labour or hardship to promote their welfare, combined with a fresh approach to the settlement of stubborn political problems, made Gandhi one of the great men of the twentieth century; yet we read in his autobiography how, on a voyage from South Africa to England, he persuaded his companion to cast his binoculars into the sea, because these aids to a wider vision were not in keeping with an ascetic life.

Although the disdainful attitude toward the natural world and all that pertains to it, including our bodies and even our minds as instruments for knowing this world, forms one of the saddest chapters in the history of religion, it is not difficult to understand how this attitude arose. The spontaneous reaction of the undisciplined human mind to anything that strongly excites its admiration is to desire to possess it. Glimpsing a colourful bird, the ignorant man wishes to shoot and stuff it to keep in his home; beholding a lovely wildflower, he plucks it; looking over a beautiful stretch of country, he covets it; if wealthy he may buy it, and if a powerful ruler he may conquer it. Similarly, exquisite works of art excite covetousness; they figure prominently among the booty of war. Since envy and possessiveness are diseases of the soul, and ownership is a fertile source of anxiety and distraction, it was natural that religions and philosophies which undertook to purify the soul should discourage them. And the surest way to avoid desire for something beautiful is never even to glance admiringly at it! In modern times, when we are encouraged from childhood to look at free animals and wildflowers without molesting them, when in public museums we see many beautiful things that are not available for private ownership, some of us seem to be learning how to enjoy without coveting.

Similar considerations account for the harsh treatment of the body and the repression of the mind. Since it is difficult to draw the line between caring adequately for our bodies and pampering them, and to indulge in luxuries is to crave them more and more, the safest course for a religion that wished to free the soul from sensuality was to encourage a rigorous asceticism. Absorption in the pursuit of knowledge of external things too frequently leads to neglect not only of our obligations but even of our spiritual development, while the reputation for great learning or skill in dialectic has often been a source of pride; hence these, too, have been frowned upon as vain pretensions by religions. Recoiling from excesses in one direction, they fell into the opposite excess. In the *Philebus*, Plato concluded that the highest good is 'measure, moderation, fitness, and all which is to be considered similar to these'. Yet the middle course that philosophy recommends is so difficult to preserve that religions have commonly been wary of it.

Despite their mistrust of the senses and all that pertains to them, religions have rarely hesitated to employ sensuous means to further their own ends. Most of them have encouraged architects and artists to lavish their talents on the construction and adornment of temples and churches and the depiction of sacred personages and scenes. Vocal and instrumental music swell through the sumptuous edifices to help uplift the soul on a surge of emotion toward its Creator. And if the monasteries have been retreats for fanatical ascetics, in barbarous epochs they have provided the only quiet havens for scholars. The convents of Christian Europe did much to preserve the treasures of Classical literature and learning through the Dark and Middle Ages, even if it was too often on palimpsests, on which modern scholars must laboriously decipher the priceless text of a Greek or Latin author which had been erased by a monk short of writing materials, so that he might cover the parchment with a copy of some devotional writer or with his own pious but banal meditations. Thus, even while we censure religions for rejecting much of the good of this earth along with its evil, we must be grateful to them for keeping alive at least a tiny flame of enlightenment in eras of intellectual decay.

From failures of appreciation and caring, we now turn to failures of aspiration. As we learned in Chapter 5, early religions recognized the survival of an unsubstantial ghost dependent upon living men for nourishment; but lacking the concept of a spiritual soul, they could not promise a blessed immortal life. In Egypt, the pharaohs and their intimates anticipated a happy existence in the afterworld long before, in the Osirian faith, similar prospects cheered the common people. The Buddha taught his disciples how to terminate the series of painful incarnations but held forth no flattering prospect of heaven—an omission which popular Buddhism, especially the Mahayana, has not failed to remedy. Even as late as the time of Christ, one powerful sect among the Jews, the Sadducees, basing their stand on the canonical books of the Old Testament, denied the soul's survival and the resurrection.

Even when, as is usually true, a religion of emancipation promises personal survival, it may fail to develop a worthy concept of heaven. It was said of the Orphics of ancient Greece that they lived temperately in this world so that in the next they might wallow like pigs in sensual indulgences, and the same remark might with equal justice be applied to some other doctrines of salvation. Mohammed's paradise of delicious fruits that never cloy, refreshing drinks that never inebriate, and an endless supply of virgin concubines, is hardly a spiritual conception. Far more inspiring is the Christian doctrine, developed philosophically by St Thomas Aquinas, that the blessed souls of the righteous dwell everlastingly in sight of God, enveloped in his love, seeing all things with unerring and unclouded vision, as he does. In Dante's poetic vision of heaven, the souls of the blessed, united with their resurrected bodies, are seated in ranks arranged like the petals of a white rose, while angels, flying constantly back and forth like a swarm of bees, bring them peace and ardour from God, whom they constantly behold. When the ranks have been filled, half of the saintly multitude will consist of those who anticipated the coming of Christ and the other half of those who accepted his teaching. Thus the beatific congregation is composed exclusively of Christians and of Jews who lived before Jesus taught; we miss the rest of humanity, and are grieved to remember that even the great philosophers of ancient Greece, whose writings gave Christian doctrine a breadth of vision that it never could have derived from the Jewish scriptures alone, are sighing in Limbo far below, yearning for God, whom they have no hope of seeing because they were unbaptized.

Indian religions are more generous, for they allow that every soul, no matter how low in the scale of being the body it now inhabits, may through a sufficiently long series of incarnations reach the highest blessedness. For the Advaita Vedanta, this is to lose all personal identity in the eternal blissful consciousness of the absolute Brahman, like a drop of rain in the ocean. Buddhism takes a similar view as to the loss of personal identity; but the more I read of Buddhist philosophy, the more I wonder what, if anything, remains of us in the Emptiness that is Full. Those who prefer a less elusive metaphysic that sticks closer to the only experience of Being that we have, our awareness of ourselves as enduring centres of consciousness, will welcome the Jaina teaching that every soul is eternal and, when purified of karmic deposits, enjoys perfect happiness, perfect knowledge, and perfect power. Yet these so splendidly endowed souls seem to exist in chilling isolation, unloving and unloved.

If these descriptions, or any of them, were factual reports, we should have to accept them as they stand. Since all are ideal visions, it is not unreasonable to demand that they be ideally satisfying. Yet in each of these eschatological doctrines we miss something: in the delectable Christian heaven as depicted by Dante, we miss the greater part of humanity; in the Vedantic and Buddhist schemes of salvation, we are reduced to anonymity with the loss of every personal accomplishment; in the Jaina view, we have all that we could wish for, except companionship and love. In truth, none of these visions of our future state can be regarded as more than a brave attempt to conceive the inconceivable; for our experience of embodied existence provides no firm clue to what a disembodied soul might experience, if indeed it can exist. If spiritual survival is above all the opportunity to continue indefinitely, in more favourable circumstances than we often encounter here, our strenuous efforts to grow in understanding, sympathy, and love, in a sort of *progressus ad infinitum*, we should have no reason to complain.

One of the gravest shortcomings of religions is their slowness to respond to changing social conditions, developing concepts, and advances in scientific knowledge. Of the innumerable instances of such archaism that might be mentioned, we must limit ourselves to a few. Although the Hebrew prophets proclaimed again and again that God demanded righteousness and mercy rather than sacrifices, which are difficult to reconcile with the concept of a purely spiritual Deity, the sacrifices, an archaic survival from a period when men were hardly capable of conceiving a spiritual God, continued until the Romans destroyed the temple of Jerusalem, where alone sacrifices to Yahweh could lawfully be made. A. C. Welch regarded the sacrificial cult at the restored temple as the rallying point of Jewry after its return from the Babylonian exile;[1] but we should also take into account the fact that if the sacrifices had been stopped, too many priests adept at butchering would have lost their jobs.

[1] Adam C. Welch, *Prophet and Priest in Old Israel*, Basil Blackwell, Oxford, 1953.

Orthodox Jews still rigidly follow ancient dietary regulations that can no longer be defended on the ground of either hygiene or humanitarianism. They oppose legislation to make compulsory methods of slaughter that are more humane than any that were available three thousand years ago, when, doubtless, the Biblical method was less brutal than, for example, the Scythian practice of slaughtering animals by strangulation.

Although modern hygiene and medicine have so reduced the mortality rate that an uncontrolled birth rate has become the greatest of all menaces to the welfare of humanity and the ecological balance of our planet, the Catholic Church is reluctant to disregard the command to 'be fruitful and multiply', made by an ancient god of war and fertility to a primitive tribe, undoubtedly with a high infant mortality, that needed to reproduce as fast as it could to replace losses in war and pursue its policy of aggression against the Canaanites. To oppose change is, of course, one of the oldest and most firmly rooted traditions of religion, which since its origin in tribal rites has rather consistently liquidated would-be innovators, first as sorcerers and later as heretics. Yet if religions could more readily adapt themselves to the changing knowledge and needs of a changing world, they would be far more successful in promoting the ends for which they exist and retaining the allegiance of thoughtful men of good will.

The final fault of religions that we need notice here is intolerance. If humility is one of the highest of religious virtues, then intolerance is one of the gravest of sins, for it springs from lack of humility. One who condemns or persecutes another for divergent views on religious questions assumes that he himself knows the correct and final answers to the ultimate mysteries, which is the antithesis of intellectual humility. The ancient Greeks were rarely intolerant; such presumption would have smacked of *hubris* and stirred the anger of gods who like mortals to know their places. Intolerance is hardly compatible with religion when we recall its origin and function: it began as man's attempt to placate mysterious forces that he could neither understand nor directly control. If the province of religion is to relate us to that which surpasses understanding, then to assume such infallible knowledge as would justify the persecution of those who hold divergent views is the negation of religion.

Intolerance was perhaps excusable in religions of preservation, which assumed that the compelling force of a petition to a super-natural power depended on the united will of the people and that any departure from a traditional rite might so offend the god that he would afflict the whole tribe. But in a religion of emancipation, of which the basic postulate is that the ultimate destiny of every man depends on his own personal conduct and inner worth, religious persecution becomes an absurdity. Yet it is a tragic absurdity that has occurred far too often, set in motion now by an ecclesiastical establishment that saw its power and privileges threatened by heterodox views, now by a fanatical preacher, now by an ignorant populace smarting under some loss or injury and looking for a scapegoat on which to vent its rage.

Probably no religion can show a record unblotted by the hideous crime of persecution, but some are more guilty than others of this most irreligious conduct. It was the intolerance of the early Christians that caused them to be persecuted by a generally tolerant paganism. Romans regarded as enemies of mankind sectarians who held that all who would not accept their faith were doomed to eternal torment, who refused to join men of a hundred other religions in paying homage to the emperor's statue, the equivalent of pledging allegiance to the flag in a modern state. After Christianity dominated Europe, the religion of love made for itself the blackest record of religious persecution and religious wars that the world has known. India, with a far greater variety of religions, has a better, although far from unblemished, record. Their wider tolerance is associated with the fine insight that a man's religious belief is a function of his mental and spiritual development. A philosopher may seek union with the Absolute Atman beyond all worship; an enlightened man may pray to an invisible personal God; while an ignorant labourer or forest-dweller prostrates himself before an idol. The omnipresent God, understanding that the idolater's clouded mind is groping for Deity, is in the idol and accepts the man's worship.[1]

Asoka, whose great zeal for the propagation of Buddhism has already been mentioned (p. 137), not only tolerated other religions within his own realm but even supported them. His famous 'Toleration Edict', carved on a rock, declares:

[1] *Bhagavad-Gita*, VII, 20–23; S. Radhakrishnan, *The Hindu View of Life*, George Allen & Unwin Ltd., London, 1927, Chs. 1 and 2.

His Sacred and Gracious Majesty the King does reverence to men of all sects, whether ascetics or householders, by gifts and various forms or reverence.

His Sacred Majesty, however, cares not so much for gifts or external reverence as that there should be a growth of the essence of the matter in all sects. The growth of the essence of the matter assumes various forms, but the root of it is restraint of speech, to wit, a man must not do reverence to his own sect or disparage that of another without reason. Depreciation should be for specific reasons only, because the sects of other people all deserve reverence for one reason or another.

By thus acting a man exalts his own sect, and at the same time does service to the sects of other people. By acting contrariwise a man hurts his own sect, and does disservice to the sects of other people. For he who does reverence to his own sect while disparaging the sects of others wholly from attachment to his own, with intent to enhance the splendour of his own sect, in reality by such conduct inflicts the severest injury on his own sect.

Concord, therefore, is meritorious, to wit, hearkening and hearkening willingly to the Law of Piety as accepted by other people. For this is the desire of His Sacred Majesty that all sects should hear much teaching and hold sound doctrine.

Wherefore the adherents of all sects, whatever they may be, must be informed that His Sacred Majesty does not care so much for gifts or external reverence as that there should be growth in the essence of the matter and respect for all sects . . .[1]

The spirit of toleration, thus early begun in India, was never extinguished. A fourteenth-century inscription at Vijayanagara in the Deccan tells how King Bukka I, himself a Sri Vaisnava, took the hands of certain Jains and placed them in the hands of certain of his own coreligionists, declaring that the Vaisnavas were to regard any loss or advancement which they caused to the Jains as their own loss or advancement. 'As long as the sun and moon endure, the Vaisnavas will continue to protect the Jaina religion. The Vaisnavas and Jains are one body; they must not be viewed as different.'[2]

[1] Vincent A. Smith, *Asoka*, *op. cit.*, p. 182–3.
[2] S. R. Sharma, *Jainism and Karnataka Culture*, Karnatak Historical Research Society, Dharwar, 1940, p. 44.

14

The Comparative Study
of Religions

We must agree with Asoka that the sects of other people all deserve reverence for one reason or another. Even the religion of the 'poor benighted savage' praying before his rude stone fetish is not undeserving of our respect, because he is trying in the best way he knows to solve some of the perplexing problems that confront him. At the same time, we are constrained to recognize that no religion is perfect; and it is hardly to be expected that anything so complex, created by beings so limited as ourselves, would be perfect. Often the best way to detect the shortcomings of one religion is to compare it, point by point, with some other religion. When we do this, it becomes evident that one religion has worked out a better solution of one problem and another has done better in some other respect, so that it would be difficult to decide which, among religions representing approximately the same cultural level, is the absolute best—nor is there any occasion to make such an invidious decision.

The comparative study of religions is a rewarding pursuit, for if done intelligently it reveals to us what are the essential features of religion and what the local accidents of a particular sect. Such a study is the best way to achieve a truly religious attitude, above all doctrinal differences and able to survive the demolition of any particular dogma. To be familiar with only one religion may be almost as unfortunate as knowing none at all, for it is apt to beget bigotry and intolerance. To one capable of study, the survey of the whole phenomenon of religion, in breadth and in depth, is far more liberating and inspiring than any self-styled infallible creed.

In estimating the value of a religion, the chief points to be considered seem to be the following:

1. The breadth of its area of moral concern.
2. Its doctrine of the individual man and encouragement of his potentialities.
3. The support it gives to our highest aspirations.
4. Its freedom from unproved assumptions.

We shall discuss these four points in turn.

1. Religions have varied immensely in their area of moral concern. The old tribal religions had one law for the treatment of fellow tribesmen and another law for everybody else. Not only were the moral restraints intended to safeguard only members of the tribe, even a fellow tribesman might be ruthlessly sacrificed for the supposed benefit of the community. The Israelite conquest of Canaan, reported in bloody detail in the book to which half the world looks for moral inspiration, was an unprovoked war of aggression that today would be severely censured by the United Nations. With the growth of civilization, the area of ethical concern widened, as is evident in the Pseudepigrapha of the Old Testament, written largely between 200 B.C. and A.D. 100. At about the same time, the Stoics were teaching that all men are brothers; there was not one moral law for the treatment of one's compatriots and another for the treatment of foreigners, but the same law held for all humanity. Nevertheless, the Stoics were censured by some of their contemporaries, of whom the gentle and compassionate Plutarch and Porphyry are good examples, for giving so little protection to animals; although some Stoic writers, such as Seneca, recommended kindness to them.

Christianity's area of moral concern is no wider than that of Stoicism, and in one respect narrower than that of Judaism, of which it is an outgrowth. In jettisoning the Jewish Law, the founders of the Church threw overboard much that was good along with much that, already archaic, encouraged a sterile ritualism. The old Law contained certain rules for the treatment of animals: they were to enjoy the sabbath rest along with their masters; the oxen that threshed out the grain were not to be muzzled; animals of different kinds, such as an ox and an ass, were not to be yoked together; a parent bird must not be taken along with its eggs or nestlings. The post-Biblical Pseudepigrapha, and even more the Talmud, repeatedly enjoin kindness to animals and threaten dire punishments to men who mistreat them. As Lecky remarked, kindness to animals 'is indeed the one form of humanity which appears more prominently in the Old Testament than in the New'.[1] Since Christianity made most of its early converts among the labouring classes of the large industrial cities of the Roman empire, rural matters were probably without interest to it. The omission from a great religion of any recommendations for the humane treatment of the diverse animals that surround and serve men has been one of the major tragedies of civilization. It left this important field to the individual conscience, which in barbarous and even in more polished ages is too often obtuse, and to tardily enacted civil laws. It is pathetic how humanitarians rummage through their New Testament for passages that might give authoritative support to their efforts to secure kinder treatment for animals. About the best they can find is Matthew 10:29: 'Are not two sparrows sold for a farthing? and one of them shall not fall on the ground without your Father.' This statement seems intended to emphasize the completeness of God's knowledge rather than his concern for sparrows.

If these compassionate people sought support for their humane efforts in Eastern religions, they would find it immediately. *Ahimsa*, or harmlessness toward all creatures, is the fundamental law in Jainism, Buddhism, and certain sects of Hinduism. Taoism is equally concerned for the kind treatment of all living things, plants no less than animals; and since this Chinese religion stresses the spiritual value of gentleness itself rather than the deleterious karma that one accumulates by mistreating creatures, its tender regard for them seems more spontaneous. These Eastern faiths have expanded the area of moral concern as widely as possible. Westerners have criticized their negative attitude, which emphasizes the avoidance of injury rather than active assistance to suffering creatures, although the latter is not absent. If we cannot have both, certainly the former is more valuable. Many people go storming through the world, careless of what they crush and bruise, only stopping here and there to apply a small fraction of their abundant energy to healing a few of the wounds caused by the major part of it. Others, more thoughtful, believe that care to harm nothing will avoid more injuries than remedial measures could ever assuage.

As to the motives for correct conduct, religions almost invariably

[1] William Edward Hartpole Lecky, *History of European Morals from Augustus to Charlemagne*, D. Appleton & Co., New York, 3rd edn., 1904, vol. II, p. 167.

promise rewards and punishments in a future existence. Philosophy, on the contrary, appealing directly to our self-respect or innate nobility, has rather consistently taught that righteousness should be cultivated for its own sake. The ancient philosophers regarded virtue as its own reward; to look for any extraneous recompense, in this world or the next, is to cheapen and degrade it. The classical philosophers commonly expressed this by saying that virtue is sufficient for happiness. One who attains this lofty viewpoint needs no metaphysical supports for right conduct; he will choose the better course, as he sees it, whether or not there is a God in heaven, whether or not his soul is immortal. But such doctrines have commonly been addressed to the select few; religions, trying to reach everybody, have typically attempted to enforce their precepts by promising rewards and penalties which, being in many cases everlasting, are all out of proportion to any good or evil we can do in our brief span of life. Yet, amazingly, many who profess to believe in the reality of these rewards and punishments are unable to control their appetites and passions for such immense stakes.

2. Not the least important feature of a religion is the kind of character it regards as ideal, which should be compared with the kind it actually succeeds in forming. Every major religion has produced admirable men of action no less than ascetics and scholars. As to which course of development is preferable, we have no answer better than that which, in the *Bhagavad-Gita*, Krishna gave to the same question put to him by Arjuna: 'In this world a two-fold way of life has been taught of yore by me, the path of knowledge for men of contemplation and that of works for men of action.'[1]

To close one's eyes to the beauty of nature and the treasures of art, to repress all natural impulses and mortify the flesh, seems a pitiful waste of a life; yet sometimes, as I judge from what I read, this course produces a character so sweet, patient, understanding, and generous that humanity is enriched thereby. More often, I imagine, a life of negations will yield a hard and narrow spirit. Certainly for the majority of men this is not the course to be recommended. For most of us, the highest ideal of personal development is that of the Peripatetic school of philosophy in ancient Greece: the balanced and harmonious development and active

[1] *Bhagavad-Gita*, III, 3.

exercise of all our excellences; a generous, responsive spirit and a sound, well-furnished mind in a strong and healthy body. Evidently the more liberal sects of a number of religions are trying to produce such people today. Christianity stresses love as a moral force; Eastern religions emphasize harmlessness; and I should want a wider personal acquaintance with representatives of a number of faiths before attempting to decide which teaching produces, on average, the more admirable character. So much depends on the temperament and innate endowment of the individual!

3. When we consider their doctrines of salvation, the advanced religions fall, as we learned in Chapter 8, neatly into two main groups, the religions of progress which believe in personal immortality, and the religions of regress which maintain that the liberated soul loses its individuality in the absolute blissful consciousness, from which its separateness was only an illusion. To the first class belong Jainism, several Hindu sects, Christianity and Islam; to the second, the Advaita Vedanta and perhaps Buddhism in its strict philosophic form. Of the two most famous Hindu theologians, Samkara taught that the released soul loses its individuality; Ramanuja, that it retains its distinctness. The former was renowned for his dialectical skill; the second, for his love of God. One who loves God intensely does not wish to have his personality absorbed by him, for love requires the duality of the lover and the beloved. Although the lover yearns for the closest possible union with his beloved, if the two became inseparably one, love would be extinguished. Love is ever a state of tension, never of final rest.

If anyone prefers to lose his little drop of personality in the ocean of impersonal blissful consciousness, that is his privilege. The objection to this doctrine is that it divests the world process of all purpose or meaning. According to it, we awake to find ourselves distinguishable individuals among countless other individuals; but this experience of individuality is often painful and, moreover, it springs from ignorance of our true nature. Our whole endeavour is to realize what we truly are, and when this realization is perfect, we become one with the primal source of all things, the only real Being. In seeking liberation then, we are striving to reverse the course of manifestation which made us, not what we are, but what we ignorantly imagine ourselves to be. If all creatures could achieve liberation, the illusion would be dispelled, and there would remain only the one absolute blissful consciousness.

Creation, or manifestation, then, seems to be just an unfortunate mistake on the part of the absolute Brahman, which creatures strive to rectify by their own strenuous efforts. Indeed, manifestation is attributed to *maya*, Brahman's sportive power or his careless dreaming. Thus manifestation is an irresponsible act that seems unworthy of the Supreme Being. On the other hand, personal immortality, at least in the theistic religions, is associated with the view that creation was a purposeful, responsible act. Thus, in the *Timaeus*, Plato, who believed in the transmigration of souls, declared that the Demiurge created the world because he was good and not jealous. According to Christian theology, God made creatures so that they might be irradiated by, and return, his infinite love. In the view of atheistic Jainism no less than of theistic Christianity, as the world process continues, Being is permanently enriched by an increasing number of beatific liberated souls.

Unfortunately, on the Christian view, as time passes not only is there an increase in the number of blissful souls, there is also an increase in the number of souls suffering everlastingly the most excruciating tortures. Since only a minority of mankind has ever embraced Christianity, the number of the damned and their tortures must greatly outweigh the number of the blessed and their bliss, so that it might have been better if the world had never been created. Moreover, the doctrine of eternal punishment is a mockery of justice. As Aristotle long ago pointed out, the central idea of justice is that of a proportion between one's merits, or demerits, and their recompense. But infinity is wholly disproportionate to any finite quantity, such as the misdeeds that even the worst criminal could do in his brief lifetime; so that punishment indefinitely prolonged could never be just. Christianity would have done better to have adopted Origen's doctrine that even devils will be saved at the last. Or if some souls, of which we have seen a number in positions of authority in our time, seem too utterly wicked ever to be washed clean, at least they might be finally annihilated. To Miguel de Unamuno, who held it better to live in pain than to cease to be, the prospect of total extinction was more terrible than that of hell itself; yet, if this place is what it is reputed to be, perhaps after five minutes there he would have thought differently. Purgatory is a morally respectable idea; hell is not.

All great goals are attained by strenuous effort; and to regard the highest goal, blessed immortality, as a state not to be won without persistent, long-continued striving is right and proper. On the other hand, the priestly expedient of using threats of punishment after death as a deterrent to wrong conduct is of dubious value. It seems that men who are not deterred from doing wrong by the prospect of its more immediate undesirable consequences are only exceptionally deterred by consideration of its more remote undesirable consequences, even though the latter are of infinitely greater magnitude. Not fear, but an ideal of excellence, should make us strive to be worthy of beatitude.

4. No religion has become popular without making assumptions that it cannot prove to the satisfaction of a critical mind, even when this mind recognizes that the whole of reality is not accessible to scientific observation and that in the realm of spirit there is no substitute for immediate intuition. The mystic's ineffable ecstasy reveals the presence of something precious within himself, but it provides no warrant for the existence of anything outside himself. The principal assumptions that religions make concern the existence and attributes of God and the nature and destiny of the soul. Except in so far as they are inseparable from these two questions, problems such as the origin of the world and of man had better be left to science, which is more competent to deal with them. Thus the theory of evolution poses no difficulties to religions that postulate the transmigration of souls between man and other animals; but to religions which claim that there is an absolute difference between human and animal souls, or which deny that animals have souls, it is more embarrassing. If they admit the reality of organic evolution, they seem to be confronted with the problem of deciding at just what stage in its evolutionary development the stock from which we descended became sufficiently manlike to contain a human soul.

The fewer assumptions unsupported by science or experience that a religion makes, the more firmly established it is. Atheistic religions like Buddhism and Jainism, which make certain assumptions about the soul but none about God, seem to demand less of our credulity than theistic religions, which have a metaphysic of the soul plus a metaphysic of deity. But the former religions uphold the dogma of transmigration or rebirth, which involves two assumptions the truth of which has not been adequately demonstrated: (i) that the soul or personality can exist apart from an organic body; and (ii) that a single soul or personality can inhabit a series of bodies. Although most of us cannot recall a previous incarnation, advanced yogis sometimes claim that they can; but in these cases it is difficult to exclude the possibility that in consequence of long brooding on the same theme they have confused imagination with memory. Likewise, rebirth has been adduced as an explanation of precocious genius: the musical or mathematical prodigy, it is suggested, has carried over abilities that he developed in an earlier incarnation. Genetic variation, however, seems a more plausible explanation of such cases.

Modern Humanism, if it can properly be called a religion, makes hardly any assumptions except the very great one that a transient existence in a Godless, purposeless universe can satisfy the human soul and prevent its yielding to ultimate despair. Lacking a doctrine of transcendence, it ignores aspects of reality that the great world religions fumblingly try to grasp; and for all its scientific caution, it may err by negation more than they do by assertion.

In all the more important affairs of our lives, such as arranging a journey, investing money, building a house, choosing a profession, or marrying, we prefer to act upon the most certain information that we can acquire. Yet religion, in a matter far more important than any of these, our eternal welfare, asks us to act upon assumptions which, viewed scientifically, are far from certain. Hence religions have always demanded faith, 'the substance of things hoped for, the evidence of things not seen'. Although faith has been extolled, by Luther and others, as the foremost of religious virtues, the one most necessary for salvation, it seems desirable to reduce as much as possible the burden it bears. Nevertheless, no one can live without it, for such is our predicament that we cannot begin even the smallest practical undertaking with absolute certainty that we can carry it to completion; so that without faith, implicit if not professed, we would do nothing. Everything depends, then, upon our 'will to believe', upon the magnitude of the part we permit faith to play in the conduct of our lives. Even if we regard religion's great promise of immortal life as far from certain, we need not for that reason become irreligious. We might at least preserve faith in our ability *to make ourselves worthy of beatitude*, and patiently, even if somewhat sceptically, await the outcome. The stronger the life within us, the more vehemently it rebels against the prospect of its own ultimate extinction, the more we shall cling to the sunnier side of doubt, the stronger our faith in the soul's survival will be. Since all the great religions help men to make their souls worthy of continued existence, they deserve our respect and allegiance.

To conclude, religions differ most importantly in the breadth of their area of moral concern, which in Eastern religions is, in general, far wider than in Western religions. As to the kind of character they tend to form in their adherents, there is greater difference between the more liberal and the more ascetic members of the same religion than between the adherents of different religions. In their eschatology, the chief difference is whether they promise the survival of the individual soul or its reabsorption into a vast, impersonal, cosmic consciousness. Of the former group, some have more spiritual views of heaven than others. Christianity developed a noble concept of heaven, but this religion is marred by the dogma of eternal suffering in hell. All religions make large assumptions incapable of scientific proof; it is difficult to decide which, if any, has the advantage in this respect, except that some can reconcile their doctrines to advances in scientific knowledge more easily than others. Although none can provide proof that the soul survives its body, all the great historical religions help men to become more worthy of eternal life, and this is a most valuable service.

Our world religions are the product of sound sentiments, which spring from the inmost depths of our being, and confused or uncritical thinking. The latter is most unfortunate, for it alienates many essentially religious people who, among other things, appreciate, care for, and aspire to, clear, coherent thinking that reflects the realities of our world.

Religion should be a bridge between the actual and the ideal. Like every bridge, it needs two firm abutments for its support. The first is a true understanding of the actual, of the world as it now is. The second abutment is an adequate ideal—one that is consistent with our inmost nature and the direction of the world process, one that would really satisfy us if we could attain it. Religions have had as much difficulty in establishing the second abutment as the first.

They have not begun with an adequate understanding of the world as it actually is, and they have rarely given us a sufficiently lofty and comprehensive ideal. Too often they have confounded the ideal with the real.

15

Rites and Sacraments

To many people, mention of religion calls to mind churches and their adornments, ceremonies and rituals of all kinds, prayer, and the like, rather than the doctrines and attitudes which these often impressive externals are intended to uphold. Yet the paraphernalia and pageantry of religion must be regarded as means for promoting its higher ends; and as always in the case of means, they should be judged pragmatically. Their whole value, other than as entertainment, lies in the support that they give to the essentials of religion. The principal function of rites and ceremonies, in the magnificent setting in which they are often performed, is to generate and preserve the emotional tone indispensable to our continued striving for high ends in circumstances that are frequently difficult. How far do ceremony and ritual promote appreciation of our lives and all that might enhance them, devoted care for all that is good and beautiful, and the aspiration to become worthy of immortal life? Unless we ascribe supernatural efficacy to rites and petitions, this is our only criterion for assessing their value.

The services commonly held in church and temple centre about the adoration of God, which consists largely in extolling his power, goodness, and glory, and, in some religions, assuming humble and supplicating attitudes in his presence. The origin of these practices is lost in the mists of antiquity, and one wonders how people ever came to suppose that this is the proper way to worship the Supreme Being. We are at once struck by the obvious similarity of the bowed, kneeling, or even prostrate attitude of the worshipper and the posture of abject submission that subjects were forced to assume in the presence of an oriental potentate—prostrations which so irked free Greeks when they were granted an audience with the Persian king, and to which they so strongly objected when Alexander of Macedonia adopted the practice in his court after his conquest of the Persian empire.

But it seems possible to trace the attitude of worship even beyond this, back to the patterns of behaviour of social quadrupeds and birds. In many species, the members of a flock or herd form a hierarchy, in which each individual dominates all those below it in the series and is submissive to all those of higher rank. Only the topmost animal domineers all the rest, and only the lowest gives way to all the others, eating last when there is a restricted source of food. In the presence of a social superior, an animal often assumes a submissive posture. Especially when there is a fight, the one that is being worsted may suddenly adopt the submissive attitude, which typically consists in exposing to the beak or fangs of its adversary the most vulnerable part of its body—the back of the head in birds, the side of the neck where the jugular vein is situated in wolves. Far from eliciting the death-blow, these stereotyped attitudes inhibit the aggression of the victor, who seems psychologically unable to press the attack so long as the intimidated adversary maintains the abject posture, but will resume the fight the moment the other lifts its head. When turkey-cocks fight, the losing bird gains reprieve by lying prostrate, his neck stretched along the ground. As Konrad Lorenz, to whom we owe these observations, has pointed out, in the heroic age the warrior who was being overpowered in single combat would sometimes cast down his shield and weapons and kneel before his adversary in a supplicatory attitude, which was not always so efficacious in preserving his life as are the corresponding postures of social birds and mammals.[1]

One who considers the history of submissive postures can hardly avoid asking whether it is fitting for the worshipper to kneel or prostrate himself in the presence of his Creator. Since God does not reveal his preferences to us, when trying to please him our only course is to do what would be pleasing to ourselves. There was a time when pompous men of power or wealth wished their inferiors to assume an abject or cringing attitude before them; but, far from being flattered, we who have grown up in democratic societies would be embarrassed by such behaviour. I believe that I am safe in saying that we prefer all men to approach us with the same respectful courtesy that we use toward them. And what ground have we for believing that God does not prefer a respectful to a self-deprecatory

[1] Konrad Z. Lorenz, *King Solomon's Ring*, Methuen & Co., London, 1952, Ch. 12.

attitude? Indeed, when we stop to consider, to assume an abject posture in the presence of our Creator is hardly flattering to him. We seem to be saying: 'You made me such a miserable creature that I am ashamed to retain my normal posture in your presence.' Ought we not rather to stand erect before him in loving gratitude, proud to be what he made us? The more worthy the creature to stand upright in the presence of his Creator, the more excellent that Creator is, the more he deserves to be praised for making noble creatures.

Although God deserves our praise, are we sure that he desires it? Praise and adulation typically consists in proclaiming God's superlative attributes in his presence; but presumably he knows what he is better than we do and does not need to be told. To be praised, even deservedly, can be embarrassing to us at times, especially if it is done in our presence. We can only conjecture what God is; but perhaps we conjecture least wildly, and have the surest foundation for regulating our attitude toward him, when we think of him as a creative artist. Such an artist would desire above all, I believe, to have his works appreciated. The truest, most fitting worship, then, is grateful appreciation of the grandeur and beauty of creation and the privilege of living in its midst. I surmise that if there is a God who watches attentively what his creatures do, nothing pleases him so much as our spontaneous delight in his handiwork and our earnest efforts to know and understand it in all its aspects. Reverently to contemplate or study any part of nature, great or small, with the thought that it is the work of some inscrutable power, is an act of worship, which can be done in the fields and forests or beneath the stars rather than in a temple. And what we adequately appreciate we will cherish, so that to care lovingly for the creation is the most fitting worship, the most adequate service, that we can give to the creative power, whatever we conceive it to be.

Prayer, which has been called 'the heart of religion', is a subject hardly less controversial than the nature of God. Dr Belden, to whom we owe this characterization of prayer, believes it to be instinctive in man, and he takes this supposed fact as evidence for the existence of the God to whom the soul is ever thus appealing; for if there were no such God, or if he failed to heed our petitions, 'it would be the first instance known to science of nature providing a universal instinct or impulse for which no possible satisfaction exists'.[1] This echo of Aristotle's dictum that nature does nothing in vain is perhaps more convincing to a theologian than to a naturalist, who can point to instinctive reactions, widespread enough in the animal kingdom, that are not only useless but in some cases injurious—reactions such as the moth's unfortunate habit of flying into a flame, which must have been fatal to large numbers of these insects that were attracted to fires set by lightning or to glowing volcanic extrusions, long before man learned how to kindle a blaze. To petition a god conceived in human form may be a rational deduction from the premises rather than an instinct. Nevertheless, in moments of extreme peril or perplexity, a social animal instinctively calls for help, and if no companion is in sight, his agonized cry is addressed to the Unseen Friend. Such spontaneous appeals to an invisible power, by people in agony or terror, depend not at all on their religious convictions and will doubtless continue to be made as long as man exists and suffers.

It has long been held by thoughtful men that to pray for specific advantages is unwise, because we do not know what, in the long run, will be best for us. Xenophon records that when Socrates prayed he asked simply for 'good gifts, "for the gods know best what things are good". To pray for gold or silver or sovereignty or any other such thing, was just like praying for a gamble or a fight or anything of which the result is obviously uncertain.'[2] Such a prayer reminds the deity of our need of divine help, leaving it to his better judgment to decide precisely what we require.

But if we believe that an omniscient God knows what is best for us, it is unreasonable not to go a step farther and believe that he is aware of our necessity without being reminded. Should we not, then, cease to importune God for anything and regard prayer simply as a form of meditation or communion with him. But if we follow our previous mode of reasoning, we must conclude that God already knows that we yearn to be illuminated by him, so that even this sort of prayer is superfluous. Accordingly, as Belden justly remarks, we must regard all these forms of prayer as in a sense petitionary; whence he concludes that, if we pray at all, it is illogical not to ask for what we most desire, trusting that the Supreme Power will grant our request if its fulfilment would be good for us. And he holds it

[1] Albert D. Belden, *The Practice of Prayer*, Rockliff, London, 1954, p. 8.
[2] Xenophon, *Memorabilia*, I, iii, 2.

proper to pray for anything that we may lawfully have, or without shame request, of the highest Power.

Although the foregoing argument seems sound enough, we may still doubt the propriety of importuning the Deity for benefits such as recovery from sickness, the birth of a son, or rain to refresh our wilting crops. In the first place, it is difficult for an educated man to believe that natural processes can be deflected or arrested by means of appeals to the unknown Power that stands behind them. And a deeply religious person often feels that to pray for such advantages is to impute to the All-knowing ignorance of our needs; to the Supremely Good, malice in withholding what he can plainly see that we require; to the Most Powerful, such weakness of mind that his purposes can be altered by the reiteration of wishes to which he could not be blind.

Furthermore, we may doubt whether it would be to our ultimate advantage to have every wayward impulse satisfied or every wish fulfilled. We are too profoundly ignorant of our source and our destiny to know what in the long run is best for us. Who can tell with certainty whether the satisfactions which he craves will not somehow be injurious, whether the afflictions he suffers may not lead at last to some unforeseen good? A modicum of experience in life, a little honest reflection upon it, convince the thoughtful man that he might be the loser if every vagrant wish were granted. Only those impulses in harmony with a trend or purpose which transcends the individual can ultimately bring felicity. Instead of praying for whatever bauble strikes the fancy or whatever appears most favourable to immediate purposes, the mature mind approaches the Deity with only a humble request for insight, for guidance amidst life's perplexities, for help in obeying the divine will. And one who has attained the summit of religious resignation asks only for strength to bear with good cheer whatever burdens are laid upon him.

When it has been sublimated to this lofty height, prayer is beyond the assaults of either science or philosophy. It becomes a discipline whereby the heart schools itself in piety and resignation. It steadies the mind by constantly reminding it of its relation to an inscrutable Whole that transcends knowledge. It holds before us the ideal of harmony with universal forces; it gives sharpness and clarity to this ideal by methodical contemplation. At the same time, it is a balm to the spirit harassed by life's vicissitudes; the familiar phrases of a prayer are like a friendly hand, which leads us gently back from the chaos of human affairs into the presence of a firm and incorruptible ideal.

When thoroughly disciplined and chastened, prayer need no longer take the form of an address to an unseen hearer. If we fix attention upon function rather than upon form, we recognize numerous ways of praying; many kinds of discourse which we do not ordinarily classify as prayer are seen to be this in essence. All earnest meditation whereby we strive to clarify our ideals, to reconcile our shifting circumstances to these steadfast aims, to plan a course of action in harmony with our highest principles, or to tame our rebellious hearts into submission to the inevitable, are in effect prayer, and of the holiest sort. Some men pray with pen in hand; their prayers, written rather than oral, may be confided to the pages of an intimate journal. Long after their death, we read the prayers of a Marcus Aurelius, or of an Amiel, and derive from them guidance for our own wavering spirit. An essay or a poem may be a prayer, if in composing it the author was striving to crystallize his ideals, to harmonize them with the realities of life, or to discipline his pious thoughts by giving them a fixed and formal dress. Or if we are blessed with that rare gift, a thoroughly sympathetic and comprehending friend, our prayer may take the form of an earnest discussion of our spiritual perplexities.

As grateful appreciation, which is the most adequate mode of worship, often leads to science and art, so prayer when most active and searching becomes philosophy. We have seen that the highest form of prayer—the only form proof against the assaults of science and criticism—is that which seeks insight, which asks for some indication of the divine will and strives to harmonize the individual spirit with the universal spirit. The attitude of the truly devout man at prayer, transformed into a more active state, becomes philosophy. Instead of simply beseeching an unseen power for illumination and guidance, the philosopher proceeds to gather such indications of the universal trend as are apparent to him, to fit them together into a logically coherent whole, then to look into himself and see what he can there find that accords with the universe as it is revealed to him, or which might by deliberate self-discipline and rational transformation be made harmonious with it. When the great intellect of Spinoza burst from the narrow chrysalis of the traditional

Jewish faith, he did not cease to feel the need of prayer. His orison took the form of a system of ontology and ethics, a mighty logical edifice that he was twelve years in erecting, fitting stone to stone with all the meticulous accuracy of the builders of Sachsahuamán. The conclusion of his prayer was that blessedness is acquiescence in the will of God. He had arrived by another road at precisely the same destination to which the teachings of his ancestral religion, liberally interpreted and shorn of excrescences, might have led him.

The contemplative man, accustomed to inward thought and silent meditation, may never feel the need to give his discourse the form of an address to an unseen hearer, in order to clarify his mind or tranquillize his spirit. For him, habitual calm reflection serves the purposes of prayer. If he prays at all, it is likely to be without premeditation, in moments of great anguish or emotional stress, which temporarily overpowers his philosophic calm and throws him passively back to an earlier stage of intellectual development. Such praying may serve as a valve of escape for overwrought feelings, but will be of less spiritual value than his customary meditation. Possibly, when the crisis has passed and he recovers his habitual temper of mind, he will be secretly ashamed of having prayed like a little child at its mother's knee.

There is another type of person, more common than the man of philosophic mind, who has never trained himself to think alone. Such a person needs a listener; when perplexed by problems too deep and intimate to be confided to vulgar ears, he finds it helpful to discuss them as though talking to someone else, as though asking advice and guidance from one wiser and more powerful than himself, even if he must indulge in the fiction that an image of wood or stone is attentive to his words. Men who have for long periods dwelt quite alone, cut off from all opportunities for conversing with others of their kind, find comfort in occasionally talking aloud to an uncomprehending animal, or even to the empty air. The modern world contains many unfortunate people who have neither learned to pray in the simple, supplicating manner of the child and the peasant, nor developed the aptitude for silent thought and devout meditation. When people of this sort are caught in an emotional tangle with no wise and sympathetic friend to guide them, their misery is extreme, and they may seek relief for their disordered mind by consulting a psychiatrist.

A recent development in psychotherapy is a belated recognition by scientists of the subjective value of prayer. The psychiatrist becomes in effect merely an intelligent, understanding, and mostly silent listener. At the first interview, he encourages the patient to talk freely and intimately, airing all his troubles. When the patient returns after an interval of several days, he is often ready to analyse his own case and point out the causes underlying his distress. At the third interview, the perplexed one may outline a course of action for the relief of his psychic tangle that he has thought out alone. The counsellor, believing it unwise to try to direct another person's life, again listens more than he speaks, perhaps asking here and there a question that helps to clarify a point on which his patient is not clear. Doubtless, in simpler and more credulous ages, many a perplexed believer, kneeling alone before an image or a shrine, prayed himself into a solution of his spiritual difficulties; just as the unbelieving modern may solve his perplexities by thinking aloud in the presence of his psychiatrist. Whether or not prayer enlists the aid of a power external to ourselves, there can be no doubt that it often taps spiritual forces hidden in the depths of our own being, so that they may rise into consciousness, giving us strength to face our daily tasks and overcome our impediments.

Another widespread and controversial religious practice is oral confession, which is found among primitive peoples such as the Melanesians no less than in advanced religions like Jainism, Buddhism, and some branches of Christianity, notably the Roman Catholic church. As with prayer, subjective advantages are claimed for this practice even by those who deny that it has any supernatural efficacy, such as obtaining God's forgiveness. It may become a sort of mental hygiene, an asepsis of the mind in an almost literal sense; the sinner reveals his fault to the priest, is given some penance to perform, and when it has been done he feels that he has been cleansed of his guilt. Thereby he is spared that sense of sin and unworthiness that has overwhelmed many a God-fearing Protestant whose church denies him the consolation of the confessional.

On the other hand, having so easily rid his conscience of an oppressive burden, the absolved penitent may the more readily repeat his transgression. By easing the conscience, confession may encourage lax conduct and lower the moral tone of a community. Possibly when confession is public, before the whole congregation rather than before a hidden priest, the greater feeling of shame may serve as a stronger deterrent to wrong-doing. According to Dr Margaret Mead, the Manus of the Admiralty Islands welcomed the advent of Catholicism because, among other things, it would permit them to confess their sins in discreet privacy instead of proclaiming them loudly to their neighbours. To these Melanesians, a sin confessed was a sin wiped out.[1] In pre-Columbian Peru, the priest generally heard confessions beside a stream; and after the sinner had completed the penance that had been assigned to him, he washed in running water so that his guilt might be borne away.[2]

Long ago the Emperor Julian, smarting under the wrongs inflicted on his family by Christianized relatives, placed these words in the mouth of Jesus: 'He that is a seducer, he that is a murderer, he that is sacrilegious and infamous, let him approach without fear! For with this water will I wash him and will straightway make him clean. And though he should be guilty of those same sins a second time, let him but smite his breast and beat his head and I will make him clean again.'[3] This bitter indictment reveals one of the most fundamental differences between the ancient philosophy that Julian loved and the salvationist religion which was superseding it. To the rank and file of such a religion, the important thing is to be forgiven by God, so that they may win heaven; to the classical philosopher, who neither confessed to a priest nor importuned God to forgive his trespasses, the essential point was to preserve his self-respect. This philosophy was for the strong, self-reliant character; to the weak, it offered no such consolation as the new religion brought. The philosopher had to bear the burden of his own shortcomings, for he had no saviour to bear them for him.

Today, no less than in ancient times, the essential question is, not whether God forgives us, but whether we can forgive ourself for being false to our principles or ideals of conduct. For one who regards an unsullied character as his most precious possession, his own conscience is the most exacting critic, and to satisfy *this* judge is more important than to be declared guiltless by any other. Such

[1] Margaret Mead, *Growing Up in New Guinea*, *op. cit.*, Appendix III.
[2] J. Alden Mason, *The Ancient Civilizations of Peru*, Penguin Books, 1957, Ch. 13.
[3] Julian, *The Caesars*, William Cave Wright's translation of the Emperor Julian's works in Loeb Classical Library, Vol. II, p. 413.

a one learns by experience, if not from wise elders, that the first point to be considered in all our acts is how they will appear in retrospect; for the pleasure that one may derive from a shameful act is fugitive and difficult to recall, but the shame persists for years as a distressing memory. To one who values above all else the priceless treasure of an unblemished life, not to stay out of prison, not to avoid the censure of neighbours, not to be forgiven by some higher power, but to keep his hands clean and his heart pure, to preserve his self-respect and avoid painful recollections of his own transgressions, is the chief consideration. Since confession cannot wash from the mind the ugly recollection of a shameful act, nor ease an exacting conscience, nor heal outraged self-respect, it seems superfluous to anyone with a high regard for his own moral integrity.

Religion might be defined as the set of practices, attitudes, and emotions which bind us to a whole greater than humanity. The chief of the religious emotions is reverence; the person who finds nothing worthy of his reverence cannot possibly be religious, no matter how assiduously he practices all the rites prescribed by his church. As a unique emotion, reverence cannot be defined or described in such a way that one who had never directly experienced it would know what it is. Among the elements included in this complex state of mind are the feelings that the revered object is supremely good; that it can be trusted absolutely, for it will do no harm; that it is too sacred to be treated rudely or with disrespect; that it is to be loved and emulated to the extent of our power. It is not so easy to account for the origin of that peculiar mental state that we call reverence as for the bodily postures so often assumed in worship, which, as we saw earlier in this chapter, are closely allied to those prescribed for an inferior in the presence of a despot or noble, and have much in common with the submissive attitudes by means of which social animals avert the fatal blow when worsted in a fight with a rival. In the presence of the great mysteries of the universe, a reverent heart is a thousand times more appropriate than a prostrated body. One of the first objects of reverence is the divinity within our own souls; but unless we absurdly assume that this divinity within us is without antecedents or connections in the larger world, reverence must extend from the self widely through the universe.

16

Religion and Deity

One who knows only religions of the type of Christianity, Judaism, or Mohammedanism might think that religion is so closely bound up with the idea of God that a book like this should properly begin with the Supreme Being. But one familiar with the history of religions and their tremendous variety, even at the present day, is forced to take a different view. Religion was not suddenly born when God revealed himself to his chosen vehicle for making himself known to mankind, or when some solitary thinker conceived the idea of a supremely perfect being who created and rules the world, and then proclaimed this grand concept to his fellows. On the contrary, religion grew out of primitive man's groping efforts to preserve his life values by any and every means that occurred to him. Utterly lacking in scientific discipline, he early conceived the notion that his life, along with everything that supported it or gave it value, were subject to the whims of beings somewhat like himself, but far more powerful and with invisible bodies. This view of the situation was inevitable, because a human or other animal body set in motion by a will was the only active agency that primitive man could somewhat clearly conceive. Following the consequences of this idea with admirable consistency, he attempted to gain the good will and support of these unseen supernatural beings by means which he knew to be agreeable to powerful men—by gifts, flattery, and a submissive attitude.

As civilization advanced and men began to think more profoundly—but still far too uncritically!—two divergent courses were open to them. One was to develop a concept of reality that made the gods superfluous, and to show how the chief goals of religious aspiration could be won without recourse to these products of human fantasy. This was the course adopted by Jainism, Buddhism, and the ancient Samkhya religious philosophy of India. These faiths, which have been the guiding light for countless millions of people for thousands of years and have held before them an ideal of conduct as noble as one will anywhere find, prove that deity is an incident in religion rather than its essence.

The alternative course was to develop the concept of Deity, by pruning away all excrescences and all those attributes of primitive gods that became increasingly repugnant to men's growing sense of decency and fittingness. The gods of the polytheistic pantheons, when too realistically portrayed in art and poetry to be consigned to oblivion, were recognized to be only so many manifestations of the one supreme God. The Zeus of the Greek philosophers, so worthy of our reverence as we behold him, for example, in the Olympian discourse of Dio Chrysostom, differs from the Zeus of early Hellenic legend no less than the Yahweh who finally emerged from the perfervid minds of the Hebrew prophets differs from the ferocious god who led the marauding Israelites to the conquest of Canaan.

This emerging concept had a peculiar fascination for the human mind. It became the fashion of a certain class of thinkers to imagine all the perfection that properly belonged to the Supreme Being on whom the world and everything in it depended. Theologians developed a concept of God so sublime that they fell in love with it, just as Pygmalion became enamoured of the statue that he sculptured. A Deity who possesses in the highest degree all the attributes which men deem most excellent and desirable, including power, knowledge, beatitude, and immortality, can hardly fail to attract strongly those who continually contemplate him. Following another approach, the mystics strove mightily for direct union with the ineffable One. The more a religion veers toward mysticism, the more it becomes a love affair between man and God.

It is understandable why those who grow up in cultures where all the religions are theistic should imagine that God is as essential to religion as a motor to an automobile, and that to profess oneself an atheist or an agnostic is equivalent to being irreligious. And yet, in defence of this point of view, it is well to recall that many people so feel the need of a supernatural being whom they can adore, and lean upon in their weakness, that they deify the very teachers, like Mahavira and Gautama, who professed to know nothing about God, and who wished to be regarded as leaders who showed the way rather than as deities to be worshipped.

Even leaving aside the hosts of gods and godlings of the more primitive religions, the concepts of God developed by more philosophical thinkers are bewilderingly diverse. To the theist, an omnipotent, omniscient God created and governs the world; to the deist, God established the laws of nature and thenceforth remained aloof, letting the universe run the course in which he set it, like a self-regulating machine. To the pantheist, the world is God or is in God; or else everything is God so far as it is real. To the panentheist, God and the world stand in a reciprocal relationship; he is not only the supreme actuality but also the supremely receptive being, who is influenced by even the least of his creatures and remembers for ever all that each does, thinks, and feels. For Aristotle, a God who neither created nor knew the world, but was eternally immersed in his own thoughts, kept the Universe in motion by his power of attraction, as the loved one attracts the lover. For Plotinus, God was the One, pure undifferentiated unity, from which the world arose as an emanation that decreased in excellence as it receded from him, and to which all things strive to return. Each of the major ways of conceiving God has had endless shades of interpretation; so that the more one studies the subject, the more he is inclined to request of anyone who professes to believe in God that he divulge just which God he recognizes. The interested reader might consult the instructive anthology *Philosophers Speak of God*, by Charles Hartshorne and William L. Reese.

God, then, has been many things to many men; but to most men, not only in the West but even in the Orient where Godless creeds have been taught, he is an all-powerful supernatural Being, who created and knows the world, the supreme Person, who hears our prayers and perhaps helps us in our direst need. Without pausing to examine all the variations of which theism is susceptible, we might say that its minimum assumption is the existence of a mind of cosmic amplitude, capable of knowing all that happens in the universe, combined with the power to put all its volitions into effect, and enjoying everlasting beatific existence. In the language of classical theism, God is a spiritual Being, without body or parts, omniscient, omnipotent, and supremely blissful. What is the evidence for the existence of such a Being?

Aside from Revelation, which must be accepted on faith and can never rank as a philosophical demonstration, the most important arguments that have been advanced to prove God's existence are three in number and are known as the ontological proof, the cosmological proof, and the physico-theological proof, more commonly called the argument from design. Of these Kant, who professed to demolish all three, regarded the ontological proof as primary. This so-called proof is an effort to discover a concept which of itself, and without any appeal to experience, provides a warrant for the objective reality of the thing conceived. Can we conceive God in such a way that his non-existence would be a self-evident impossibility?

Certainly no scientist would ever try to demonstrate the existence of anything in this fashion, but the project is challenging to the metaphysical mind. Apparently the first to attempt such a proof was St Anselm, an Italian monk who became archbishop of Canterbury in the eleventh century. He told how he sought long and earnestly for a single argument which, alone and without any other supports, would demonstrate that God truly exists; how again and again the desired proof seemed to be just within his reach but always evaded him, until he was about to give up in despair; how when he tried to think of other things his problem intruded upon his consciousness, until at last, one day when he was exceedingly weary of resisting its importunity, illumination came. God, he recognized, was the being than which nothing greater can be conceived, the greatest possible object of thought. Such a being cannot be conceived as non-existent; for in this case you can think of another in every respect similar which is conceived as existing; and this, because it actually exists, would be greater. Therefore, the greatest object of thought, which is God, necessarily exists.[1]

Some five centuries later, Descartes propounded this argument in essentially the same form. Kant, however, rejected it, pointing out that existence adds nothing to the content of a concept. Whether or not your concept corresponds to some independently existing thing is a fact about the concept that can be ascertained only by experience, not by examining the concept itself. If the actually existing thing contains more than your concept of it, your concept is inadequate and needs revision. A hundred real dollars, he said, contain no more than a hundred possible dollars. To convince yourself of this truth,

[1] Charles Hartshorne & William L. Reese, *Philosophers Speak of God*, University of Chicago Press, 1953, p. 96–106.

imagine what you can buy with a hundred dollars, then earn or borrow this sum and take it to the shops. If you knew the correct prices, the real goods that you buy will correspond exactly to the goods you hoped to purchase while your money was still a dream.[1]

In answering the argument of Anselm and Descartes, Kant overlooked the distinction which each made, after the first formulation of his argument had been criticized, between necessary and contingent existence. God, the most perfect being, they claimed, cannot be conceived not to exist, because the very possibility of non-existence is incompatible with the highest perfection; whereas all created things, such as men, houses, or trees, may be thought of as either existing or not existing. God exists necessarily; creatures, contingently. But is not this ascription of necessary existence to God a high-handed procedure, a dogmatic assertion of the very point which was to be proved? The answer to this question involves the consideration of the cosmological proof.

Whereas the ontological proof is an attempt to provide a factual foundation for an intellectual construction, the cosmological proof is, in a sense, just the reverse, for it is an attempt to provide an intellectual foundation for the facts of experience. Take anything you know, your chair, your house, the planet beneath your feet, or your very self, and you will find, if you attentively investigate its origin and mode of being, that its existence depends upon something else. You exist because your parents lived; they owed their lives to their parents; and so on indefinitely. The earth owes its existence to the primal nebula out of which it condensed, along with the sun and the other planets. Everything that owes its existence to something else, so that with a slightly different course of events it might not have existed at all, is said to exist contingently. Behind every contingent being stand other contingent beings, and you can trace this series back and back into the dim past until, like a tired swimmer who yearns to feel his feet on solid ground, your weary mind seeks a place where it can stop, not simply from exhaustion, but because it has reached a point where further regress is impossible. Such a natural resting place, the desideratum of every mind that seeks a solid foundation for its interpretation of experience, can be found only if, behind the procession of con-

[1] Immanuel Kant, *Critique of Pure Reason*, Transcendental Dialectic, Book II, Ch. 3, 'The Ideal of Pure Reason'.

tingent beings, there stands a necessary being, a first cause, a being whose existence depends upon itself alone, so that it might continue to exist if everything else were annihilated.

If we analyse this quest of a first cause or necessary being, we find that it has two aspects. The objects which surround us consist of matter with a more or less definite form. To account for the form, we always go backward into the past: the form of an animal or plant was transmitted to it by its parents; the form of an artifact, such as a table or a jar, was given to it by the artisan who made it; the form of a mountain is due to the forces within the earth that heaved it up and to the erosion of its surface by rain and frost and wind. If the universe of interacting forces is not eternal, if the chain of causes ever had a beginning, the first cause that set it in motion was far in the past.

When we consider not the forms which things present to us but their substance or the matter of which they are composed, we penetrate in depth rather than travel backward in time. Since your body is composed of atoms, your existence is contingent on their existence. In the view of the old atomism which regarded the smallest particles as uncreated and indestructible, they existed necessarily, so that in this direction the quest of necessary being soon reached its goal. In the modern view, the existence of atoms is contingent upon that of the electrons, protons, and neutrons of which they are compounded; and since even these appear not to be indestructible, their existence is in turn contingent upon something else, which is probably space. If space is indeed ultimate, uncreated and indestructible, depending on nothing else for its existence, it represents necessary being. But whether this or something else is ultimate, it must act unremittingly to support contingent beings. Our existence from moment to moment depends upon something other than ourselves, so that existence is, in a sense, creation incessantly renewed.

What can be said for this doctrine of necessary existence? As to the first cause in the sense of a Creator of the universe, it seems a barren hypothesis. In the view of some thinkers, including Aristotle, the universe has existed without beginning, which makes it unnecessary to postulate a Creator. If, in our insistent demand for explaining origins, we assume a creative Deity, we merely push our problem farther back without bringing it any nearer solution, which is an intellectually wasteful procedure. A God who could create the universe would, it seems, be greater than the universe, so that his origin poses a problem even more perplexing than that of the universe. If, to escape this difficulty, one suggests that God is self-created, or else eternal, we must ask why the universe could not equally well be self-created or eternal. If, on the other hand, we seek necessary being not in the remotest reaches of time but in depth, we seem to be on firmer ground. This pageant of ever-changing forms which we call the universe evidently depends upon something eternal and indestructible, a first cause or necessary being. Although this is a necessity of thought, we have no assurance that our intellectual necessities always correspond to reality.

The ontological proof and the cosmological proof agree in pointing to something which exists necessarily. Although neither is con-clusive, the cosmological argument seems stronger. In itself, however, it tells us nothing of the nature of that whose necessary existence it claims to have proved. To learn more about this being, we must turn to the ontological proof, which pretended to establish that the necessary being was the greatest, most perfect being the human mind could conceive, but failed to convince a number of cautious thinkers. If, however, we accept the cosmological proof while rejecting the ontological proof, we are left with the conclusion that beyond, or beneath, all the contingent beings that make up the phenomenal world stands a necessary being, the nature of which we can learn, if at all, only by other means. Philosophers who find great satisfaction in the establishment of abstract principles may rest content with this; but the simple, pious man, yearning for something to revere or worship, may well ask whether this necessary being possesses such attributes that he could call it 'God'.

Of all the means that men have used to prove the existence of God, the physico-theological proof or argument from design has, ever since men began to philosophize, been the most popular and convincing. This argument rests on an analogy. The artifacts that we employ to support our lives and satisfy our desires did not come into existence by chance; all, from great ships and aeroplanes to the simplest tools and household furnishings, were first conceived in somebody's mind, then created out of appropriate materials. Living things, especially the higher animals, are far more complex, more perfectly adjusted to their natural environment, more admirably self-regulating, than the most intricate machines that men have yet succeeded in constructing. They live on a planet which supplies everything necessary for their existence, which travels around the sun, in equilibrium with its sister planets, in a manner that always excites the wonder and admiration of thoughtful people. Could all these complex creatures, all these marvellous adjustments that make the world a fit place for their habitation, have arisen by chance? If all the things that men make for their own convenience require a designer, is it not absurd to suppose that the far grander things that nature presents to us could have come into existence without a mind far greater than ours to plan and create them?

If we consistently follow out our analogy, we see that it points to the existence, not of a Deity who created the world from his own substance or perhaps from nothing, but to that of an architect or superhuman artisan who, working with materials already present, moulded them into the forms, and impressed upon them the motions, which so excite our admiration—just as the human designer works with materials he did not create. Even with this limitation, a being who established the planets in their courses around the sun, and set up the circulations which enable the earth to support life, and filled it with living creatures, seems great enough to be the God of religion, although there are certain aspects of life on this planet which might make one doubt whether he was good enough. And those insatiable mystic spirits who demand nothing less than the All might not be satisfied with a God who is not the ground and support of the universe but merely its architect.

Until a little over a century ago, no one could convincingly refute the argument from design, because there was no alternative explanation of the origin of the structures and functions of living things so well established that it commanded widespread assent. Already in the fifth century B.C., Empedocles suggested that existing animals might represent a selection of the viable types resulting from the chance combination of parts; but it remained for the inexhaustible patience of Charles Darwin to present the theory of evolution in such a form that thoughtful men were forced to take it seriously— biologists, as an incentive to fertile investigations that were to establish it ever more firmly; churchmen, as the most powerful threat to their dogmas. Today, scarcely anyone competent to pass judgment believes that animals and plants were created in the forms in which we now find them. Far from holding that the earth was designed as an abode for living things, we are now convinced that life, arising from the simplest beginnings, adapted itself to the circumstances it found here, as the indispensable condition of its survival; just as a guest must conform to the customs of his hosts' household, however strange they may seem to him, if he wishes to be asked to prolong his visit.

From Alfred Russel Wallace, Darwin's great co-worker, to the present day, there have been those who believed that, although all other organisms have evolved by natural means, man's development has, in at least some respects, been divinely guided. To a naturalist, the means adequate for the origination of all the other animals, with their marvellous organization and their admirably integrated patterns of behaviour, seems adequate to account for man and all his faculties. One who denies this should explain how it happens that the superior power who is supposed to be guiding our development has left us with such glaring imperfections, especially in the moral sphere. Wallace's hesitation to accept the theory of evolution by natural selection, while it was still in its infancy, as adequate to account for man's moral nature is understandable; but some recent expressions of this view seem due to man's stubborn pride and arrogant refusal to recognize his brotherhood to the rest of the living world.

Even if we still believed in the fixity of species, the argument from design would be confronted with a perplexing difficulty. As a rule, one who designs some intricate piece of machinery does so not merely to demonstrate his skill as an inventor by creating a mechanism that works perfectly; he makes it to serve some purpose. For what purpose, then, were this earth and its inhabitants designed? If one answers that the world was created so that sentient beings might live in joy, we must ask him why so many were made to prey upon or to parasitize others, thereby bringing an incalculable amount of fear and suffering into the realm of life. If, in the spirit of the ancient philosophers, he answers that the world was created for gods and men—or perhaps only for men, since the gods, with one possible exception, appear to have abandoned it—our objection remains: Why are men afflicted with countless ills, from diseases, parasites, predatory animals, natural catastrophes and, above all, their own passions and appetites so difficult to control?

Unable to allay these doubts, the apologist for God might demand that we change our point of view, looking to the good of the whole rather than that of individuals. By means of endless conflicts between organisms, that wonderful thing, the balance of nature, which certain contemporary ecologists regard almost as something holy, is preserved. But the purpose of creation, if it has one, must be sought in conscious beings able to enjoy their existence, not in a vast, impersonal complex of relations like the balance of nature, incapable of thought or feeling. We shall never cease to ask why a supposedly wise, benevolent, and extremely powerful Creator could not devise a means for preserving the balance of the whole without such unfeeling treatment of the parts.

The Judeo-Christian tradition has long overemphasized the creative function of Deity, to the neglect of other functions of equal importance. If creativity were a sufficient indication of God's existence, no thoughtful person could be an agnostic, and far less an atheist. Not only does creativity pervade the world; it seems everywhere, and at all levels, to be present to an excessive degree. It produces far more living things than the earth can support, thereby giving rise to that competitive strife for space and nourishment that is, directly or indirectly, the principal source of our woes. It drives us to write more books than can be published, to paint more pictures than the public will buy, to invent more machines and gadgets than are needed, thereby becoming responsible for all the distress of wasted effort and disappointed ambition. And on a vastly larger scale, who can say that creativity has not produced an excessive number of galaxies, solar systems, and life-bearing planets—more than can be properly supervised by the creative power?

When we survey religions widely, it becomes evident that man's quest of God has not been, primarily, a search for a creator—that has been the preoccupation of philosophers and theologians—but for a guardian and protector, a God who cares. Religious India builds temples, not to Brahman the Creator, but to Vishnu the Preserver, and other more intimate deities. Hellenic Zeus was in no sense a creator but a late-comer on Olympus, whose function was to govern gods and men and provide the life-giving rain. With his sure insight into what matters in religion, Jesus stressed the paternal care of the Father in heaven rather than his creative function. In the human world, we honour an adoptive parent who lovingly nurtures a child he did not beget; we revile the actual parent who neglects his offspring. Creation that is not followed by adequate care of the creature, especially if it be one capable of joy and suffering, is not only a careless but a wicked act—whether done by man or God. It is time that we tone down this exaggerated cult of creativity and give more attention to other aspects of divinity. Even an infallible proof that God created the world and everything in it would fail to provide an object for religious devotion, unless we were also assured that this God cares lovingly for the least of his creatures.

Thus the classical arguments for God's existence leave us unconvinced. The cosmological proof points to a necessary being, or mode of being, beneath the flux of contingent events, but it fails to throw light on the attributes of this being. There are strong reasons for believing that this being is not the God of theism, or any benevolent being that can know and effectively control the whole universe. The objections to this notion come from four sources, from methodology, from science, from morality, and from experience. We shall consider them in this order.

1. Theism in most of its varieties, as well as panentheism and some forms of pantheism, postulate a God who knows the whole universe in all its details. In classical theism, God is held to be omniscient, knowing at a single instant all that was, is, and will be, seeing the whole temporal sequence as an eternal Now. Even when these exorbitant claims are pruned down, for all these theological doctrines God is, above all, a mind or spirit of cosmic amplitude.

This concept is inadmissible from the point of view of methodology. Every type of organization that we know has limits which it cannot exceed. The type of organization represented by insects, in which the soft and vital parts of the body are enclosed in a hard, chitinous exoskeleton, soon reaches an upper limit of size; insects are rarely more than a few inches in length, and the giants of the order hardly attain one foot. The vertebrate type of organization, in which rigidity is achieved by means of articulated bones within the flesh, can achieve much greater size; but an upper limit is set by various factors, one of the most obvious of which is that the cross-sectional area of the bones, and accordingly their strength, increases as the square of the linear dimensions of the organism, whereas the mass that they must support increases as the cube of these dimensions, so that, with increasing size, the bones become inadequate to support the animal's weight. When it lives in a supporting medium like water, it may become larger; but even so there is a limit which it cannot surpass. Similarly, machines cannot exceed a certain size without becoming unwieldy; and large associations of people become unmanageable unless they are divided into smaller co-ordinated units.

Such examples, which could be indefinitely multiplied, forbid us to assume that, because some type of organization is practicable on one scale, it could exist on a far different scale. But this is exactly what theism has done. Taking as a model our little finite minds, which know a limited number of things, most of them imperfectly, and can give attention to only one or two of them simultaneously, it has conceived a mind of cosmic amplitude which can know perfectly an infinite number of things and, what is more, hold them all in attention simultaneously. This, if one stops to consider, is even more ludicrous than supposing that there could be a mammal the size of the earth, or an aeroplane with a wing-span of a thousand miles. If the theists retort that God's mind is not an infinitely magnified human mind, and his knowledge is not of the same type as our knowledge, we must challenge them to imagine a mind organized differently from the only mind they know, and ask them if they can conceive of any mode of knowing fundamentally different from their own.

God's mind is often said not to be in space; but if it is to know, or exert any influence upon, a spatially extended universe, it must be somehow in contact with it. The divine mind must either pervade the universe throughout, or be restricted to certain regions of it, or be concentrated at one point. How could a mind co-extensive with the universe preserve that coherence which in our own minds is indispensable for effective thinking, that unity without which we develop a dual or multiple personality, as in certain pathologic cases? How could a thought in one part of a mind so vastly extended be effectively associated with a thought in another part, thousands of light years away?

If, to preserve the unity of God's mind, we suppose that it is not itself spatially extended but makes contact with space at a certain point, then, unless we also suppose that some signal travels faster than light, millions of years must elapse before God learns what is happening in the more distant reaches of the universe, or before he can make his will effective there. The theologian seeks to escape these difficulties by asserting that God knows simultaneously all the past, present, and future of the universe; he sees the whole pageant of time *sub specie aeternitatis*, so that his perfect knowledge is not dependent upon the receipt of information from any part of it. But if he sees the whole temporal sequence as simultaneous, if this year his thoughts are exactly the same as last year, how can he know what is happening now, at this instant? I, for example, may be thoroughly familiar with the novel you are reading for the first time, so that the ideas that are entering your mind successively are, in a sense, simultaneously present in mine. But unless I further learn, by peeping over your shoulder, which chapter you are now perusing, I cannot tell whether you are sorrowing over the hero's misfortunes, or breathlessly expecting the outcome of a perilous situation, or chuckling over his jokes; my mind is not in rapport with yours. A God without the time-sense, who sees as simultaneous what we experience successively, lives, like Aristotle's Unmoved Mover, in splendid isolation from a temporal world. To pray to such a God is an absurdity.

In fairness to classical theism, we should recall that it took shape when the known universe was far smaller and neater than it has since become. Indeed, the all-seeing deity was originally no more than a tribal god, who watched sharply to make sure that the people obeyed his commands. So long as the population remained small, his task was perhaps not impossibly great. A universe billions of light years in extent would seem to demand some revision of time-honoured beliefs. The force of the foregoing objection to the concept of Deity would be greatly diminished if, instead of one God, we might have many, each responsible for the care of a certain aspect of the world, or of a certain region, as in the old polytheisms. Each god, then, would not need to know so much; his mind would not be such a monstrous exaggeration of the only kind of mind we know. In extolling the Hebrew prophets for having developed an ethical monotheism, we should place the emphasis, I believe, upon *ethical* rather than upon *monotheism*. The trouble with the old gods was, not that they were many, but that, far from moral themselves, they did not consistently demand righteousness of their worshippers. I see many advantages in a plurality of truly moral gods. The moral problem, for us, consists largely in learning how to live in harmony with our fellows; a number of perfectly moral gods might provide a shining example for us to follow, as a single God without a peer cannot. There are even those who claim that this God is beyond morality, although it seems to be a Creator's moral responsibility to ensure the happiness of the beings he creates.

In view of the far more efficient and compassionate administration of this immense universe that a plurality of conscientious gods might provide, I believe that if thoughtful creatures could choose the manner in which their universe is governed, they would vote overwhelmingly in favour of polytheism. Man is an incurably polytheistic animal. In praying to the local patron saint, or to the maternal Virgin, the Catholic peasant finds a comfort he could never derive from addressing the remote and baffling triune Deity, himself a compromise between monotheism and polytheism. The chief objection to a polytheistic religion is that, in our prevailing ignorance of supernatural beings, it permits the imagination to run wild, multiplying gods and their attributes without any control by experience. The great advantage of monotheism is its economy. It reduces the number of costly cults of deities, and places some restraint upon the imagination, but far from enough.

The foregoing discussion leaves open the question whether there may be, diffused throughout the universe, consciousness not organized into the unity of a thinking, knowing, foreseeing mind.

2. The scientific objection to theism is that it neglects the problem of how a spiritual being could put his volitions into effect in the realm of matter. The prevailing notion, that God's fiats are automatically executed, was obviously inspired by the old oriental despot, who had merely to utter his decree to have it fulfilled. But the monarch gave his commands through a material mouth, and had many ministers, officials, and slaves to execute them, with the prospect of dire punishment if they displeased his majesty. When we follow the only safe course, that of keeping close to experience, we must admit that mind or spirit can cause changes in the material world, or even communicate effectively with another mind, only by means of an organic body. We accomplish what we will either

directly by means of our limbs or indirectly by using our bodies—as in writing, speaking, or pushing buttons—to set other bodies or machines in motion; and aside from these methods, we cannot make the smallest perceptible change in the external world. How a disembodied God could create matter, or shape it into a world, or cause anything to happen in this world, is a scientific problem which remains in utter obscurity. No one, to my knowledge, has suggested any solution more plausible than the old notion of the fiat. Although theism claims that God is omnipotent, able to accomplish everything, it fails to show how he could accomplish anything.

3. The moral objection does not touch the notion of an omniscient, omnipotent being; but the God of religion is also held to be perfect or supremely good, and here moral considerations enter. We cannot escape the ancient enigma: If God is good, whence cometh evil? The commonplace answer is that evil comes from man's free will. We now know that essential evil, the conflict of creature with creature, resulting in their mutilation, suffering, and destruction, arose on this planet long before man appeared, because the excessive fecundity of living things threw them into fierce competition for food and space. In this unrelenting strife, animals developed those strong passions, including anger, hatred, greed, lust, and fear, which we inherit from our pre-human ancestors, to our own great distress, because they are so difficult to control and they goad us into acting in ways that we afterward regret—they are the source of moral evil, which depends on the will. Accordingly, those philosophers who have considered the problem most profoundly allow 'free will', or, more correctly, metaphysical freedom, not only to man but to creatures far lower in the evolutionary scale. Indeed, some have discerned the foundation of freedom in the 'uncertainty principle' or 'principle of indeterminacy' in the behaviour of the subatomic particles; just as, long ago, the Epicureans derived the freedom of the will from the inexplicable sideward swerve of the atoms falling through the void.

This problem of free will has been the course of heaving oceans of muddy thought, into which one hesitates to voyage even a little way, lest one's vessel founder. Suffice it to remark here that the only precise meaning that I can find in the term 'free will' is indeterminacy in the origination of our volitions. And if a volition is not a determinate or necessary consequence of what we are, in the circumstances in which we find ourselves, I fail to see how anybody could be held responsible for what he does. Not only would it be most unjust to punish anyone for the crime he committed when his volition escaped from the control of his whole character, but punishment would be futile even as a deterrent, because in exactly the same circumstances the same person might, on another occasion, act in a quite different manner.

A man with any considerable degree of free will would behave like a car with a defective steering gear that did not obey the steering wheel. However, even some of the most strenuous advocates of free will and its moral necessity allow us so little of it, and are so uncertain of the circumstances in which we exercise it, that it is like having a cent in one's pocket when he enters a store where the cheapest article costs a half-dollar. From the ethical point of view, it is not moral freedom that we should worry about, but moral efficacy. If our moral decisions help us to become better and to act more righteously, what difference does it make whether they are, in some abstruse metaphysical sense difficult to understand, free or not? And everyone can answer for himself whether his moral determinations are effective.

The problem of free will, or metaphysical freedom, is complicated by its superficial similarity to the problem of political freedom, which stirs up men's passions to obfuscate their judgment as scarcely any other question does. We begin by demanding to be free from the arbitrary commands of a despot, and end by insisting upon being free even from our own past and what we essentially are! There is, however, more than superficial similarity in the occasions on which the question of freedom arises. So long as men are happy, they care little whether they live under a democratic government or a benevolent monarch; it is only when they groan under heavy taxes, and are unjustly punished, and find their active impulses too frequently thwarted, that they begin to agitate for liberty—unless they are stirred up by ambitious trouble-makers, as has too often happened in recent times. Similarly, when our lives run smoothly and contentedly and we avoid major perplexities, we rarely bother about the problem of free will. It is chiefly when we find ourselves in troubled waters and make decisions that we soon regret, that we begin to question whether our will is free, whether it would not have been possible for us, at certain critical junctures, to have reached different, and better, decisions.

What we really want—unless we foolishly permit selfish schemers to persuade us to the contrary—is happiness rather than freedom, be it political or metaphysical. Men of the deepest religious feeling have commonly held that blessedness consists, not in the free exercise of our little capricious will, but in perfect conformity to the will of God, so that his will becomes our will, in which case our will also becomes his will. Hence if a benign Creator had infused a portion of his own righteous will into each of his creatures, and placed them in such circumstances that by the exercise of this will they would be happy, they would never have suspected that their volitions were not a perfectly free and unconstrained expression of their own souls—as indeed they would be, if God had made it so. If in truth creatures have free will in the metaphysical sense, and this is the cause of the countless ills from which they suffer, then, for the sake of giving us a bauble so elusive that we are not even certain that we possess it, we have been deprived of a priceless heritage. Was this a worthy course for an omnipotent God to take?

However, it is not necessary to reach a decision on this perplexing problem of metaphysical freedom in order to be convinced that the ills from which creatures suffer are not wholly, or even chiefly, their own fault. Innate in many people are appetites and passions so strong that they struggle futilely to restrain themselves from illicit acts. Whether our volitions are 'free' or strictly determined, without greater wisdom and foresight than the Creator has given us, our choices, even if made with the best intentions, will often bring sorrow to self and others. Indeed, it is a common experience for the best of men to find themselves in such a predicament that any choice they can make, whether to act or not to act, will fail to conform to their vision of absolute rightness. One who believes that he is surrounded on every side by God's perfect creations would wish so to live that not the least of them would be injured. Yet this is impossible, for we can hardly take a step in the fields or woods without crushing some marvellously organized creature; even if we decide to subsist wholly on fruits, the diet most consistent with harmlessness, we cannot produce them without sometimes waging war on the creatures that attack our fruit trees; and if in despair we resolve not to eat anything, we still destroy one of God's creatures—ourselves. Unless it can be proved that the excessive abundance of living things results from their metaphysical freedom, then it is evident that it is not the free will of creatures, but the Creator's failure to set limits to their excessive multiplication, which is responsible for most of the ills that they suffer.

Man, feeling guilty because his passions so often escape from his control, has shown a pathetic eagerness to exonerate his Creator, by taking upon himself the blame for the world's vast evil, as is well expressed in those sly, trenchant lines of Emily Dickinson:

> O Lord, we beseech thee,
> Forgive us thy iniquity.

We judge the quality of any creator by that of his creations, refusing to call a painter perfect unless his pictures are perfect, or a cabinet-maker perfect unless he makes perfect furniture. This method of judging, fair in all cases, is especially applicable when the creator is known to us chiefly or only by his works, as in the case of the Creator of the universe. A perfect God, if he undertakes to create, should produce a perfect universe; and if he fails to do so, we cannot call him perfect.

It is no less wickedly perverse to refuse to recognize and condemn all the evil in the world, than to refuse to recognize and gratefully appreciate all the good and beautiful things it contains; it is just this mixed character of the world that is the source of most of our perplexities. A wholly benevolent and moral God might fail to create a perfect world if he lacked omnipotence and was obliged to work with recalcitrant materials—as Plato recognized in the *Timaeus*. We cannot, without being false to ourselves, save both God's omnipotence and his perfect goodness. If a God who is omnipotent and omniscient has permitted so much evil to arise in his world, then we must conclude that he is morally inferior to the best men; for they will to cure the world's ills but cannot, whereas he can cure the world's ills but will not. And morality is, in the first instance, a matter of the will.

4. The empirical objection to admitting God's existence is that we have so little direct and unequivocal experience of it. Man's religious quest has been largely a game of hide-and-seek with Deity. Even mystics who claim to have been in communication with God

give us, at best, accounts that are fragmentary and difficult to interpret, and our most complete delineations of the divine nature were simply spun out of the heads of theologians. A God who could permit men to entertain such revolting notions of his character, productive of so much suffering, as have often been held, without promptly correcting these views, must, if he exists, be not much better than the more bloodthirsty religions have depicted him. He must be the Arch-misanthrope.

The reasons alleged for God's failure to reveal himself more unequivocally are man's unworthiness and his inability to understand anything so immeasurably greater than himself as God is supposed to be. Doubtless we are incapable of encompassing intellectually the whole nature of Deity, just as an infant child is incapable of understanding its parent. Nevertheless, the loving parent makes his presence known to the infant in such a way that it cannot doubt his existence, thereby comforting the child and helping it to grow into an understanding of the motives and thoughts of an educated adult. And certainly it should not be beyond the power of God to reveal himself to even a simple-minded person in a manner that left no doubt of his existence and his will.

Some have held that imperfect creatures are not worthy to behold their perfect Creator. To this we must reply that a finite creature is not necessarily imperfect. Quite the contrary, perfection is more easily attained in little things than in great. It would never have occurred to the Greek philosophers to compliment God by attributing infinity to him, for to them that which is infinite must always remain incomplete and ill-defined, and only the finite could be perfect. It seems unworthy of God to make a creature so paltry or defective that it is not worthy to behold its Creator; as though an artist painted a picture so bad that he was ashamed to be seen standing before it in a public exhibition. A creature might be unworthy to know some other, and better, God, but it could hardly be unworthy to gaze upon the God who created *it*. If men are too wicked to be granted a direct revelation of God, perhaps the reason is that he has remained so effectively hidden from them; with a more adequate communication of his presence and his purpose with us, we might be vastly better. One might suspect that God prefers to remain aloof from men, in which case it is irreverent to try to intrude upon his privacy. A divine Person, I have little doubt, would be as evident to all his creatures as the sun, which some nations have believed to be God. The strongest reason for doubting that God exists is that it is possible to doubt that he exists. If he existed, and wished us to know him, he would not permit us to doubt his reality.

It has been widely held in the Christian tradition that God himself moves us to seek him, so that the very desire to find him is evidence of his existence. Thus Jesus declared (John, 6:44): 'No man can come to me, except the Father which has sent me draw him.' The discussion of grace in the *Summa Theologica* of St Thomas Aquinas supports the view that to approach God, or carry out his will, we must in the first instance be moved by God himself. If this be true, God has been most unkind in implanting in many good and earnest men an intense desire to know him, without revealing himself in a satisfactory and unequivocal manner. If, however, instead of assuming the existence of a complete and perfect God, a divine Person who might make himself known to us, we postulate the existence in the universe, and in each creature, of a seed or spark of divinity that is striving to fulfil itself through the world process, this unsatisfied yearning to know God becomes explicable. In this case, it is indeed the divinity within us that stirs us to seek God; but we do not find him, not because he is perversely hiding from us, but because he is still coming to be, and we, his creatures, must help to create him. To this matter we shall return in the final chapter.

The foregoing strictures have reference only to those anthropomorphic doctrines which make God a human person immeasurably enlarged, with our human faculties of knowing, willing, and the like. Scarcely helping us to understand the order and beauty of the universe, which is otherwise explicable, these views of God make the world's vast evil utterly incomprehensible. For that an intelligent being, as perfect and powerful as God is supposed to be, should permit a child or a bird or even a worm to suffer, is a shocking notion, revolting to all our finer sentiments. Moreover, to view God as a person is not helpful, for persons are external to each other. How often do we hear people lamenting their intrinsic loneliness, their vast spiritual distance even from those nearest and dearest to them! Such externality seems to be an inevitable limitation of personality, applying to it wherever it occurs. To be closer to us, the inmost soul of our souls, God must be an immanent spiritual power, not a transcendent Person. To the pragmatic contention that only an anthropomorphic God can satisfy the religious sentiments and serve as an object of devotion to people incapable of understanding high metaphysical concepts, the answer is that theologians have made God so grandly remote and forbidding that simple devout people turn from him to figures that are more intimate and approachable, the saints and incarnate gods and deified teachers of every religion.

God is the faith that at the beginning of the world lay a benevolent purpose; the trust that beyond the mixture of good and evil brought forth by the world process lies something that is wholly and changelessly good; the hope that everything precious will be saved at the end—what else do we know about God, what solid content has the idea beyond this aspiration?

It would be wrong to regard theology as a barren pursuit, because it can provide no convincing proof of the reality of the Deity whose attributes it so painstakingly elaborates. No undertaking that has engaged the earnest thought of so many good and intelligent men can be quite worthless. Despite its often dry and crabbed language, theology is more closely allied to poetry than to science or even to critical philosophy; and this is the reason why it appeals most strongly when given the poetic dress that properly belongs to it, as in Dante's *Divine Comedy* or Milton's *Paradise Lost*.

As an expression of man's effort to conceive the summit of perfection, the Being who exemplifies his highest aspirations, theology is ever worthy of our respect. In the changing pattern of theological concepts, we may read the growth of man's moral vision and the expansion of his sympathy. The dipolar God of recent panentheism, who interacts with his world and is responsive to it, is a nobler concept than the monopolar God of the old classical theology, who remains grandly aloof from all that he has created. It is only when theology becomes dogmatic, insisting that it has proved what it has not proved, that it deserves the censure of every conscientious thinker. And it must be added that the notion of God or the gods, by diverting man's attention from the search for valid explanations of natural phenomena and claiming a vast amount of mental energy that might have been more profitably employed, has from primitive times been a major obstacle to understanding the universe.

As we began this chapter by pointing out that religion does not stand or fall with the demonstration of God's existence, so it seems proper to end it by pointing out that religion's highest aspiration, immortal life, need not be abandoned along with belief in God. In the West, God has been called the guarantor of immortality; but certain Eastern religions have long held it to be possible without him. Since both God and the released human soul are conceived as spirits without bodies, proof that either exists would strengthen our faith in the possibility of the other. But the assumptions made by the doctrine of individual immortality are to those made by theism as a mole's hill to Chimborazo. A disembodied spirit of the magnitude of the human soul may exist even if a disembodied spirit of cosmic magnitude does not exist. The two assumptions are interdependent only to the extent that it is hardly possible to believe in the existence of a truly just and benevolent Creator, without also being confident that we shall not wholly die; for to have implanted in the human soul a burning desire for everlasting blessedness that could never be fulfilled, would be satanic cruelty.

Belief in immortality seems, therefore, to be more fundamental to religion than belief in God. To the moral consciousness, this belief carries, as its corollary, belief in the moral order of the universe; a universe so ordered that it preserves the precious things that have arisen in it must contain a moral principle, whether it be immanent (as in karma) or transcendent (as in theism). But a universe that preserved nothing, in which everything was destined to final dissolution, would encourage belief in neither a moral principle nor God.

17

Religion in the Modern World

The major religions of the world are very old. The newest of them, Mohammedanism, was founded over thirteen centuries ago, by a prophet who borrowed much from the far older ethical monotheism of the Jews. Each of the ancient religions has split into many sects, which usually differ only on minor points of doctrine, while preserving the fundamental beliefs of the original faith; and in addition some new religions, still with few adherents, have sprung up in recent times. The old, well-established religions contain dogmas which were incredible to the most critical minds of the age in which they arose, and have become increasingly difficult to reconcile with our modern, scientific concept of the universe. It is hardly possible for a clear thinker, familiar with this concept, to believe in them literally without dividing his mind into two well-insulated compartments, one containing religious beliefs and emotions, the other containing scientific facts and theories. This is a most unsatisfactory procedure, for the coherence, in one self-consistent pattern, of all our experiences and beliefs is our strongest warrant for the truth of any of them. If the contents of the compartments are irreconcilable, our minds are in a precarious state. Some day an insistent thought may slip through a fissure in the partition and enter the wrong compartment, bringing turmoil into this alien world and spiritual agony to the person who hoped to preserve peace of mind by preventing his incompatible beliefs from confronting each other.

It is not surprising, then, that the old religious certainties are weakening and the churches are losing their hold on the people. If the present wave of economic prosperity continues and higher education becomes ever more widespread, will this process continue until the old faiths die away or are confined to the remote, backward regions of a scientifically enlightened world? Is religion indeed decaying? What is its future in a scientific age? Is its only hope of survival a catastrophic global war which will destroy civilization and reduce the few survivors to a state of primitive barbarism, in which case they will doubtless revive the crude religious beliefs and cruel rites which, the world over, have been associated with this cultural level? Before attempting to answer these questions, it will be helpful to analyse religion into its elements. It may be that all the constituents of religion as we now know it are not so organically connected that all must live or die together; and if this be true, knowledge of which parts are more viable may help to keep religion alive.

Religion, in its whole range and scope, has three parts or aspects, which may be symbolized by the heart, the head, and the hand. To the heart correspond all those emotions and spiritual cravings commonly associated with religion: fear of a higher power; gratitude for life and its supports; yearning for union with transcendent goodness; the aspiration for immortality. To the head correspond the dogmas and precepts of a religion: its concept of God; its cosmogony or account of creation; its doctrine of the soul and its destiny; its moral code; its special revelations. To the hand correspond all the activities prompted by religious emotions and directed by the beliefs of some particular faith: the building of temples and shrines and images; ritual and worship; the practice of religious precepts.

It is, as has long been recognized, the second part of religion, consisting of its doctrines and dogmas, that is most vulnerable in a critical, scientific age. Aware that their whole elaborate doctrinal edifice was attacked at its very foundation by the theory of evolution, the Christian churches opposed Darwinism with all their resources. But neither argument nor vituperation could arrest the accumulation of evidence, by biologists and geologists, that organisms, far from being originally created in their present form as told in Genesis, have gradually evolved from simpler ancestors over a period vastly longer than tradition allows. Liberal churchmen have somehow managed to reconcile their doctrines to the scientific view, in some cases by regarding the Biblical account as allegory; but Fundamentalists still cling stubbornly to the ancient account in the face of mountains of contrary evidence. This scientific development seems to have presented no grave difficulties to Indian religions, such as Hinduism, Buddhism, and Jainism, which in any case regarded the universe as immensely old and placed no formidable chasm between man and the other animals, whose souls they hold to be interchangeable. Since religion is an effort to achieve a satisfactory relationship with a larger whole, both the parts that are seen and the parts that are unseen, until we achieve a correct understanding of this whole we can have no firmly established religion. Accordingly, religion cannot brush aside, as irrelevant to its purposes, such things as evolution.

Recognizing no God, Jainism and Buddhism, in their pure forms, are hardly affected by attacks upon the concept of Deity. As these faiths attest, more essential to religion even than God is a soul able to exist without an organic body, belief in which has been seriously undermined by modern developments in biology and psychology. If consciousness, far from being an attribute or the very essence of an independent substance, is merely an activity of the material brain, how can it survive the decay of this organ and how can immortality be possible? Curiously enough, the Buddha anticipated by more than two thousand years David Hume's contention that the so-called soul is not a substance but only a sequence of psychic states, a doctrine agreeable to the Buddha's goal of the ultimate extinction of the individual but hardly compatible with the dogma of rebirth that he so firmly held. To Jainism and Christianity, which each in its own way teaches the indestructibility of the soul, the dissolving criticisms of modern philosophy and psychology are more damaging. Yet these religions may find support in the views of so able a psychologist as William McDougall, who believed that the unity of consciousness points to the existence of a unitary soul that is more than a function of the body.

Then there is the whole question of the validity of special revelations for a scientific age which has become accustomed to demanding evidence. If a mystic experiences the Divine, or a prophet receives a message from God, that is doubtless valid for him; but to convince others, he should be able to show them how to obtain the experience or to hear the message. It is the same in everyday life, as in science. One with keener eyesight than mine may point out something that I overlook; but unless I finally discern it where he asserts it to be, I shall hardly believe him. To be credited by his colleagues, a scientist must explain how he conducted his experiments, and at least some of these men must repeat these experiments and obtain the same results. A God who plays favourites, revealing himself to some and hiding from others, seems not to be everybody's God. To the objection that one must be very good to be in direct communication with God, I should reply that a God who more freely revealed himself and his will could make a great many people a great deal better.

The foregoing are only a few of the many considerations which lead to the weakening and decay of the second aspect of religion, that corresponding to the head, in a scientific age. But doctrines, and belief or faith in their truth, are, as we have learned, by no means the whole of religion; and before we conclude that religion is doomed to eventual extinction, we must ask how it fares with the other aspects. Let us begin with that numinous state of mind which Rudolf Otto recognized as a peculiarly religious sentiment, and analysed at painstaking length in *The Idea of the Holy*. 'This mental state', he wrote, 'is perfectly *sui generis* and irreducible to any other; and therefore, like every absolutely primary and elementary datum, while it admits of being discussed, it cannot be strictly defined.' Otto despaired of conveying the exact quality of this unique feeling to one who had never directly experienced it; but to help the reader understand the numinous state of mind he employed such terms as 'creature-feeding', and the '*mysterium tremendum*', which contains such elements as 'awefulness', 'overpoweringness', and a sense of the 'wholly other'. It is the feeling of the infantile helplessness and dependence of the creature in the awful presence of a mysterious Creator infinitely more powerful than himself—a feeling of blank wonder, an astonishment that strikes us dumb, amazement absolute.

Although qualitatively different from natural fear, such as one might feel in the presence of a menacing wild animal or during an air raid, this feeling of the numinous resembles natural fear. But it seems more akin to the way we felt as, while still young and impressionable, we listened to a well-told ghost story around a dying campfire; or when, with shaking limbs, we ventured into an

[1] Rudolf Otto, *The Idea of the Holy: An Inquiry into the non-rational factor in the idea of the divine and its relation to the rational*, translated by John W. Harvey, Oxford University Press, 2nd edn. 1950.

abandoned house reputed to be haunted, to prove to taunting companions that we were not afraid.

Such numinous emotion, evidently once a powerful element in the whole complex of religious feeling, seems to be greatly attenuated, if not extinguished, in the more enlightened adherents of advanced religions. The whole tendency of philosophy and rational theology, such as that of Aquinas, is to substitute other feelings for that of trembling self-abasement in the face of an overwhelming, incomprehensible power. By conceiving of God as the benevolent, loving father, the source of all things good, the final goal of all our effort, we drive into the background of consciousness the unfathomable character of an infinite power. We come to think of God, not as the 'wholly other', but as the being allied to the best that is in us, as indeed somehow present in the inmost depths of our soul; so that the more we cultivate this divine aspect of ourselves while purifying ourselves of everything incompatible with it, the more godlike we become.

The higher religions encourage the substitution of such Apollonian feelings as love, reverence, gratitude, and cheerful obedience for the Dionysian attitude of trembling stupor in the presence of the highest power. Or else, by dismissing the idea of God, religions like Jainism and Buddhism seem to remove the very source of the numinous feeling; and if the adherents of these religions, hungry for something to worship, substitute for the creator God the wise and benevolent teacher, the Tirthankara or Buddha who showed the way to salvation, grateful love rather than trembling submission should be the feelings inspired by such deified men. As for myself, I cannot recall having experienced the numinous emotion in a notable degree since I was a small boy listening to a superstitious nurse; yet I do not deem myself less religious than I then was.

Just as, in the long course of religious history, concepts of Deity have undergone immense transformation without destroying religion, so it seems possible for religious sentiments to alter without making us irreligious. While, with our changing concept of the universe, some religious feelings are weakened or even destroyed, others surge up to replace them in the breast of an animal that is naturally religious. Of these, one of the most fundamental is appreciation, without which religion can hardly exist. Among the more encouraging developments of recent times is the growth of appreciation of the natural world, which thoughtful men will always view as the manifestation of some great creative power, however this power is conceived. An increasing number of people visit the still unspoiled areas of the globe to enjoy their beauty, often travelling thousands of miles in a way that was impossible a generation or two ago. Not only do they seek such spectacular phenomena as snow-capped peaks and thundering waterfalls; to watch free animals of all kinds leading their natural lives in their ancestral habitats, all undisturbed by the spectator, has become for many a precious experience, a generous reward for a long journey. Far from wishing to secure the animal's skin or the bird's plumage, as was formerly the custom, many people are now satisfied if they can obtain a photograph, or merely a view to treasure in memory.

In such encounters with the creatures that share the earth with us, we have one great advantage over them. We can participate sympathetically in the joys of other beings as, in all probability, they cannot participate in ours. By contemplating their graceful forms and beautiful colours and curious habits, we enrich our lives; although they seem to derive no comparable benefit from observation of the other creatures that surround them, including ourselves. Not by the ease with which we can slay animals of all kinds, but by our appreciative response to their presence, do we demonstrate our superiority over them. To experience joy in the contemplation of other beings and sympathetic participation in their joys is the sign of a truly spiritual nature, which sets it apart from the bestial nature that derives pleasure only from the satisfaction of its own appetites. Spirituality has its darker side, for those who enter sympathetically into the joys of other creatures are also oppressed by their pains. Such distress arising from the sight of suffering may be lightened by doing whatever we can to help the sufferers.

Growing appreciation of the beauty and wonder of the world in which we live is accompanied by a growing sense of responsibility for its preservation. More than ever before, thoughtful men care about their planet, not only its nearer but also its more distant regions. This increased concern cannot be attributed wholly to improved communications which promptly convey to us, in words and pictures, what is happening in remote lands; there has been a true spiritual awakening which makes us feel more keenly for our fellow creatures in another continent than our ancestors, a few short generations ago, felt for those close at hand. Many of us are distressed by the decimation of free animals in distant countries that we have little hope of seeing, by the destruction of stately forests whose beauty we never expected to enjoy; we give our time and wealth to preserve them. Others labour valiantly to alleviate the sufferings of domestic animals, those unfortunate creatures who contribute so much to man's welfare at such a fearful price of pain, mutilation, frustration, and death to themselves.

Similarly, there is increasing concern for the welfare of people in all parts of the earth. This growth has been so rapid that it is difficult for us to realize that not until the nineteenth century was chattel slavery abolished in the British Empire and the Americas. The merciless exploitation of labourers and native populations, which not long ago would have passed unnoticed, today raises a storm of protest even in distant countries. We rush from the four corners of the earth to succour the victims of a disastrous earthquake, volcanic eruption, or other natural catastrophe. Nations cooperate to improve the living conditions and education of the people, to abolish disease and hunger. Although once such philanthropic efforts were undertaken chiefly to win converts for one's own faith, now they are often made regardless of the religion of the beneficiaries.

These endeavours to improve the situation of mankind are, unfortunately, not always as wise and foreseeing as they might be. All the irresponsible talk about the dignity of man leads the ignorant to believe that it is their natural endowment, like their ability to walk and to see, rather than a state that each of us must attain by his own efforts to acquire virtue and wisdom, without which a man has less dignity than an animal equipped at birth with integrated patterns of behaviour adequate for its guidance in its ancestral environment. Flattered by demagogues, the petty-minded imagine that they already possess that high worth which wise and pious men of all epochs have held before themselves as an ideal to be striven for all their lives. Likewise, too much insistence on human rights diverts attention from human obligations, the conscientious discharge of which alone gives rights their foundation. And unless people take a more responsible attitude toward begetting children, their condition will deteriorate, economically and spiritually, despite all that their own governments and international agencies can do to improve it—as is happening in those countries where the growth of the population is most rapid.

Some people care only about improving the condition of their fellow men, while others are concerned above all for the preservation of the natural world; but those who view the situation broadly are aware that these two endeavours are so closely connected that, unless both succeed together, both will fail together. Although the problems that confront us are vast and for effective work each must concentrate upon some small field, without the coordination of our efforts little will be accomplished. What each of us can *care for* is very limited, but unless we *care about* the whole earth with all the life that it supports, we do not care intelligently about anything.

Unless, by the widespread elevation of the intellectual and spiritual quality of men, more of them develop a responsible attitude toward humanity and the earth that supports it, the natural world will be devastated by the rising flood of people hungry for its products and unconcerned about its future. Who could be inspired by the prospect of billions of men living in vast cities or a ravished countryside, cut off from all those beneficent influences by which nature has through the ages enriched and ennobled the human spirit; who could care whether such teeming masses of hurrying, worrying, self-centred people flourish or vanish from the earth that they have so impiously afflicted? Just as, if mankind tried to exist on an exclusively cannibalistic diet, there would be a constant diminution of the mass of human flesh, until the last man died of starvation after having devoured the next-to-last; so, if men tried to live only on the spiritual sustenance they can offer to each other, without reaching into the vaster environing world for renewal, there would be a continuous decline in their spiritual quality. The truth that no animal can long survive on its own secretions applies to its spiritual no less than to its physical aspect. Man, for all his vaunted superiority over the natural world and his proud efforts to control it, is inseparably a part of it, so that he cannot dislocate its rhythms without suffering spiritual starvation and eventual extinction.

By what path do we most surely reach that universal sympathy and concern for the earth as a whole which is the truest expression of the religious spirit? We recall that primitive man, far from regarding all men as brothers, looked with hostility, or at least with suspicion, on all people beyond his own family or clan. Likewise, as little children we feel strange and uncomfortable in the presence of all who are not intimates of our own household. From this primitive condition of the individual and the race, the first step toward developing a sense of fellowship with all life, we would suppose, would be to become conscious of the brotherhood of all mankind. This seems the natural course in the expansion of one's sympathy to embrace all things under the sun, to attain cosmic consciousness. Yet this course frequently proves to be a blind alley, leading no farther than man. For the person who first develops a strong sense of the unity of mankind and a brotherly feeling toward all men, is apt to have his mind so filled with pride in the magnitude of human achievements, with pity for human suffering, or with perplexity in the face of man's many unsolved problems, that it remains fixed within humanity and fails to expand beyond it—except possibly to reach toward a God who is a magnified image of man.

The identification of self with a whole far more comprehensive than humanity is, therefore, not so likely to be attained by first developing a strong consciousness of the multitudinous ties that bind us to mankind as by shrinking away from humanity, with all its absurdity, cruelty, and ugliness. Repelled by his fellow men, the solitary spirit seeks to identify himself with nature, finding his greatest joy, his most meaningful experience, in communion with the living world in spots where it has been least abused by man's destroying hand. Here he has the satisfying sense of being in contact with something far older, vaster, and more stable than humanity. Some stop at this point. Others go farther, realizing at last that the sympathy which embraces all things with the exception of mankind is only somewhat less narrow than the sympathy which is concentrated on humanity and at most thinly diffused beyond it. For the wider view shows us that man, too, belongs to nature, and that the manifold crudities which repel us from him—his aggressiveness, cruelty, destructiveness, greed, and lust—all have their roots in the animal world whence he arose, even if they have grown ranker and more noisome in him. Nature is greater and more wonderful when we recognize that it includes man, and man greater and more understandable when we recognize that he belongs to nature, than either could be without the other.

Thus, to the mind capable of broad sympathy and the general

view, the most certain road to the feeling of oneness with all life and true cosmic consciousness appears to be that which leads through the larger natural world to mankind, rather than that which might pass through humanity to the larger natural world but too often loses its way in the maze of human affairs and never passes beyond them.

Neither appreciation nor caring is new in the world. If primitive men had not, at least dimly, appreciated their lives, they would never have developed the religious rites whereby they sought to safeguard and prolong them. The ancient philosophers were eloquent in their expressions of appreciation of the beauty and order of the heavens; the very term by which they designated the universe as then conceived by them—*kosmos*—was a recognition of the admirable order they detected in the movements of the celestial bodies. It is difficult, after so great a lapse of time, to decide whether their glowing passages owe more to deep personal feeling or to a literary tradition. Be that as it may, there is little doubt that recent generations have witnessed a widening and deepening of appreciation of most other aspects of the natural world, especially the wilderness and all the living things it contains, and the smaller creatures that surround us in our gardens and fields, such as plants, insects, and birds. This growing appreciative interest is due in part to the superior means we have for viewing and studying them.

Similarly, care for the living world, human and otherwise, is by no means new. There never lived a ruler more concerned for the welfare of all the inhabitants of a great realm, to whatever animal or vegetable species they belonged, than the Indian emperor Asoka. But today more people are more actively interested in the welfare of the creatures of many kinds that share the earth with them, at whatever distance they live, than ever before. This increase in the number of those who care is due only in part to the vast multiplication of the earth's human inhabitants during the last century. There has been a genuine widening and deepening of concern which is a gain for religion, even if the organized religions are not alert enough to recognize and foster it.

In the contemporary world, many of the most truly religious people belong to no church. One may well ask who is more religious, the mystic who closes his eyes to the world while bending all his efforts to achieve an ecstatic vision of God; the parent who cares lovingly for his children, regardful of their spiritual no less than their bodily development; or the conservationist who loves the natural world and does his best to prevent its spoliation? I doubt whether the mystic can rightly be considered the most religious of these three.

In that part of religion symbolized by the heart, aspiration is, as a rule, closely associated with appreciation and devoted care. How does it fare with aspiration in the modern world? With the advent of modern science and the vast power it soon demonstrated to control natural processes for the benefit of men, the more hopeful spirits began to anticipate a sort of terrestrial paradise. Science was heralded as the New Messiah that would bring heaven down to earth; and the prospect of a greatly prolonged and more rewarding life, free from many of the toils and pains that afflicted our ancestors, solaced those whose belief in spiritual survival was weakened or destroyed by the rationalistic-mechanistic outlook that spread over the Western world.

Although science and its offshoot, technology, have brought us many benefits, in transforming human life they have given rise to a host of new perplexities. Just as, for the early Christians, Christ's promised second coming to usher in the Messianic Era receded farther into the future with each succeeding generation; so, in this harassed modern age, the promise of technological democracy to bring peace and happiness to the earth seems even farther from fulfilment than it did to our grandfathers. We see ever more clearly that what chiefly stands in the way of such limited felicity as we can rationally expect to enjoy on this earth is not the difficulty of controlling natural processes so much as the difficulty of moderating our inordinate appetites, controlling our vehement passions, and learning to work unselfishly for the welfare of our world—which is the truth that all the higher religions and religious philosophies have proclaimed with surprising unanimity.

And even if science succeeded in creating an earthly paradise and enabling us to live as long as Methuselah, this would not still that yearning for immortal life that has ever stirred the human heart. The more richly rewarding life is, the more bitter the final quenching of consciousness appears to us. It would be wrong to regard this as a failure of gratitude for life's many gifts, for with the extinction of memory all the precious experiences we ever had seem reduced to zero; the gifts are all taken back. As the spotty recollections which others have of us fade to nothingness with the passing of the generations, it will be almost as though we had never existed. Although it is difficult to believe that any healthy mind is so thoroughly reconciled to the prospect of its own annihilation that it does not cherish, in its inmost depth, a timid little hope that death is not just what it appears to be, many educated people seem reluctant to reveal an aspiration that they regard as incompatible with prevailing scientific or philosophic views. Like the fox who could not reach the grapes, some cynically disparage what they have no hope of attaining.

We should be grateful to Miguel de Unamuno for so candidly confessing, in *Tragic Sense of Life*, his own horror of spiritual extinction, and so expertly portraying the plight of the modern man who yearns for immortal life yet doubts its reality. In Chapter 12 I gave some reasons for believing that spiritual survival is not impossible; a more thorough treatment of the subject, which I hope some day to make, involves the discussion of difficult ontological problems that are beyond the scope of this book. But however nagging our residual doubts, we can at least bend all our effort *to become worthy of immortal life*. As in Pascal's famous wager, by this course we have everything to gain and nothing of consequence to lose. Although it seems possible to have a religion that does not promise a blessed immortality to the righteous, such a religion would be tragic. A religion that provided indubitable proof of immortal life would be triumphant.

In an age when appreciation and devoted care are growing and aspiration is far from dead, the prospects of religion cannot be regarded as gloomy. These are the lifeblood of religion, coursing through its living heart, providing the vital energy for those manifestations of religion that correspond to the head and the hand. These, above all, have prompted men to build temples and elaborate ritual and try to fathom the nature of God. Suppose all the churches and temples were to crumble into dust, the ceremonies to cease, the theological dogmas to be proved false—would that (except for the loss of artistic treasures) be a calamity? Unless the old established religions can somehow shake off the archaism which has been the bane of religion and adjust their doctrines and practices to our present understanding of the world and its needs, their dissolution might be far from regrettable.

With the passing away of these works of the head and the hand, religion would live on, so long as the true religious spirit flourishes in the heart. Religion belongs to the individual man, not to any church. The organized religions deserve our allegiance only in so far as they incorporate, and make effective, our innate capacities for appreciation and devoted care. If the churches fall to ruin, we can more fittingly take as our temple this whole wide earth, with its carpet of living green, its heaving seas, its vaulted canopy ceaselessly changing from azure to sable studded with a myriad moving points of light. Any narrower fane seems inadequate for the worship of the power that rounded off our planet, set it coursing around the sun, and filled it with multitudinous life. And what form of worship is more proper than grateful appreciation of the beauty of the earth, the wonder of the heavens, and the privilege of living in so fair a world beneath such a sky? As to the nature of this creative power, we can begin to understand it only by combining, in a single comprehensive view, what science teaches us about the external world with what we learn by probing the inmost depths of our own being, which eludes the scrutiny of objective science. And since our religion would be incomplete if it found no use for our hands as well as our hearts and our heads, how better could we serve it than by doing all we can to preserve the beauty of our planetary temple and shield from harm all its varied inhabitants?

The religions of the past have been more successful in providing consolation and hope for the downtrodden than in providing inspiration, guidance, and spiritual stability for the prosperous, well-educated, critically intelligent class of society. The whole history of civilizations shows that ignorant and barbarous peoples somehow acquire higher culture, often largely by their own efforts, but that high culture and prosperity cannot maintain itself for lack of proper motivation—hence the decline of advanced civilizations. Success is often a greater peril than adversity: the latter stimulates our efforts; the former often brings fatal relaxation. The great challenge to religion is to provide motivation that will keep high cultures going. A religion for the strong and prosperous is at least as necessary as a religion for the weak and downtrodden.

Although we have reason to hope that a religion which satisfies the spirit without embarrassing the intelligence with outworn dogmas will arise and continue long to flourish among mankind, we have no ground for a comfortable complacency. If the forces of good have been growing stronger in the modern world, so have the forces of evil. Indeed, both are present in every man's breast, as was recognized by the sages of old; although, without understanding the evolutionary history of mankind, they could give no adequate explanation of this paradox. According as one or the other prevails within us, we join the ranks of those who fight to preserve the beauty and fertility of the earth, along with the nobility of the human spirit; or else we join the opposing army of those who stop at nothing to satisfy their lust for pleasure, power, or wealth.

This aeonian struggle, symbolized in the old Persian religion by the conflict between the powers of light led by Ormuzd and the powers of darkness headed by Ahriman, has increased in violence through the years, and today is waged on a vaster scale, with more destructive weapons, than ever before. We have now reached that stage in our evolution at which we can, in some measure, fulfil the world process by knowing and appreciating its accomplishments; and in so doing we give purpose and significance to our own lives. Or, by senseless destruction, we may largely cancel the accomplishments of the world process on this planet; and in so doing we will make our lives paltry and meaningless. The choice belongs to the present generation.

18

Religion and the Emergence of the Divine

A number of attempts have been made to interpret the world process, or that small part of it comprised in the history of mankind, as the expression of some hidden purpose. The Jews of old regarded history as the manifestation of Yahweh's will with Israel. St Augustine is credited with having developed, in *The City of God*, the first comprehensive philosophy of history. For him, the significance of the whole human drama, from the creation of Adam to Christ's expected second avatar and the Final Judgment, was man's redemption from the original sin and the segregation of the souls of the elect from those of the damned. For Hegel, history was the self-expression of the Absolute Idea. Herbert Spencer took the widest possible view, regarding the whole course of universal evolution as the emergence of ever wider, more harmoniously integrated patterns, which at the higher levels are exemplified by human social institutions and moral conduct, and which will finally result in the establishment of the greatest perfection and most complete happiness. Eventually, however, evolution will probably be succeeded by dissolution, when the universe will revert to that undifferentiated pristine state whence it emerged—a notion as old as Heraclitus and the Stoics. For Bergson, the goal of the *élan vital* was to produce forms of life that achieved the maximum amount of indeterminacy, which to him meant freedom.

A few generations ago, optimists read history as man's continuous progress toward a richer, happier life by means of ever greater control over nature and an ever more perfect social state. Today, we do not doubt our ability to extend our control over natural processes almost indefinitely; and this is just what makes us fearful; for the moral and social advances which should have kept pace with this increasing power and made it safe have been far from satis-factory.

The growth and consolidation of large national states has almost put an end to the petty inter-tribal and inter-city conflicts that were rife in the earlier epochs of human history; yet for several decades the world has not been without a war, and periodically the whole globe is convulsed by an armed conflict which for magnitude and destructiveness makes all previous wars seem like petty skirmishes. By enabling one nation to attack another separated from it by mountain chains or wide oceans, almost instantaneously and without warning, modern advances in transportation have destroyed the sense of security that the more isolated countries once enjoyed.

Although in the more developed countries even humble people have luxuries such as kings hardly dreamed of in ancient times, we pay for these things with mounting nervous tension and an increas-ing feeling of futility. In stark contrast to the great material prosperity of the highly industrialized nations, a large part of the world's population still lives in precarious misery, wretchedly housed, undernourished, ill-educated. To cap the gloomy picture, the flood of population is rising faster than provision can be made for its support and threatens to inundate the globe with a degraded and impoverished humanity. Although it is easy to point to progress in certain respects, the whole advance appears most precarious, leading we know not where, and of doubtful value.

If, from viewing such external aspects of the human situation as technological and political developments, we turn to the examination of religious sentiments and ideals, we get a more heartening picture of significant progress. Religion, we cannot too often repeat, is dedicated above all to the preservation and advancement of the fundamental life values; this has been true from its groping infancy, and the changes in its form and content have been due chiefly to the growing spiritualization of these values and the means of securing them.

For a conscious being, the worth of existence must ever be expressed in words signifying some satisfying state of consciousness: terms such as happiness, joy, fulfilment, blessedness, bliss, in all their varying shades of meaning. Such psychic states belong, as far as we know, only to individuals, and they are the persistently sought goal of every individual, not only of men and the higher animals but, most likely, every sentient being. All the advanced religions—certainly all those that have appealed to many people for many generations—have recognized this striving; and it is to their everlasting credit that they also recognized the equal right of every man to try to win blessedness. Thus, long before Kant taught us, in knotty philosophical language, to regard every man as an end in himself rather than merely an instrument to be used by others, the great historic religions had, each in its own idiom, proclaimed the same doctrine. Certain Eastern religions, notably Jainism, Buddhism, and some branches of Hinduism, early went much farther than this, regarding every sentient being as an end in itself, a soul whose claim to blessedness is as valid as any other's. This is the true spiritual significance of the doctrine of metempsychosis, which visualizes a means whereby the least embodied soul may rise to the highest state; and even if we reject the dogma of transmigration as resting upon inconclusive evidence, we honour the generous spirit that inspires it.

Not only did the great religions recognize the universality of the longing for a happier and more prolonged existence, they pointed out clearly the means for attaining serenity here and preparing oneself for blessedness in the hereafter. Harmony is the foundation of happiness, harmony in every aspect of our lives, in the functioning of our bodies, in our thoughts and emotions, and in our relations with the living things of all kinds that surround us. One of the chief obstacles to the attainment of harmony is the strength of those appetites and passions which, indispensable to the survival of an animal in a state of nature, become hypertrophied under the conditions of civilization, like weedy wildlings in a sheltered garden. The more prosperous a society or a social class becomes, the more people can relax from the daily struggle to fill their vital needs, the more rankly these appetites and passions grow, unless strenuous efforts are made to control them, which is best accomplished by directing vital energy to ideal ends. Not only do they keep the soul in a state of ferment destructive of inner peace, they make it impossible for us to dwell in concord with our neighbours.

Like a good physician who points unerringly to the cause of a disease, the sages of old diagnosed the malady of the human soul and prescribed the one certain method for its cure. Appetite must be controlled, passion subdued, hatred replaced by love, selfishness by generosity, vengefulness by forgiveness. By these means, and these alone, could a man live in peace with himself and those around him, thereby replacing the violent alternations of exaltation and depression typical of a passionate nature by a calm, abiding joy, and developing the kind of soul which alone seems worthy of eternal life. Just as, in the earlier stages of medicine, doctors frequently prescribed too drastic a cure, so these physicians of the soul sometimes advocated too radical a suppression of our emotional life by a harsh and sterile asceticism. Nevertheless, the whole experience of our race approves the basic soundness of their method.

The ideals and principles of all the great religions took shape, and were given adequate expression, in the six or seven centuries ending with the crucifixion of Christ or, we might say, the death of St Paul. This interval, long in itself but only a small fraction of the whole period which has elapsed since man first began to live in societies, fashion tools, develop language, and form his first crude religious concepts, saw the composition of the principal *Upanishads*, the life and teaching of Mahavira, Gautama Buddha, Laotse, Confucius, Pythagoras, Socrates, Plato, Zeno the Stoic, many of the Hebrew prophets, Jesus, and his apostle to the gentiles, Paul of Tarsus.

None of these great teachers developed his peculiar doctrines from the ground level of primitive savagery; each owed much to his predecessors and the spiritual and intellectual atmosphere of his age, as historical and archaeological research make increasingly clear. Thus the *Upanishads* were an outgrowth of the *Vedas*; Mahavira was the last of a long line of Jaina Tirthankaras, some of whom appear to be legendary; the moral concepts of Judaism owed much to the far older and greater civilization of neighbouring Egypt, whose slow spiritual development was traced by Breasted in *The Dawn of Conscience*. Jesus, if not himself an Essene, was certainly influenced by their doctrines, which have become better known to us since the recent discoveries in the caves at Wadi Qumran above the Dead Sea. There is the strongest contrast between the ideals of all these great teachers and those which prevailed, at least among the warrior chiefs who ruled Greece and northern India, in the preceding Heroic Age, when wealth and power were sought above all else, prowess in arms was the most admired accomplishment, and unbridled passions governed the course of human events, as we learn from such epic poetry as the *Iliad* and the *Mahabharata*.

One who considered only the most revered names in the history of religions might conclude that there has been no continuous progress to the present time, but on the contrary religion rather suddenly attained, in the period indicated, a peak which it has never been able to surpass. He might even reach the distressing conclusion that there has been a general decline in the quality of humanity, which has lost the capacity to produce men of the spiritual height of some who lived two millennia ago. This would be a lamentable error. In certain respects, indeed, the precepts given to mankind in distant ages are unsurpassable. It seems impossible to enunciate a principle of conduct more succinctly adequate than the Golden Rule, proclaimed independently in Israel and China, or the law of absolute harmlessness in thought, word, and deed, India's great contribution to universal ethics. Once such supreme maxims have been formulated, they preclude the highest originality in the field of religious morality. We can only repeat these lessons that the past has handed down to us; one who claimed to have made an independent discovery of the Golden Rule would be mocked as a presumptuous plagiarist.

Yet in men such as Mahatma Gandhi and Albert Schweitzer, the modern age has produced people who compare favourably with the spiritual giants of a distant past. In comparing the moderns with the revered men of antiquity, we must allow for the probability that tradition has exaggerated the virtues and conveniently forgotten the weaknesses of the latter, whereas the former have lived in the full glare of a too-prying publicity. Moreover, when assessing the religious development of mankind, we must remember that no biological species is composed of identical individuals, and the more highly evolved the species, the greater the apparent individual variation in every character. In man, the difference between the level of the spiritual élite and that of the general population represents thousands of years of evolutionary progress. This is as true today as it was in ancient times.

Progress in any field must be measured not only by the development of principles or ideals but also by their practical application. Anyone who tries earnestly to live by the Golden Rule or the Law of Ahimsa will soon encounter perplexing problems which these high precepts, in their succinct expression, fail to solve for him. The proclamation of these comprehensive ethical maxims left much work to be done in the clarification of their implications and the working out of social arrangements and economic practices that are compatible with them. This immense task has been proceeding steadily, if haltingly, through the centuries. The Golden Rule, for example, seems to forbid social inequalities, for no one likes to be treated as an inferior; yet it was not until the late eighteenth century that a nation destined to become great was established on the principle, enunciated long before by the Roman jurist Ulpian, that 'All men, according to natural right, are born free and equal'. Likewise, slavery is clearly incompatible with the teachings of the great religions and religious philosophies; but this abominable practice was so firmly entrenched in all the ancient societies that even Stoicism, one of its most outspoken critics, got no farther than recognizing that slaves could be the moral equals of their masters, and insisting upon their humane treatment. It remained for modern times to witness the abolition of slavery in all but the most backward corners of the earth. Similarly, the subjection of women to the whims and lusts of men is inconsistent with the recognition that they, too, have souls to be perfected and saved. The Stoics believed that women should be treated as equal partners in wedlock; and noble wives, such as Arria and Fannia, figure prominently among their heroes. The Buddha was persuaded to admit women into his monastic order, although not without certain misgivings as to their effect upon its stability. Nevertheless, the legal recognition of woman's equal status has only tardily been achieved in the more enlightened countries.

In these and other ways, ideals which religions first proclaimed to the world have been slowly coming to realization in secular societies, and in many instances written into civil law. Without overlooking the origin of ideals now professed by many people who do not consider themselves religious, we cannot fail to recognize steady and significant progress in the things for which religion has stood. At the same time, it would be disastrous to forget the tremendous amount that remains to be done before the ancient ideals of the great religions are somewhat adequately realized, and the life values which are their chief concern are properly safeguarded.

To appreciate the full sweep of that evolutionary advance of whose nature the religious sentiments of mankind are such a significant expression, we must look not only forward but also backward from that period, in the centuries immediately preceding the death of Christ, in which the founders of religions lived. These men and their doctrines did not suddenly descend upon the earth but are culminating points in an immensely long development. First it was necessary to form a solar system, containing at least one planet massive enough to retain a gaseous envelope and at such a distance from the central sun that it was neither too hot nor too cold for vital processes which require liquid water as a medium. Then life arose, at first in the simplest, most inconspicuous forms, and slowly through the ages evolved into organisms of increasing size and complexity. Animals acquired sensory organs, which gradually improved in sensitivity and discrimination; they developed means for propelling themselves through the water or over the land or through the air; they perfected nervous systems to coordinate and direct their movements in response to external stimuli. In the higher animals, the apex of the nervous system enlarged into a brain that became the seat of memory and intelligence and enabled them to adjust their lives more adequately to varying circumstances. These animals learned to communicate with each other by visual signals, sounds, or scents. Some of them united into more or less closely integrated societies.

At long last, a terrestrial branch of the ancient and mostly arboreal Primate stock developed language, whereby one individual could convey ideas to the minds of its companions instead of merely calling their attention to present objects by means of signals, as in other animals. This more adequate communication permitted closer cooperation between individuals and favoured the growth of societies. Social intercourse, together with the possession of hands that could make ideas effective, stimulated the development of intelligence to a point far beyond that reached by any other animal; and with the increasing ability to think, this terrestrial Primate, which we may now call man, became more conscious of himself and concerned for his own future. Feeling himself threatened by a thousand forces, seen and unseen, that he could neither understand nor control, man developed magic and religion to protect himself from the perils that menaced him, effect results unattainable by natural means, and propitiate the unseen powers on which his life depended.

Despite these novel expedients—untried, as far as we know, by any other animal—to stabilize their lives and control their destiny, men continued to suffer; and in the measure that they became more thoughtful, they recognized that a large share of their ills sprang directly from the unrestrained play of their own strong appetites and passions. At the same time, they yearned ever more for a happy life beyond the grave. With deepening moral insight, they began to suspect that there was a close connection between the control of those impulses and appetites which can bring so much misery here on earth and the quality of the existence they could expect after they had passed to the great beyond. The higher religions grew out of this dual effort to bring harmony into society while preparing us for a blissful immortality.

Such, in briefest outline, is the long course of evolution, from the primal nebula to man and his institutions, which has been treated in great detail, and from various points of view, in countless books. What common feature can we find throughout this whole long development? What principle unites its earliest and latest stages? From first to last, creative advance consists in increasing organization; in uniting discrete elements into coherent patterns; in harmonizing the myriad particles that the universe contains; in bringing unity into multiplicity. In the genesis of a solar system, a vast cloud of diffuse material is condensed into nearly spherical bodies of definite form, which circulate rhythmically around the central sun, in a pattern of masses and movements so balanced and stable that it persists for an immense period of time. In the formation of the various kinds of atoms, much the same thing seems to occur on an infinitesimal scale: protons and neutrons unite into a central nucleus, around which a definite number of electrons rotate or vibrate somewhat in the manner of planets around the sun. Molecules are formed by the union of few or many atoms in definite and often exceedingly complex patterns, which in favourable circumstances persist indefinitely. Crystals are produced by the lining up of atoms or molecules, layer upon layer, with the precision of well-drilled soldiers, in formations that delight us by their delicacy or brilliance. Living protoplasm grows by the union of a great variety of usually complex molecules into a functioning pattern able to transform energy and react to stimuli. Multicellular plants and animals are composed of many cells conjoined, often with beautiful regularity, into tissues, which in turn make the organs of which the organism is formed. A healthy living plant, and even more one of the higher animals, consists of many organs, composed of innumerable cells, which in turn contain a vast number of molecules, each made up of few or many atoms; and all these so diverse constituents are closely integrated into a harmonious whole that is able to act as a unit in all the diverse activities which support and fulfil its life.

Doubtless the discerning reader has already recognized the place of religion and morality in this aeonian process. Animals composed of diverse parts conjoined in one harmoniously functioning whole frequently band together in a society, which is never so closely integrated as the individuals who compose it. Many kinds of social animals are innately endowed with impulses and modes of behaviour which reduce friction and help them to live in concord with their companions. Man, whose innate patterns of behaviour disintegrated in the measure that his intelligence and capacity to learn from his elders improved, is by nature adapted to neither a solitary nor a social life. He needs the assistance of his fellows; he is unhappy away from them; yet his egoism, his greed, his pride, his jealousy, his strong passions, his tongue difficult to control, and a hundred other maladaptations bring him into frequent and often violent conflict with his neighbours. Unlike many other kinds of animals, he lacks innate, ritualized, nonviolent methods for settling his differences with his fellows. And these disharmonies in the social body are but the external manifestations of disharmonies in the soul of each of its members. We are torn by contrary passions and desires; we quarrel with our best friends and then regret it; we sin or commit crimes and are overcome by remorse. The community, acting through its elders or chiefs or, in more advanced societies, through the whole ponderous mechanism of the law, can punish public infractions; but neither customary nor written law can cure the private disorders of the soul which are the cause of transgressions.

This is where religion steps in. By appealing to that principle of harmony that lies at the core of every man and indeed of every organized being including the most ferocious, it brings a measure of concord into society, at the same time that it gives to the individual soul peace and a sense of worthiness to pass to a higher mode of existence or to meet its Creator. Thereby it carries a step farther that some process of harmonization which began when the solar system took shape and atoms were formed from the ultimate particles, which is manifest in the growth of a crystal or an organic body, which joins men into societies and takes this means to improve societies and the character of those who compose them. Nowhere is there discontinuity, but one unbroken movement sweeps creation forward from its prime foundations to its highest manifestations in the spiritual realm. We have no warrant for dividing things into the natural and the supernatural; there are only earlier and later phases of natural process. Immortality, if it can be achieved, is as natural as the crystallization of a snowflake or the birth of a child.

The process which brings order into the universe by building up its primary elements into patterns of increasing amplitude, complexity and coherence, also brings an increase of value. By value we mean that which enhances existence, that which makes life precious, that which makes us cling passionately to our conscious existence and shrink with horror from the thought of its extinction. In a universe devoid of value, no creature would care whether it continued, or ceased, to exist. Value is inseparable from consciousness, for we cannot imagine that a creature wholly insentient would find any satisfaction in its existence. Yet we can imagine, although with difficulty, a state of awareness, and indeed a comprehensive knowledge of the world, accompanied by neither joy nor sorrow, neither satisfaction nor dissatisfaction—a wholly neutral or valueless consciousness. Value is that aspect of experience which makes us appreciate the world and our life in it. Without it there could be no religion, for we should find nothing worth our care, no foundation for our aspirations; and with neither appreciation, devoted care, nor aspiration, religion would not exist.

Increase in organization and increase in value are complementary aspects of the same process, the first appearing when we view the world objectively, the second in our subjective experience. If we believe that life is richer and more rewarding for us than for an amoeba or some other one-celled organism, we must also believe that this is because in us vastly more cells, arranged in all the complex patterns of our tissues and organs, are cooperating closely together to make it so.

While on one side increase in value depends upon the organization of conscious beings, on the other side it depends on the external situations to which these beings respond. The chief forms of value are, in the Western tradition, beauty, truth, and goodness; and if we analyse any of them, we find that each depends upon the union of separate elements into a harmonious whole. A lovely flowering plant or a beautiful animal is itself a complex organism, just as are we who delight in beholding it. Moreover, there must be a certain correspondence or harmony between its appearance and our aesthetic nature, without which we would fail to respond with pleasure to its presence. When we reflect that its life, no less than ours, depends upon the earth which supports us, the air that we breathe, and the sunlight which furnishes energy for its vital processes and makes it visible to us, we begin to realize how many different things, distributed over how vast a space, work harmoniously together to give us a value-experience so frequent as the sight of a flower or a bird. In such an experience, many separate existences are bound together into an ideal unity which gives significance to all of them and to the process that created them.

The pleasure we find in surveying a wide landscape depends upon how all its distinguishable features—hills and trees and fields and buildings—fall together into one satisfying whole. It is a commonplace to say that the value of a painting or other work of art depends upon how well the artist has succeeded in combining all its features into a balanced and harmonious unity. The same principle applies to music, in which many aerial vibrations, many distinguishable sounds, blend together and carry out a single movement which must harmonize with the listener's mood, lest he be distressed or annoyed rather than uplifted by it. Every experience of beauty, visual or auditory or depending on the operation of several senses simultaneously, springs from harmonies far more extensive and subtle than those which we detect in the beautiful thing itself. Such an experience is the focus at which countless contributing factors come to fruition.

A thorough demonstration of how truth depends upon harmony would involve the exposition of a whole theory of knowledge and lead us too far afield. Here it will perhaps suffice to ask the reader to consider what criterion he uses to determine whether a supposed fact or a theory is true. Is it not just that it fits coherently into the whole body of his knowledge, that it is contradicted by no experience, no accepted fact, no well-tested theory? An alleged fact that clashes with our convictions troubles us like a pebble in our shoe until we can either find grounds for its rejection as false or else, perhaps by revising our conceptions, reconcile it to the other contents of our mind. It is above all the satisfaction we feel in the harmonious integration of all our cognitions, and our faith that our knowledge somehow corresponds to the external world, that make truth precious to us. This feeling of adequacy could hardly be achieved if there were not some concord, difficult to analyse, between the way our minds work and the way nature operates in the world about us. Truth, like beauty, is above all a manifestation of harmony and order in the world.

To be convinced that goodness depends on the harmonious adjustment of one thing to another, we need only consider the occasions when we use this word and the corresponding adjective 'good'. Depending on our point of view, goodness may be either internal or external. A good machine is one of which all the wheels, levers, and other parts are so adjusted to each other that they work harmoniously together to make the machine run smoothly and efficiently. Similarly, a good animal body, which is a healthy body, is one of which all the cells and organs function together in perfect harmony to support the life of the body and its appropriate activities. The internal goodness of any compound object depends on the external goodness of its parts. However carefully made a certain part of a machine may be, we do not consider it good unless it is properly adjusted to all the other components. Similarly with the organs of a body: the lens of an eye, for example, may be perfect when considered in isolation, but we do not call it good unless its curvature is properly adjusted to its distance from the retina, so that it may focus images sharply upon the latter.

To call an isolated object, alone in space, either good or bad would be meaningless, unless it were compound and we referred to its internal coherence. The external goodness of any thing depends on its relations to other things; we commonly qualify it as good or bad by considering it with reference to our own needs, desires, or ideals. A good tool or machine is one which performs well the work we require of it. A good man is one who lives in harmony with his

THE GOLDEN CORE OF RELIGION

neighbours because he treats them with justice and consideration. We say that such a man is morally good, and we esteem such goodness above every other kind. Moral goodness, however, differs from other forms of goodness only in so far as it depends upon the will. It manifests itself by bringing harmony into human relations; and since the inner life of other individuals is hidden from us, this is the criterion by which we commonly recognize its presence. Whether we contemplate an animal whose structure and activities are admirably adapted to its environment, or watch a machine perform its work supremely well, or consider a man of outstanding moral excellence—a neighbour, or perhaps a personage in ancient history—we derive satisfaction or value from the contemplation of goodness, and above all from that of moral goodness. And when the goodness, of whatever kind, contributes directly to our own well-being and happiness, we value it far more.

That which has value for us, we love. The highest love is excited by goodness, beauty, and truth. The most perfect love would be generated by the most perfect synthesis of values, which is an ideal never realized. The experience of loving is one of the most precious that life can bring to us, but it is not a primary value because it depends upon the recognition of the more fundamental values of beauty, goodness, and truth.

We are parts of the world, composed of the universal substance, formed by universal processes. Moreover, we are the only parts which we can know intimately—although far from adequately—from within rather than from the outside. Unless we can regard ourselves as small but significant samples of the whole, we shall never begin to understand the world; for only when we combine the internal view with the external view does it acquire meaning for us. When we survey objectively the evolutionary history of our planet, we find that it consists in building the primary components into patterns of ever increasing coherence, complexity, and amplitude. Corresponding to this on the subjective side, there is an enhancement of existence or increase in value, which we experience directly, and which, by taking ourselves as samples of the whole, we infer to be present at earlier stages of the process.

The principle that underlies the world process seems to be that value increases by the union of parts into a harmonious whole. It is a social principle, the principle of love, which Empedocles of old took to be the great constructive force in the universe. If this principle was originally present as an idea, it was an idea worthy of the highest mind, of God. But to know the origin of this principle which underlies the world process would be equivalent to knowing how nature acquired its laws, by which we mean no more than those courses which it habitually follows; and this is a matter hidden in the deepest obscurity. Yet we may recognize that there lies at the heart of the universe a principle, a power, a striving—we hardly know what to call it—which we may reverence as divine. This spark or, more correctly, leaven of divinity, pervades the whole and is present in every part. It is this divine spark or leaven, working in the inmost being of every man (although often obscured by ugly passions) that makes us seek the highest good, which we call God. Unless there had been a seed of divinity at the beginning, the world would never move Godward.

If the world process is set in motion by a principle such as might have been conceived by a loving, benevolent God, how does it happen that our actual world contains so much ugliness and evil? Unhappily, to have a correct, even a divinely conceived, principle is not enough. A sea captain who knows only the principles of navigation will never bring his ship into port. To reach his destination, he must also know details of latitude and longitude, winds and currents, and the like. Similarly, a world set in motion by a great constructive principle will inevitably run into trouble without continuous supervision by a divine mind with an infinite capacity for details. A great difficulty might have been avoided if the centres of organization had been so remote from each other that the harmonious patterns growing up at each of them could never collide; but such isolation of organized beings would have precluded their forming an environment for each other, uniting in higher syntheses, or engaging in fruitful cooperation.

Matter has a strong tendency to organize itself; at moderate temperatures and pressures it does so with a rush. The impulse toward vital organization is so intense that, after this planet became favourable for life, organisms sprang up in such excessive numbers that they were inevitably thrown into conflict for the means of subsistence. As, with growing complexity, animals developed more effective means for destroying each other, the internecine struggle was intensified; ugliness and suffering increased along with beauty and the capacity for enjoyment. Beings with a principle of harmony within them became so charged with the fierce passions necessary for their preservation in a world of conflict that their inmost nature was largely obscured. The slow passage of geologic epochs has brought forth many wonderful and admirable things on our planet, there has been a great increase in value, but at the price of incalculable strife and pain.

All this evil is a secondary effect or by-product of the same process which, primarily or directly, brought forth all the order and goodness on this earth. The very uncontrolled intensity of a beneficent creative process has been responsible for involving the world in strife and suffering, so that we may truly say that if the impulsion toward goodness or harmony had been weaker, there would be far less disharmony or evil. The recognition of this paradox makes it unnecessary for us to postulate any principle or power of evil, an Ahriman or Satan, as the author of the world's sorrows. At the same time, the divine guidance which might have repressed excesses and given a new direction to dangerous trends has been conspicuously lacking. Even if we concede that God started the world and infused it with its grand constructive principle, we can hardly believe that, either directly or through auxiliary deities that he might have created, he has continued to give the careful supervision by which alone lamentable developments might have been avoided. Either he found this problem too vast even for him, or after setting this world on its way he turned his attention to others beyond our ken. Deism is more easily reconciled with the present state of our planet than is theism.

Yet, despite the weakness of the proofs of God's existence and the powerful objections that have been raised against the concept of a cosmic mind, we yearn for God. Religion, a natural development of the world process at its more advanced stages, focuses our gaze upon some ultimate perfection of which Deity is the most adequate symbol. The seed of divinity within us will allow us no rest until we find God; yet reason makes us doubt his existence, and the more sensitive our conscience becomes, the more vehemently we reject the notion that a perfect being should permit so many imperfections to arise in the world that he created. Where shall we turn in our dilemma?

Long ago, one of the most acute thinkers of all time pointed out the way. Instead of placing God at the beginning of the world, as its source or creator, Aristotle concluded that the perfect timeless being was its objective, its goal, the supreme object of desire that keeps the universe in motion by its attractive power, as the loved one attracts the lover. By this novel solution of a perpetually perplexing problem, Aristotle avoided all the difficulties involved in deriving the imperfect from the perfect, evil from goodness—difficulties which, a few centuries later, gave rise to the Gnostic doctrine of a step by step decline from the perfect God to a degenerate demiurge who created our evil world. The wonder is that Aristotle's solution, made at a time when the only available theory of evolution—that of Empedocles—was far too crude for acceptance by so careful a thinker, has not found greater favour in an age which explains nearly everything by a theory of evolution that has been worked out in detail; for to place perfection at the end rather than at the beginning is in accord with the notion of development. Almost alone among recent philosophers, S. Alexander regarded Deity as emergent from the world process rather than its source; but his Deity is very different from Aristotle's Unmoved Mover.

We can follow Aristotle's lead without adopting his too-intellectualistic concept of the Unmoved Mover's perfection as consisting in nothing but timeless absorption in his own abstract thoughts, never touched by awareness of the transient events in the world that ceaselessly seeks him. Professor Hartshorne's panentheism has done much to cure us of this lopsided view of perfection. 'To believe in God', wrote Unamuno, 'is, before and above all, to wish that there may be a God.' To the higher sort of man, an ideal may be far more attractive than anything that already exists; and the God whom we seek may be an ideal rather than an actual being. Indeed, God has always been an ideal, if by this we mean something that we wish to find rather than something of whose existence we are assured by experience. And since we who cherish this ideal, and the religions which encourage us to support it, are outgrowths of one continuous process that began when the solar system condensed from the primal nebula, it is hardly going too far to say that God, the ultimate perfection, is the world's ideal, the goal toward which it has been steadily groping through all the difficulties which beset a vast, unsupervised creative process.

A valid ideal differs from a mere idea, such as that of a centaur or a unicorn, in the compulsion it exerts upon us to make it real. Yet we need not expect to realize it fully; the ideal that is too easily fulfilled is hardly high enough to be worthy of us, and we learn to be satisfied if we can advance steadily if slowly toward it. Far from being discouraged if our ideals remain ever above our grasp because they rise higher as we approach them, we should welcome this as an indication of our intellectual or moral growth. It would be folly to expect that God, the highest perfection, could be realized by imperfect man in the foreseeable future. Yet it would be pusillanimous not to strive toward our ideal because it seems so remote. If there is no God in heaven, we regret his absence but can do nothing about it; if there is no God in our own soul, that is an even more grievous lack which it lies in our power to remedy. One may be agnostic about the heavenly God, but no one can be agnostic about the God within him.

What can we, puny creatures that we are, do to bring God into the world or, what amounts to the same thing, the world nearer its ideal God? Before we can answer this question, we must ask another: What is it that men have most expected of their God and most sorely missed? That which more than all else makes thoughtful people doubt that he exists is the absence of any indubitable indication that an intelligent being, far more powerful than man, cares lovingly for his creation and all that it contains, repressing the occasional violence of physical nature, restraining the strife that convulses the living world, bringing peace and joy everywhere. If there were a little more loving care in the world, we would feel that God, whom the most poetic of the founders of religions conceived as a loving father, were closer to us. And is this not a defect which it lies in our power to remedy? Devoted care is the very heart of religion, that which alone gives substance to its aspirations; and to become more religious is above all to care more deeply about our world.

The most effective way to serve God as an ideal is to intensify our care, first for ourselves, so that we may become fit agents for the work to which we dedicate ourselves, then for our neighbours, and finally for the planet as a whole, with all its living cargo. Nothing so truly reveals the divinity in man as his capacity to care about, and to work unselfishly for, not only his own children but a distant posterity, not only his own kind but living things of many kinds, not only his own neighbourhood but his planet as a whole. It is above all this God-like quality within us that encourages us to believe that we can, in some measure, create the God of our ideal.

One person's love seems a weak and timid thing to confront the world's vast indifference; but love breeds love; and if we could only make a good start, it would grow like a swelling cloud, until presently we found ourselves in an atmosphere so saturated with love that it would hearten all our efforts. If humanity could generate enough unselfish love, we should feel a divine presence hovering over the earth; and although it would be unreasonable to expect that this world afflicted with decay and death could become paradise, it would become immeasurably happier than it has been.

To care lovingly for anything, we must appreciate it. Appreciation is the beginning of religion; if men had not valued their lives on this earth, they would have no desire to safeguard and prolong their conscious existence, and they would never have developed all those rites and beliefs, intended for this purpose, of which religion objectively consists. The more a thoughtful person admires or loves anything, the more gladly he exerts himself to protect it.

It is perverse to permit the world's vast evil to spoil our enjoyment of the still vaster amount of good and beautiful things that it contains. Failure to recognize and approve the good is no less a symptom of spiritual and moral blindness than failure to recognize and condemn the evil. The very presence of the ugly and the evil should intensify our appreciation of the good and the beautiful, by reminding us of the enormous difficulties that had to be overcome in the production of the latter. Optimism and pessimism, in their exact meaning, are equally puerile in the face of a world that is so obviously neither the best nor the worst that might exist. To know and appreciate, to the extent that they deserve to be known and appreciated, all the excellent things that the world contains gives significance not only to our own lives but likewise to the whole aeonian process that formed them. We should wish so to take unto ourselves all the good and lovable things that the world has pro- duced, to seize them so firmly with our mind, to engrave them so indelibly on it, that if this whole planet were to be destroyed with the exception of the appreciative souls that it has nurtured, its finest accomplishments would be preserved in memory for ever.

What a single soul might preserve is little, but what many souls might preserve is much.

By striving ceaselessly toward that ideal of perfection which we call God, by caring devotedly for our inmost selves and all things worthy of our care that we have the power to protect or to improve, by appreciating everything beautiful and good which the world presents to us and storing our memories with it, we make our souls worthy of that immortal life which religions promise to their faithful. If immortality is, or will become, attainable by the human soul, it must be within the possibilities of that great, all-embracing, infinitely varied, and still imperfectly explored system of orderly, interrelated events which we know as nature. Only by regarding spiritual survival as natural, in the same sense that our birth, our thought, our aspiration, and our body's final dissolution are natural, can we who have been nurtured on science and philosophy hold faith in it. If the spirit survives its body in the course of nature, as in the course of nature the light from a beacon on a hilltop goes coursing through outer space long after the fire has died, then it is reasonable to believe that its survival depends upon such intrinsic qualities as the intensity of its love, the unity of its aspirations, its coherence and the absence of passions that tear it asunder.

If we preserve faith that the soul's destiny depends upon its intrinsic strength alone, then we can dispense with all those special, more or less magical, beliefs and practices on which religions have relied to ensure a blessed immortality, and in which they differ so strikingly one from another, while we carefully follow those directions for purifying the soul of its baser inclinations and making it worthy of immortal life, on which the higher religions are in substantial agreement. Thus, by regarding the most cherished and persistent of human aspirations, immortal life, as a condition to be achieved, if at all, by the natural and obvious means of nurturing and purifying the soul and making it fit to survive, we can rise above those sectarian differences that have brought so much strife and bitterness to mankind and move toward a universal religion. All the greatest religious teachers seem to have entertained some such thought, and it is chiefly their more narrow-minded and fanatical followers who have insisted that their church offers the one possible way to salvation.

When religions are in substantial agreement, it is probable that they have grasped, or are on the track of, some important truth; whereas those dogmas on which one differs from all or most of the others are probably either false or unimportant. Since all religions recognize the necessity of faith but differ as to the beliefs in which faith is needed, we may conclude that faith is indispensable to religion, but not faith in tenets peculiar to one of them. The one indispensable article of faith seems to be that by caring devotedly, and with such intelligence as we possess, for our own souls, and for the good and beautiful things around us, we increase the total sum of good in the world, and all will be well with us in the end—even if we cannot foresee in detail just how this will come about. If we hold fast to this ultimate faith, and regulate our lives by it, we possess the golden core of religion. All the rest is accessory to this central treasure.

Epilogue

It seems proper to conclude this book by answering, as well as we can, a question that was raised in the Introduction: Has religion made an adequate return for the immense amount of time, effort, and wealth which, since prehistoric times, men have lavished upon it? Can it justify its vast expenditure of human resources, mental and material?

More than any other human institution, religion has taught us to care, for our own souls or characters, for our fellow men, for the living world that surrounds us. Primitive religions directed men's care above all to the natural foundations of the tribal life; the advanced religions have been more concerned about caring for one's soul. In their totality, religions have directed our capacity for caring to nearly everything that needs, and is worthy of, our devoted service. In promoting and guiding this capacity, which more than all else gives us a claim to superiority over our brother animals, religion has made a priceless contribution to our spiritual growth and, indirectly, to our material prosperity.

Religion, more than any other institution, has persistently nourished our quenchless aspiration for a richer, more significant conscious existence, indefinitely prolonged. There is, it is true, no incontrovertible evidence that religion's promise of spiritual survival has been fulfilled even in a single instance. Nevertheless, by encouraging us to become worthy of everlasting happiness, religion has, in countless instances, made us better parents, neighbours, and citizens, more considerate of the living things that surround us. This is no small service to humanity.

One of the special offices of the advanced religions has been to bring consolation and hope to the downtrodden, reconciling them to their deprivations and sufferings. In times of adversity, sickness, and bereavement, religion has been for many people a soothing balm. This is one of religion's functions that has been most severely criticized. Not to reconcile the downtrodden to their hard lot, but to goad them into rising up and shaking off their oppressors, seems to some thinkers the proper course. To solace the afflicted by persuading them that a supernatural Power has laid their burdens upon them for their own ultimate benefit, that their sufferings on earth will be compensated in heaven, is a course hateful to the strong, self-reliant man who insists above all on intellectual honesty. Just as aspirin mitigates physical pain without removing its cause, so has religion through the ages relieved a vast amount of spiritual suffering that it cannot abolish. For a spiritual analgesic, as for a physical, men have often paid dearly and thought their money well spent. Even from this point of view, religion may claim to have justified itself, although the claim may not pass uncontested.

The vast effort expended upon religious edifices, even in communities where the majority of the people are miserably housed, sometimes appears a lamentable misapplication of resources. The value for religion of these costly, often lavishly ornamented constructions, along with the impressive ceremonies and solemn music that fill them, must be measured by their capacity to generate massive emotional support for religion's endeavours. This in many cases is considerable; the magnificent setting, the pageantry, and the music may conspire to uplift even the unbelieving to seldom-experienced emotional heights. And quite aside from their religious value, the nobler religious structures may be held to justify their existence as architectural gems. They are monuments to man's capacity for caring.

In my youth, I believed that the world needed a new religion, which would provide inspiration and guidance without embarrassing us with unprovable dogmas. Now I am convinced that, although we need more religion, we already have too many religions. Religion, in its essence, serves to unite men; whereas religions, with the dogmas peculiar to each, have long been a divisive force. What we most need is deeper, more grateful appreciation of the wonderful world in which we dwell; the broadening and intensification of our capacity for caring; the heightening and steadying of our aspirations. The education that does not undertake to do these things is a most defective education, unworthy of the name; so that education in these fundamental elements of religion should become an integral part of every curriculum, even in schools supported by a State that guarantees religious freedom.

A society which in some measure realizes our most cherished

hopes must be so permeated by religious motives that the distinction between religious and secular dies away; and this can be accomplished only by adequate education. If, in addition to the fullest cultivation of their capacities for appreciation, devoted care, and aspiration, people feel the need of those special dogmas which in every advanced religion have been a fertile source of schism, their freedom to hold them need not be restricted; but the State must remain aloof from them.

That an animal so richly endowed by nature as man, dwelling in a world so splendid as ours, should so rarely realize his possibilities for joyous and meaningful existence, is one of the most distressing facts of human life. It is to the everlasting credit of religion that it has rather consistently tried to overcome the obstacles to life's fruition, whether they occurred in the form of hostile forces in the external world or the evil tendencies within us. Science has proved itself far more capable than religion of confronting and overcoming the external obstacles; but, long before psychiatry arose, religion pointed with a sure finger to the disorders of the soul and showed us how to correct them. For this reason, if for no other, we cannot dispense with its teachings.

Index

Aeneas, 63

Agriculture, origin of, 68–70; and religion, 75; influence on treatment of animals, 85–6

Ahimsa, 117–20, 188, 246–7

Ahriman, 86–7, 153

Akbar, 89–90

Alacaluf Indians, 39

Alexander, S., 257

Alexander the Great, 141, 196

Allen, Grant, 62 n., 68–9, 74

Almsgiving, international, 134–5

Altar, origin of, 73

Amiel, Henri-Frédéric, 201

Anaxagoras, 145

Animals, care of self, offspring and companions by, 35–7; attitude of primitive man toward, 80–3; changes caused by agriculture, 85–6; in Persian dualism, 86–7; protected by Asoka, 88–9; by Akbar, 90; by Burmese and Tibetans, 91; by Chinese, 92; destruction of, in North America, 92; Jains' treatment of, 118; in Jewish law, 187; in Eastern religions, 188

Animism, 76–80, 91

Anthesteria, feast of, 68

Antigone, 63

Antisthenes, 175

Apocalypse, 21

Apollonius of Tyana, 44

Appreciation, as a basic element of religion, 13; analysis of, 17–18; in the Psalms, 18–9; by Ikhnaton, 20; by Jesus, 21; by Greek philosophers, 22–5; lack of, by ascetics, 26; in nature mysticism, 27; of our bodies and minds, 29; imparts purpose to the universe, 30–1; by a Buddhist monk, 33–4; as a mode of worship, 198; modern growth of, 231–3, 237

Arapesh of New Guinea, 48–54, 108

Archaism, in Arapesh culture, 53; a fault of religion, 182–3

Arda Viraf, Book of, 87

Aristophanes, 72

Aristotle, 24–5, 28 n., 78, 86, 124, 141, 146, 191, 208, 257

Arjuna, 146, 189

Arnold, E. Vernon, 127 n.

Art, 9–10, 164–5

Asceticism, 26, 133

Asoka Maurya, 88–9, 137, 184–5, 237

Aspiration, as a basic element in religion, 14; for everlasting life, 152–72; in the modern world, 238–9; for God, 257–60

Athens, cult of dead in, 67–8; protection of sacred olive trees in, 78; result of giving wheat to, 134–5

Atman, 112

Atomism, Democritan, 156, 158

Attachment and detachment, 145–51

Australia, kangaroo hunt in, 82

Avalokitesvara, 138

Aztecs, 15, 72

Beauty, 28–9, 252

Belden, Albert D., 198–9

Benedict, Ruth, 41 n.

Bergson, Henri, 242

Bhagavad-Gita, 128, 146, 184 n., 189

Bodhisattva, 138

Body, human, as object of appreciation, 29; abuse of, 41–3; as the spirit's temple, 44

Book of the dead, Egyptian, 113–15

Brahman, 111–2, 191, 215

Brahmanas, 87

Breasted, James H., 19–20, 115 n., 245

Buddha, Gautama, 12, 32–3, 88, 112, 116, 136, 178, 180, 230, 245, 247

GEORGE ALLEN & UNWIN LTD

Head office:
40 Museum Street, London, W.C.1
Telephone: 01-405 8577

Sales, Distribution and Accounts Departments
Park Lane, Hemel Hempstead, Herts.
Telephone: 0442 3244

Athens: 7 Stadiou Street, Athens 125
Auckland: P.O. Box 36013, Northcote, Auckland 9
Barbados: P.O. Box 222, Bridgetown
Beirut: Deeb Building, Jeanne d'Arc Street
Bombay: P.O. Box 21 103/5 Fort Street, Bombay 1
Calcutta: 285J Bepin Behari Ganguli Street, Calcutta 12
Dacca: Alico Building, 18 Motijheel, Dacca 2
Delhi: 1/18B Asaf Ali Road, New Delhi 1
Hong Kong: 105 Wing on Mansion, 26 Hankow Road, Kowloon
Ibadan: P.O. Box 62
Johannesburg: P.O. Box 23134, Joubert Park
Karachi: Karachi Chambers, McLeod Road, Karachi 2
Lahore: 22 Falettis' Hotel, Egerton Road
Madras: 2/18 Mount Road, Madras 2
Manila: P.O. Box 157, Quezon City D-502
Mexico: Libreria Britanica, S.A. Serapio Rendon 125 Mexico 4 D.F.
Nairobi: P.O. Box 30583
Rio de Janeiro: Caixa Postal 2537-Zc-00
Singapore: 36c Prinsep Street, Singapore 7
Sydney, N.S.W.: Bradbury House, 55 York Street, Sydney, N.S.W. 2000
Tokyo: C.P.O. Box 1728, Tokyo 100-91
Toronto: 145 Adelaide Street West, Toronto 1

Theology and Meaning

A CRITIQUE OF METATHEOLOGICAL SCEPTICISM
RAEBURN S. HEIMBECK

Dr Heimbeck's argument for the cognitive nature of religious discourse is twofold. First, he shows that such discourse can qualify as cognitively significant without having to satisfy the verification requirement. Secondly, he shows that it does in fact satisfy such a requirement because it is firmly rooted in the empirical realm. He shows that while religious language bears several similarities to non-cognitive discourse, its strongest affinities are with cognitive discourse.

This study should be of great interest to teachers and students of contemporary philosophy of religion as well as to the general reader familiar with basic philosophical distinctions. Though he reasons with minute care, Dr Heimbeck uses everyday examples to illustrate his argument. As a result, his book is both easily comprehensible and highly readable, although the discussion of philosophical and theological points is conducted at an advanced level.

Demy 8vo.

Psychology's Impact on the Christian Faith

C. EDWARD BARKER

The deep hunger for a religious faith that works is apparent everywhere. But the Church is failing to meet this profound need because it is still bound up with the obsessions, the masochism and the sexual distortions concealed in the writings of the Early Fathers and other authorities in Christian history. These same 'nervous' traits and distortions are much in evidence in Christian belief and practice today, and make, not for health and integration of personality, but for confusion, neurosis and immaturity.

As for the Founder of the Faith, Jesus himself was remarkably free from any trace of obsession, masochism or sexual bias. Nineteen hundred years before psycho-analysis was born, Jesus showed himself a penetrating psychologist. As the truth he taught is freed from the obsessive preoccupations and interpretations in which tradition has bound him, the real intentions of his teaching—whether about guilt and forgiveness, the cross, the Kingdom, disease and calamity, the family or divorce—emerge with the impact of a fresh revelation, psychologically valid, therapeutically sound and highly pertinent to the cry of modern man for a workable faith.

Demy 8vo.

GEORGE ALLEN AND UNWIN LTD